TODAY in HISTORY

Elvis

John Boertlein

Copyright © 2006 by John Boertlein

All rights reserved. No portion of this book may be reproduced in any fashion, print, facsimile, or electronic, or by any method yet to be developed, without express premission of the copyright holder.

For further information contact the publisher at

Emmis Books
1700 Madison Road
Cincinnati, OH 45206
www.emmisbooks.com

Library of Congress Cataloging-in-Publication Data
Boertlein, John, 1957-
Today in history : Elvis / by John Boertlein.
   p. cm. -- (Today in history series)
   A day-by-day guide of facts and trivia about Elvis Presley.
ISBN-13: 978-1-57860-264-3
ISBN-10: 1-57860-264-5
   1. Presley, Elvis, 1935-1977--Chronology. 2. Presley, Elvis, 1935-1977--Miscellanea. I. Title. II. Series.
ML420.P96B66 2006
782.42166092--dc22
                         2006002509

Cover and Interior Designed by Carie Adams
Production Design by Katie Riley
Edited by Jack Heffron

Distributed by Publishers Group West

For Kyla and Stewart
And most of all, for Mary Carol

INTRODUCTION

Looking back into Elvis Presley's life on a "day-to-day" basis is like re-reading a favorite novel, listening to a CD you've owned for years and still play once a week, finding yourself unable to change the TV channel when you find a certain film playing on cable, or better yet, getting a phone call from a friend you haven't heard from in years. Everything about Elvis has the potential to inspire fascination. His mere presence and involvement was, and is, enough to spark the generations since the 1950's to an affinity with the man and his many talents.

Perhaps that's why it's nearly impossible to separate the "flesh and blood" Elvis from an almost mythical image. Rock 'n' roll creator and ultimate-superstar-entertainer aside, Elvis's off-stage life has all of the elements of a heartwarming melodrama fit for a forum of its own. The classic "rags to riches" small town roots, the never-ending road trip with his buddies, charm capable of enchanting most of the world's female gender, and a genuine respect for his fellow human beings, set Elvis apart from any other cultural icon of our time. Indeed, facets of Elvis's life mirrored a fairytale story. There are hiss-able villains (Colonel Tom Parker), beautiful princess brides (Priscilla), knighthoods bestowed (by the United States army and law enforcement agencies coast to coast), a castle at Graceland, and a fleet of chariots too numerous to count.

How then does a random sampling of important (and some not-so) dates in Elvis's 15,197 days on God's Earth give us an idea of why Elvis was *Elvis*?

I think it is in looking into the mine, seeing the diamond-in-the-rough, watching its excavation and eventual transformation into a shining gem that allows the only true appreciation of its beauty, value, and durability.

And so it is with Elvis. True legends aren't born that way. They don't achieve spectacular presence overnight.

No, Elvis's talent, charisma, and earned popularity remain intact. It's only by looking at milestones of the journey along the way that perhaps we can experience a glimpse into the man, the legend personified.

January

History

1 January

(1956) With his career taking off, Elvis flies from Shreveport, Louisiana, where he was appearing on a country and western variety show *Louisiana Hayride*, to St. Louis's Kiel Auditorium to appear in a New Year's Day Grand Ole Opry Show. Accompanied by high school friend-turned-bodyguard/driver Red West, Elvis appears as a feature act along with country and western singer Webb Pierce. The show is headlined by Nashville favorite Hank Snow who, coincidentally, is a former client of Colonel Tom Parker.

quote of the day

"We were the only band in history that was directed by an ass."

—Scotty Moore, Elvis's guitarist, about having to take his cue from Elvis's derriere because he couldn't hear over fan's screams.

KING COMPOSER

Q: Of the many songs Elvis recorded and performed, he composed only one. What's the name of the song and who are the co-writers?

A: Along with Red West and Charlie Hodge, Elvis wrote "You'll Be Gone," which he recorded in 1962 and appears as the "flip side" of 1965's "Do The Clam," and on the LP *Girl Happy*.

Today in

January

(1967) Elvis and Colonel Tom Parker's contract agreement, acknowledging they are engaging in what is recognized as a partnership, goes into effect today. Colonel Parker continues to collect 25 percent of all of Elvis's movie salaries and guaranteed record company advances. But now the Colonel also receives 50 percent of any profit or royalties over the basic payment of film and record contracts. Parker also benefits 50 percent of any "special" deals, like television appearances, promotions, or endorsement appearances.

quote of the day

"It was Elvis who really got me hooked on beat music. When I heard 'Heartbreak Hotel,' I thought, 'This is it!'"

—Paul McCartney

BY THE NUMBERS

There are at least ten separate sites on the World Wide Web dedicated to instructing visitors on designing a home shrine to Elvis.

---History---

(1967) Elvis's love of horseback riding comes to light when he begins a buying spree involving everything to do with the sport. Besides equipment and apparel for him and the entourage, Elvis buys himself a favorite palomino named "Midget's Vandy." He promptly changes the name to "Rising Sun." He also buys a horse for his father, and a Tennessee Walker named after Robert E. Lee's "Traveler."

3 January

quote of the day

"I ain't no saint, but I've tried never to do anything that would hurt my family or offend God.... I figure all any kid needs is hope and the feeling he or she belongs. If I could do or say anything that would give some kid that feeling, I would believe I had contributed something to the world."

—Elvis Presley

A COLORFUL KING

Q: Only three of Elvis's motion pictures were filmed in black and white. Can you name them?

A: 1. *Love Me Tender* 2. *Jailhouse Rock* 3. *King Creole*

4 January

(1957) At 1:00 P.M. today, Elvis drives to the Kennedy Veteran's Hospital in Memphis for his army draft board pre-induction physical, which is performed by Dr. (Captain) Leonard Glick. Elvis is accompanied by Dottie Harmony, a striking Las Vegas dancer who's been visiting at Graceland, and Cliff Gleaves, a rockabilly singer and close friend to Elvis. The trio ride in style in a cream-colored Cadillac.

Elvis passes the physical and is issued Selective Service Number 40 86 35 16, but no draft rating is assigned.

quote of the day

"He taught white America to get down."

–James Brown

BY THE NUMBERS

From 1969, when Elvis returned to live performances after years of making movies, until his death in 1977, Elvis made a remarkable 1,128 personal concert appearances!

History

5 January

(1955) Elvis's new manager, Bob Neal, who replaces first manager and current band member Scotty Moore, flies to Shreveport, Louisiana, to confer with *Louisiana Hayride* promoter A.M. "Pappy" Covington regarding upcoming bookings for Elvis on the popular Southern country and western show. The bookings are crucial for the *Hayride* show and Elvis.

Neal's choice of using an airplane, as opposed to a twelve-hour round trip in an automobile, for the trip from Memphis to Shreveport suggests the trip was too important to chance for a phone conference as Elvis is becoming more and more in demand.

quote of the day

"Elvis had a range of about two octaves and a third. Most pop singers have about a one-octave range. He was a high baritone. He could nail high G's and A's full-voiced. That was just his natural ability. But in the army, practicing with Charlie (Hodge), he made his voice stronger. He sang more from the diaphragm, and with some power, rather than just from the throat. He'd say, 'It's the same music, just with more balls.'"

~Billy Smith, Elvis's cousin, from Elvis Aaron Presley: Revelations from the Memphis Mafia

KING STUFF

The former Soviet Union declared Elvis's music subversive and banned it from use of any kind for decades. The ban was finally lifted in 1988.

Today in

6 January

(1957) Elvis makes his third appearance on *The Ed Sullivan Show* in New York City performing, at the network's request, "Peace in the Valley." The show's standard "waist up" shots are used for "Don't Be Cruel." For the performance, Elvis wears a gold lamé vest given to him as a Christmas present by Barbara Hearn, a girl Elvis began dating in high school and saw on and off through the '50s and '60s. At the conclusion of the show, Ed Sullivan thanks the young entertainer, telling the audience, "This is a real decent, fine boy...We want to say that we've never had a pleasanter experience with a big name than we've had with you."

quote of the day

"I resented that. She was assuming that I slept with him and I never did. I wish I had....but I never did!"

—*Nancy Sinatra, commenting on Mary Tyler Moore's statement that Elvis slept with all of his leading ladies except her.*

YOU AIN'T NUTHIN' BUT A CHOW CHOW

Elvis thought so much of his 18-year-old chow chow dog, "Getlo," that in 1975 he paid for the ailing pooch to be flown to Boston from Memphis for expensive treatment for kidney disease at the New England Institute of Comparative Medicine. When Getlo wasn't at the hospital, his owner arranged for a two-night stay at Boston's Fairmount Copley Plaza Hotel.

7 January

(1967) Earlier in the week in Memphis, Elvis's uncle, Johnny Smith, and Elvis's cousin (and Johnny's daughter), Brenda, are in a serious automobile accident. Johnny suffers a deep laceration on his forehead, and Brenda has a fractured skull. It is assumed by members of the family that Johnny was drunk when the crash occurred. Johnny, who had been employed by cousin Elvis as the gatekeeper at Graceland, promptly loses his job. The replacement gatekeeper becomes inner-circle "wannabe" James Caughley, who had hung around Elvis for about a year.

quote of the day

"...and now I can't even feed my chickens. It's supposed to be bad for his image."

—Gladys Presley on Elvis's career vs. the live chickens she kept at Graceland

Elvis Auto

Q: Before Elvis developed his penchant for cars (and could afford to pay for them,) the Presleys had pretty basic transportation for their trip from Tupelo to Memphis. What kind of car did they own?

A: A green 1937 Plymouth Coupe.

Today in

8 January

(1935) On Old Saltillo Road in East Tupelo, Mississippi, in a house he built himself, Vernon Presley summons Dr. William R. Hunt to assist Mrs. Gladys Presley in giving birth to twin boys. The first, Jesse Garon, named for Vernon's father, is delivered stillborn at 4:00 A.M. The second, named for Vernon's middle name, Elvis Aaron Presley, is born at 4:35 A.M. The next day, Jesse is buried in an unmarked grave in the Priceville Cemetery, near Tupelo. Elvis becomes the Presleys' only child as the only survivor of several miscarriages and Jesse's stillbirth.

quote of the day

"I can never forget the longing to be someone. I guess if you are poor you always think bigger and want more than those who have everything."

—Elvis Presley on the occasion of his 30th birthday.

ELVIS'S GRAMMY TIME

Q: Of the 14 times Elvis was nominated for a Grammy Award, how many did he actually win?

A: Three

History

9 January

(1971) An announcement comes from the Junior Chamber of Commerce of America that Elvis will receive the honor of being named one of the nation's Ten Outstanding Young Men of the Year for 1970. The Jaycee awards have been given out since 1939 and have been awarded to men of achievement in all fields. Previous recipients include Leonard Bernstein, Orson Welles, Jesse Jackson and Ralph Nader. All recipients must be 35 years of age or younger. Elvis was nominated for the honor by former Shelby County, Tennessee Sheriff Bill Morris, whom Elvis had presented with a Mercedes-Benz automobile the prior Christmas. Joining Elvis in the ten were Ronald Reagan's press secretary, Ron Ziegler, and Tom Atkins, a civil rights activist from Boston.

quote of the day

"Without preamble, the three-piece band cuts loose. In the spotlight, the lanky singer flails furious rhythms on his guitar, every now and then breaking a string. In a pivoting stance, his hips swing seriously from side to side and his entire body takes on a frantic quiver, as if he had swallowed a jackhammer."

—TIME *magazine, May 15, 1956*

ALOHA, PLANET EARTH

Q: 1973's *Elvis: Aloha From Hawaii* garnered an estimated record audience globally. Approximately how many people enjoyed the show "via satellite?"

A: One billion people in forty countries.

Today in

10 January

(1962) The IRS begins looking into Elvis's 1955–1960 tax returns, trying to determine how income tax laws apply to Elvis's multiple contracts with RCA, the movie companies, Sun Records, the *Louisiana Hayride* and others. The IRS ultimately takes issue with large sums of money designated as "expenses" rather than "salary" regarding the movie contracts. Alterations in the contracts fix the problem.

(1970) At the RCA studios in Los Angeles, Elvis begins rehearsals for an upcoming Las Vegas engagement. He changes his repertoire from his first Las Vegas appearance because another live album is planned and to keep up with contemporary tastes in music. To the show he adds: "Proud Mary," "Polk Salad Annie," "Walk a Mile in My Shoes," and "Sweet Caroline," among others to augment his own recently recorded work.

quote of the day

"Elvis Presley was a weapon of the American psychological ward at inflicting a part of the population with a new philosophical outlook of inhumanity.... to destroy anything that is beautiful in order to prepare for war."

–Youth World, *a Cold War-era East German Communist Newspaper*

ELVIS IN YOUR POCKET

Promoters reportedly raked in over half a million (1956 dollars) by introducing: Hound Dog Orange Nonsmear Lipstick- "Keep me always on your lips!" The Elvis Brooch- "Wear his signature close to your heart." And the Elvis Presley Doll- "He'll be your companion- morning, noon, and nighttime too!"

History

(1975) Around this time, two coeds from Mississippi, nineteen-year-old Patsy Haynes, and seventeen-year-old Areecia "Honeybee" Benson, ship themselves to Graceland in a crate marked "Russian Wolfhounds." REA Express delivers the box to the gate-house at Graceland and the gatekeeper, Elvis's uncle Vester Presley, calls the mansion to report its arrival. Uncle Vester is told Elvis doesn't need any more dogs, and he orders the parcel returned to the truck, at which point the girls are discovered inside. They never get to see Elvis despite their effort.

11 January

quote of the day

"I felt a responsibility toward him and toward the whole world, too. I felt that this is someone the world loves. I adored him beyond description, but I also felt so many other people loved him that I wanted to take good care of him for everybody."

—Linda Thompson, in an interview for
The Inner Child by Peter Whitmer, Ph.D.

RANKING ELVIS

Q: Elvis was inducted into the United States army in 1958 and honorably discharged in 1960. What was the highest rank Elvis obtained in the army?

A: Promoted to Sergeant, January 20, 1960.

Today in

12 January

(1957) Not willing to travel to Nashville to record, Elvis goes to Radio Recorders in Hollywood to begin his first session in four months. He completes five songs including, "Don't Be Cruel," "All Shook Up," and the pop inspirational number "I Believe."

(1967) NBC announces the signing of a contract for Elvis's first television appearance since 1960. The agreement, including a feature film as part of the deal, pays Elvis $250,000 for the Christmas special, $850,000 for the film, and $25,000 for the film's music. Colonel Parker once again exceeds his benchmark $1,000,000 total.

(1973) At the International Convention Center Arena in Honolulu, Hawaii, the first performance of *Aloha From Hawaii* is held, being billed as a "dress rehearsal." The show is taped in case problems arise with the satellite transmission the next night.

quote of the day

"The first time I appeared on stage, it scared me to death. I really didn't know what all the yelling was about. I didn't realize that my body was moving. It's a natural thing to me. So to the manager backstage I said, 'What'd I do?? What'd I do?' And he said, 'Whatever it is, go back and do it again.'"

—Elvis Presley in MGM's 1972 documentary Elvis On Tour

DIVERSE FAN BASE

Q: In the 1950's who was the only black radio disc jockey that played Elvis records on a regular basis in Memphis from radio station WDIA?

A: Rufus Thomas

History

13 January

(1973) Tonight and early tomorrow morning, Elvis makes entertainment history with his televised concert from the Honolulu International Convention Center. Beamed live via Globecom Satellite, *Aloha From Hawaii* is broadcast to most of the Far East, including Australia, South Korea, Japan, Thailand, the Philippines, and South Vietnam. Ratings for the show are the highest ever recorded. The show is even beamed from Hong Kong to Macao on the Chinese mainland, where it is viewed by thousands in Communist China. The show is seen on a delayed basis later in the day in thirty European countries. The total estimated audience is over one billion! At an estimated cost of 2.5 million dollars, this is the most expensive entertainment production to date.

quote of the day

"You above all make all of it work by being the leader and the talent. Without your dedication to your following it couldn't have been done."

—Colonel Tom Parker in a 1973 letter to Elvis about the success of Aloha From Hawaii.

PAYING THE TAB

Q: On April 4, 1973, *Aloha From Hawaii* was broadcast in the U.S. at 8:30 PM on NBC. The show accounted for most American viewers in the time spot. What American product sponsored the famous concert telecast?

A: Chicken of the Sea

Today in

14 January

(1976) Elvis is in Colorado with his entourage for a Vail vacation. Late in the afternoon, an Elvis associate telephones Denver's Kumpf Lincoln Mercury car dealership to make an appointment. Elvis and company arrive at the salesroom about 9:00 P.M. where he purchase five Lincolns for a cool $70,000. The lucky recipients are Denver police vice squad Captain Jerry Kennedy and his wife, Denver police doctor Gerald Starkey, and Denver police detectives Ron Pietrofeso and Robert Cantwell. Elvis reportedly becomes very irritated at Cantwell when he overhears the officer comment he's never "gotten anything for nothing."

quote of the day

"Elvis is the greatest cultural force in the twentieth century. He introduced the beat to everything. Music, language, clothes, it's a whole new social revolution—the '60s come from it."
—Leonard Bernstein

HAPPINESS HOTELS

There are twenty-two motels and hotels in the United States that have "Elvis Rooms." Where the King slept, so can you.

History

15 January

(1955) Colonel Tom Parker arrives in Shreveport, Louisiana, to catch the *Louisiana Hayride* show. He's there to see a new talent named Elvis Presley perform. Rumor has it the young man "gets the girls excited the way Frank Sinatra used to do it." Parker is not disappointed. Elvis, wearing a rust-colored suit, black-dotted purple tie, and pink socks does "Hearts of Stone," "That's All Right," and "Tweedle Dee."

quote of the day

"His kind of music is deplorable, a rancid smelling aphrodisiac...it fosters almost totally negative and destructive reactions in young people."

—Frank Sinatra, 1950's

PREMATURE SELLOUT!

Elvis's "That's All Right" sold over 7,000 copies in Memphis during the first few weeks of its release—and Sam Phillips hadn't even had that many copies pressed yet!

16 January

(1971) Elvis and Priscilla attend day-long Junior Chamber of Commerce ceremonies in Memphis, during which Elvis receives one of the Ten Outstanding Young Men of the Year Awards for 1970. United Nations' ambassador-appointee George Bush is in attendance. During a press conference Elvis tells reporters, "I don't go along with music advocating drugs and desecration of the flag. I think an entertainer is for entertaining and to make people happy."

quote of the day

"When I was a child, ladies and gentlemen, I was a dreamer. I read comic books, and I was the hero of the comic book. I saw movies, and I was the hero of the movie. So every dream that I ever dreamed has come true a hundred times."

—Elvis Presley, 1971 *upon acceptance of one of the JCC's Ten Outstanding Men of the Year Awards*

BONJOUR MONSIEUR PRESLEY

In Paris, France, the Folies-Bergere, the Casino de Paris, the Lido, and the Moulin Rouge all identify themselves as having been patronized by Elvis.

17 January

(1959) Elvis is in Booneville, Mississippi, for a show the local newspaper hails as "the fastest rising country music star in the nation will be performing in his own top-notch manner." Colonel Parker is reportedly, "trying to get a booking at one of the big resort hotels in Nevada. Negotiating a deal that is terrific to say the least."

(1967) After buying the Circle G Ranch about ten miles south of Graceland near Walls, Mississippi, for his growing horse herd, Elvis continues a truck-buying spree. Today he purchases one 1967 Chevy custom El Camino, two Dodges, and five Ford trucks for family and friend use around the ranch.

quote of the day

"Husbands still scoffed. Wives still screamed. He kissed a few never-to-be-forgotten kisses, tossed a few perspiration-soaked scarves, graciously accepted the proffered lingerie. Crouched and karate-chopping, he teased the audience into perfectly controlled, orderly, well-behaved hysteria."

—Linda Winer in a 1972 concert review for the Chicago Tribune

ELVIS LINGUISTICS

Q: Elvis recorded eleven songs in languages other than English. Can you name them?

A: "Alla en el Rancho Grande," "Aloha Oe," "El Toro," "Guadalajara," "Havanagila," "Ku-u-i-Po," "Marguerita," "O Sole Mio," "Santa Lucia," "We'll Be Together," and "Wooden Heart."

18 January

(1964) This month Elvis is the high bidder in an auction for President Franklin Delano Roosevelt's yacht, the *U.S.S. Potomac*. Colonel Parker issues a press release that Elvis will donate the sixty-five-foot yacht, which brought $55,000, to the March of Dimes to be used as a possible National Shrine. F.D.R. suffered from polio, the primary concern of the March of Dimes Society.

quote of the day

"Using endearing terms like 'little us' was his way of being affectionate. His mother had raised him on this sweet talk and Elvis spoke it with those he cherished.... In moments of intimacy he would switch to third person address: Him yuvs you and her yuvs him."

—Priscilla Beaulieu Presley, from Elvis And Me

TEDDY BEAR OR TIGER?

Elvis studied and practiced karate for many years, often incorporating karate moves into his show. Elvis's inner circle all had karate names provided courtesy of Elvis. The King's karate moniker was "Tiger."

History

19 January

(1976) RCA releases *Elvis—A Legendary Performer, Volume Two*. *Billboard* calls the album "another fun set for the collector, young fans who may not have the older things, and fans in general." Featured on the album are an alternate take of "I Want You, I Love You, I Need You," in which Elvis reversed the lyrics, unreleased live versions of "Blue Suede Shoes" and "Baby What Do You Want Me to Do" from the *Elvis TV Special,* and an unreleased version of "Blue Hawaii" from *Elvis: Aloha From Hawaii.* Eventually, RCA produces four of the "Legendary Performer" series which is considered to be an all-encompassing outline of Elvis's career pieces.

quote of the day

"Do you promise to adopt each other's hound dog, and never to step on each other's blue suede shoes, and to always be each other's teddy bear?"

—Elvis Impersonator/Justice of the Peace Ron DeCar, offering wedding vows at the Viva Las Vegas Wedding Chapel in Las Vegas.

PAYING WITH ELVIS

Q: Elvis was the first to appear on an American institution's vehicle of business, although today the practice is very common. What item was Elvis the first to adorn?

A: Elvis Presley was the first person ever featured on a credit card when Leader Federal Savings and Loan of Memphis issued an Elvis card in 1988.

Today in

January

(1958) Principal photography begins for Elvis's second picture for Paramount, *King Creole*. While working on the film, Elvis has the opportunity to meet one of his idols, Marlon Brando, in the studio commissary.

(1960) In the army and three days after returning from Paris on leave, Elvis is promoted to acting sergeant.

(1961) The Colonel lands an agreement with MGM for a four-picture deal at a salary of $400,000 plus $75,000 for expenses and $25,000 for musical expenses per movie. Elvis will also receive 50 percent of the profits after the first $5,000,000 is recouped. The motion pictures made under this contract are: *It Happened at the World's Fair*, *Viva Las Vegas*, *Kissin' Cousins*, and *Girl Happy*.

quote of the day

"When I met him, he only had a million dollars worth of talent. Now he's got a million dollars!"

—Colonel Tom Parker

BEST MAN WITH BULLETS

Elvis was the best man at Sonny West's wedding to Judy Morgan in Memphis. What some didn't know was that Elvis was also the Best-Armed Man. During the ceremony he was packing two gold-plated .45 caliber pistols in shoulder holsters, one pearl-handled pistol in his waistband, one pearl-handled pistol in the small of his back, and one Derringer in his boot.

History

21 January

(1963) This week, production begins for *Fun in Acapulco*, Elvis's thirteenth film. Although the movie is set entirely in Mexico, all of Elvis's scenes are filmed at Paramount Studios in Hollywood. A second movie crew already traveled to Acapulco to film background scenes, using a double for Elvis and other principal characters when necessary. Even Elvis's scenes at the hotel and swimming pool are filmed on studio sets. *Fun in Acapulco* marks Ursula Andress's American movie debut, although she's appeared in Italian films since 1954. It's well known in Hollywood that Elvis usually dates his costars. However, he avoids a relationship with Ms. Andress, who at the time is married to actor John Derek. For Elvis, romantic involvement with a married woman is out of the question.

quote of the day

"He (Elvis) never contributed a damn thing to music."
— Bing Crosby

"The things that he did in his career, the things he created, are really important."
— Bing Crosby at a later date

TELEVISION VETERAN

Q: Elvis appeared on television many times. His last appearance (while alive), *Elvis: Aloha From Hawaii*, made television history and remains a modern classic. What was Elvis's television debut?

A: Elvis's first appeared on television on March 5, 1955, on a regional broadcast of *Louisiana Hayride* on KWKH TV, the CBS affiliate in Shreveport, Louisiana.

---— Today in ——---

January

(1955) Elvis receives a booking to appear on the Hank Snow Tour from February 14 to 18. He receives an advance check for $425, which is 50 percent of his pay for the tour.

(1966) Four inches of snow fall on Memphis, inspiring Elvis and his troupe to have a snowball fight and built a snowman at Graceland.

(1969) Elvis records "Suspicious Minds" at American Sound Studios in Memphis. After only four takes, he feels it's ready to go to press.

quote of the day

"It's a duty I've got to fill, and I'm gonna do it. I guess the only thing I'll hate about it is leaving my mama. She's always been my best girl."

—*Elvis, on becoming a GI*

THE ORIGINAL COLONEL OF CHICKEN?

Before becoming a "performer's manager," Tom Parker earned a living by barking at a stall in a circus. One of his most famous attractions was "Colonel Parker's Amazing Dancing Chickens."

History

(1957) Steve Sholes, the Country Music Hall of Famer responsible for signing Elvis to the RCA Victor Label in 1955, sets up a session at Radio Recorders in Hollywood for Elvis to cut "Loving You" as a single. Characteristically, Elvis instead concentrates on other material during the 10:00 A.M. to 6:30 P.M. session. Sholes, being credited for allowing Elvis to "run" his own recording sessions, allows Elvis to make his own decisions on what to record and how to record it. "I Beg of You" and "One Night" result, with each a potential candidate for single release.

quote of the day

"Elvis Presley is like the 'Big Bang' of rock and roll. It all came from there and what you had in Elvis Presley is a very interesting moment because, really, to be pretentious about it for a minute, you had two cultures colliding there. You had a kind of white European culture and an African culture coming together—the rhythm, okay, of black music and the melody chord progressions of white music—just all came together in that kind of spastic dance of his. That was the moment. That's really it. Out of all that came the Beatles and the Stones, but you can't underestimate what happened. It does get back to Elvis."

—Bono

STAYS FRESH—EVEN ON STAGE

When Elvis's patented jumpsuits got too tight around the waist and couldn't be let out anymore, Elvis needed a way to shrink. The fix fell upon his staff who, equipped with giant rolls of Saran Wrap, tightly bound his midsection—a "quick fix," albeit one that made it hard to breathe.

Today in

24 January

(1965) A hasty session is arranged in Nashville by producer Sam Katzman for a soundtrack to accompany MGM's new film, *Harum Scarum*. Because of the hurried schedule, Elvis's regular accompanying musicians are not available. Stand-ins become Grand Ole Opry house band member Charlie McCoy on guitar, Henry Strzelecki on bass, and Kenny Buttrey on drums. A flutist and oboist join in to achieve a Middle Eastern flavor to the soundtrack. Elvis has not recorded in a studio for eight months, and the musicians notice his distraction and disinterest in the material. The first night, Elvis ends the session after only four hours of doing 38 elongated takes of "Shake That Tambourine."

quote of the day

"It was Elvis that got me interested in music. I've been an Elvis fan since I was a kid. Ask anyone. If it hadn't been for Elvis, I don't know where popular music would be. He was the one that started it all off, and he was definitely the start of it for me."

—Elton John

FAMOUS JELLY ROLLS

The first commercial Elvis did was for the Southern Made Donut Company, for a radio broadcast during one of his *Louisiana Hayride* appearances. The donut company distributed baked goods throughout the southeastern United States.

History

(1957) Colonel Tom Parker announces a deal with MGM for Elvis's third film, tentatively titled "The Rock." Parker hails it as "the biggest deal ever made in Hollywood." Though the deal only allows for $250,000 and 50 percent net profit, Hollywood producer Hal Wallis receives the Colonel's unspoken message. *Jailhouse Rock* becomes Elvis's third film. Several items made for the production of *Jailhouse Rock* became rare collectibles. The most interesting is the picture sleeve for the single record of "Treat Me Nice"/"Baby I Don't Care" on Laurel Records (No. 41, 624) by Vince Everett (Elvis's character) There were about 100 picture sleeves printed. Also, in the scene at Geneva Record's office, the poster hanging on the wall of singing star "Mickey Alba" actually bears a likeness of Elvis.

25 January

quote of the day

"I'm definitely gonna do a record with him. You'd be surprised what we could do together. You ask me if I think he's good. How many Cadillacs was it he bought? That boy's no fool."

—Louis Armstrong, 1957

PAYING RESPECTS

When the late President John F. Kennedy's then nineteen-year-old daughter Caroline showed up at Graceland after hours at Elvis's funeral, the Presley family admitted her, not realizing she was interning for *Rolling Stone* magazine. Her subsequent article was published in the issue devoted to Elvis's death. Caroline reported she was stunned by Graceland's décor, and she described Elvis with the words "his face seemed swollen and his sideburns reached his chin."

―――― Today in ――――

January

(1970) Elvis opens a four-week engagement at Las Vegas International Hotel's showroom. The invitation-only affair is attended by everyone from legendary rock musician Fats Domino to screen-star Zsa Zsa Gabor. The show draws rave reviews. The *Los Angeles Herald-Examiner* gushes, "The new decade will belong to him." The show includes karate moves and jumpsuits showing Elvis's sometimes-forgotten ease of movement.

quote of the day

"I love his music because he was my generation. But then again, Elvis is everyone's generation, and he always will be."

—Margaret Thatcher, former prime minister of Great Britain

MAKES THE BLUE GRASS GROW

Q: January 1970 brought the release of one of Elvis's enduring gold record singles which mentioned a place in the South. Can you name the location that lent its name to this popular ballad?

A: Kentucky. The song is "Kentucky Rain"

History

27 January

(1971) It is the beginning of a monthlong stand at the International Hotel in Las Vegas. Beginning with this engagement, Elvis's show opener changes to something he will keep until the end. When Elvis returned to the stage in 1969, James Burton and the TCB Band opened the show with a lively version of the intro to 1957's "Baby I Don't Care" from *Jailhouse Rock*. This allowed Elvis to come on stage and then choose either "That's All Right" or "C.C. Rider" to start the show. Beginning this year, a dramatic instrumental, played by the full orchestra, is used to usher Elvis on stage. The piece is patterned after the Richard Strauss tone poem "Also Sprach Zarathustra," now commonly known as the theme from *2001: A Space Odyssey*. Variations of the theme were used in the past to send Elvis into an intermission, but future shows will almost inevitably use it as an opener.

quote of the day

"When I was thirteen, I saw him (Elvis) perform live and I suddenly understood what sex is all about. I was screaming at the top of my lungs."

–Raquel Welch

PUPPY LOVE

Q: Before Priscilla, Elvis had a close call on the marriage front only once. Who was the gal Elvis thought could be "Mrs. Right?"

A: Dixie Locke, one of Elvis's Memphis sweethearts, whom he met in church in 1954.

Today in

28 January

(1966) There are rumors flying about that Colonel Parker may sell Elvis's contract to Beatles manager Brian Epstein. *Today* columnist Dorothy Manners reports: "You could have knocked Elvis Presley over with a beetle when he read in his Memphis newspaper a rumor out of London that Brian Epstein is buying up his contract as well as Colonel Parker's interest in it. Elvis got the Colonel long distance as fast as possible. 'No,' drawled the good Colonel Tom. 'Not unless they want to pay us enough so we can retire and not have to work anymore. If they want us under those conditions I strongly suggest our selling.'"

quote of the day

"I remember Elvis as a young man hanging around the Sun Studios. Even then, I knew this kid had a tremendous talent. He was a dynamic young boy. His phraseology, his way of looking at a song, was as unique as Sinatra's. I was a tremendous fan, and had Elvis lived, there would have been no end to his inventiveness."

–B.B. King

WEIGHTY ROLLER COASTER

Elvis's battle with weight is infamous. When Elvis checked into a Nashville motel while preparing for a recording session, the motel staff commented on his food requests, "The first night he ordered cheese omelets, four orders of bacon and six sweet rolls. The next thing you know he's demanding soup. No wonder his weight goes up and down like a balloon."

History

29 January

(1975) Elvis's then-girlfriend Linda Thompson awakens in the early morning hours in their Graceland bedroom to find the singer desperately struggling for breath. Elvis is taken to Baptist Memorial Hospital where he is admitted. He stays on the eighteenth floor of the Madison East Wing. It is first reported Elvis is undergoing a "general medical work-up," because he is suffering from "liver problems." Rumors have it Elvis is hospitalized in an attempt to lose weight. In fact, Dr. George Nichopolous, better known as "Dr. Nick," is trying to get Elvis's use of prescription drugs under control. Elvis neither loses weight nor kicks the drug use. The official reason given for the hospitalization is "hypertension and an impacted colon."

quote of the day

"If life was fair, Elvis would be alive and all the impersonators would be dead."

–Johnny Carson

JUST SAY NO!

Between January 20 and August 16, 1977, "Dr. Nick" prescribed to Elvis 5,684 narcotic and amphetamine pills, an average of 25 a day!

Today in

30 January

(1956) Elvis records for the first time at RCA's New York studio at 155 East 24th Street. Steve Sholes, the RCA executive who signed Elvis to the RCA label in 1955, has concerns about the potential failure of "Heartbreak Hotel." Sholes has Elvis do a cover recording of Carl Perkins's recent Sun Records hit "Blue Suede Shoes," assuring Sun's Sam Phillips he will not shadow Perkins's success by putting it out as a single. Sholes is concerned because some of the top people at RCA fear they made a mistake in signing Elvis. At the session, the only addition to Elvis's regular band members is pianist Shorty Long who is in New York performing in a Broadway musical.

quote of the day

"This boy had everything. He had the looks, the moves, the manager and the talent. And he didn't look like Mr. Ed, like a lot of us did. In the way he looked, the way he talked, way he acted—he really was different."

–Carl Perkins

ELVIS IN LITERATURE

The Tennessee Williams play *Orpheus Descending* is reputed to be about Elvis Presley. The play is about Orpheus, the young god who captures the affections of the masses with his music. Ironically, the book concludes with Orpheus's destruction by way of idolatry and corruption.

History

31 January

(1955) Acting as both Elvis's first manager and lead guitar player, Scotty Moore tallies the earnings Elvis and the band have made during January, 1955. Moore's accounting reveals the group made $2,083.63 after the past month of touring. The proceeds are split, after expenses, with Elvis receiving 50 percent and Moore and bassist Bill Black each getting 25 percent.

quote of the day

"I'm sitting in the drive-through and I've got my three girls in the back and this station comes on and it's playing "Jailhouse Rock," the original version, and my girls are jumping up and down, going nuts. I'm looking around at them and they've heard Dad's music all the time and I don't see that out of them."

—Garth Brooks

ROCK 'N' ROLL PASTURE

Glenna Anderson, a fourteen-year-old 4-H Club member from San Diego, California, won "Best Steer" ribbon at the East San Diego County Fair with her bovine "Elvis." She took first place over competing steers "Royal" and "Fats Domino."

February

― History ―

(1968) Lisa Marie Presley is born today to proud parents Elvis and Priscilla Presley! It is nine months to the day after Elvis and Priscilla were married. Priscilla is admitted to Baptist Memorial Hospital's fifth floor of the east wing. Six hours and nineteen minutes later, Dr. T.A. Turman delivers a baby girl weighing six pounds, fifteen ounces, measuring 20 inches long. Lisa Marie, whose middle name is in honor of Colonel Parker's wife, Marie, also takes on the nicknames "Buttonhead" and "Yisa" by her proud daddy.

1 February

quote of the day

"You'd hear him before you'd see him. You'd hear these noises at the top of the staircase. He'd slowly make his way down, and there he was. The thing about my father is that he never hid anything. He didn't have a façade. Never put on airs."

—Lisa Marie Presley from Elvis by the Presleys

TERRIBLE TWO'S

Q: Elvis had his own nicknames for Lisa Marie, but Memphis Mafia Member Lamar Fike and one-time girlfriend Linda Thompson had nicknames for Lisa Marie too. What were they?

A: Lamar Fike: "Little Führer," Linda Thompson: "Gumbernickel"

Today in

February

(1956) Elvis's popularity continues to rise. His contract for appearances on *Stage Show*, a CBS television variety series hosted by big-band musicians Tommy and Jimmy Dorsey, is increased from four performances to six. Problem is, Colonel Parker can't deliver Elvis on show night for over a month as Elvis has prior commitments to continue appearances on the show where he made his television debut, *Louisiana Hayride*. The "strong audience reaction" accounting for the increased bookings is satisfied as Elvis sings "Tutti Frutti," "Heartbreak Hotel," "Blue Suede Shoes," and "I Was the One" on subsequent shows.

quote of the day

"...I realized that there was nothing hipper or cooler than Elvis. He had created cool with that withering sneer of his, and anybody who said Elvis wasn't cool was like a rebel priest denying the God that gave him life."

–Chet Williamson, from his essay *"Double Trouble,"* in The King Is Dead

JAILHOUSE ROCKED!

Vernon Presley was convicted of forgery by Tupelo Superior Court Judge Thomas J. Johnson in 1938. Sentenced to three years in prison, Vernon was sent to Parchman Penitentiary, a brutal Mississippi state prison located two hours from Tupelo. Parchman was on a 1,600-acre farm where the prisoners were forced to work every day. It was rumored that Vernon received whippings from prison guards, leaving scars on his back.

―――――――――――― History ――――――――――――

(1956) Elvis is back in RCA's New York studios for another recording session. He cuts two rhythm-and-blues classics, "Shake Rattle and Roll," and "Lawdy Miss Clawdy." Although not generally credited, Elvis later claims he played piano on "Lawdy Miss Clawdy."

(1976) Elvis is recording at his Graceland estate in hopes the relaxed, home-like setting will enable him to concentrate on his music. It doesn't work out that way, however, as Elvis appears more and more distracted, even to the point of retreating to his bedroom to plot with Sonny and Red West the violent assassinations of all Memphis drug dealers. He appears on the verge of delusional paranoia.

3 February

quote of the day

"The only possibility in the United States for a humane society would be a revolution with Elvis Presley as leader."

–Phil Ochs

WHO DID YOUR DECORATING?

Elvis's private bathroom in Graceland was decorated with pink and orchid colors. The shower doors were etched with the initials "EP" on the glass panels.

Today in

4 February

(1973) Elvis is performing an engagement for several weeks in Las Vegas at the Hilton. At some point Elvis meets heavyweight boxing champion Muhammad Ali, who is in Vegas training for a title defense bout against Joe Bugner. Elvis presents Ali with an elaborately sequined robe bearing "The People's Champion" across the back. Ali recollects about Elvis, "I felt sorry for him because he didn't enjoy life the way he should. He stayed indoors all the time. I told him he should go out and see people." Ali later reciprocates the gift by presenting Elvis with his boxing gloves. The gloves are autographed with, "You're the greatest" on the left, and, "To Elvis, my main man, from Muhammad Ali" on the right.

quote of the day

"I want to count Elvis's hound dogs twenty years from now. Only time will tell if Elvis is collecting Cadillacs in 1976."

—Spike Jones in 1956

GREASY KIDS' STUFF?

Dixie Peach Pomade was Elvis's favorite hair dressing in the late 1950's. Elvis also liked Presto hairspray and Lustre Crème Concentrate shampoo.

History

(1959) While serving with the army in Europe, Elvis learns of the airplane crash that took the lives of Buddy Holly, Richie Valens, and J.P. (the Big Bopper) Richardson. Elvis sends condolences to the fellow rocker's families. Elvis had met Holly in the latter's hometown of Lubbock, Texas, in 1955 while Elvis was performing at a place called the Cotton Club. Legend has it Elvis told Holly that if he came down to the *Louisiana Hayride* show, he'd get him on. But when Buddy and a partner, Bob Montgomery, showed up, Elvis wasn't there, and they were turned away.

5 February

quote of the day

"Without Elvis none of us could have made it."

–Buddy Holly

STAR STUDENT

On October 3, 1956, Elvis's teacher from L.C. Humes High School, Mildred Scrivener, appeared on a game show called *Twenty-One* in New York. When host Jack Barry asked Mildred about Elvis Presley, she mentioned that she knew him and that he had been a student of hers. On the show, Ms. Scrivener lost to a writer from Oneonta, New York.

Today in

6 February

(1955) Elvis is appearing in a Sunday concert at Ellis auditorium in Memphis, with Faron Young, Martha Carson, Ferlin Huskey, and the Wilburn Brothers. Between the 3:00 P.M. and 8:00 P.M. shows, Elvis has a chance to meet with Colonel Tom Parker at Palumbo's Restaurant. Also at the meeting are Sun Records president Sam Phillips, and Parker associates Bob Neal, Oscar Davis, and Tom Diskin. Scotty Moore and Bill Black are also present. The apparent purpose for the meeting is to discuss young Elvis's future, a subject everyone in the group has a stake in. Neal is very much encouraged by the Colonel's enthusiasm. But when the Colonel explains to Sam Phillips that Elvis is going nowhere on a small-time label like Sun and that he has already suggested to RCA that they buy the contract, Phillips takes offense and the meeting is, for all reasonable intents, over.

quote of the day

"It isn't enough to say that Elvis is kind to his parents, sends money home, and is the same unspoiled kid he was before all the commotion began. That still isn't a free ticket to behave like a sex maniac in public."

—Eddie Condon in Cosmopolitan, *December 1956*

DO NOT PASS GO...

The first Elvis Presley game was manufactured by Teen-Age Games, Inc., in West Springfield, Massachusetts, in 1957. There were five levels in The Elvis Presley Game: "Getting To Know Him," "Learning To Like Him," "Can't Do Without Him," "Let's Go Steady," and "Get The Preacher."

History

(1963) Elvis and Priscilla have spent the past three years trying to persuade the Beaulieus to permit Priscilla to move to Memphis where she can finish high school. Joseph Beaulieu and his daughter fly to Los Angeles to meet Elvis and receive a tour of the city. The three later fly to Memphis where Priscilla enrolls in Immaculate Conception High School. Immaculate Conception is an all-girls Catholic Academy, run by nuns, located on the corner of Central Avenue and Belvedere Boulevard in Memphis. The press is told Priscilla will be living with Vernon and his second wife, Dee, and Dee's three sons in their home next to Graceland. But, according to Priscilla, she moves into Elvis's bedroom the moment her father leaves town.

7 February

quote of the day

"As the lad himself might say, cut my legs off and call me shorty! Elvis Presley can act.... Acting is his assignment in this shrewdly upholstered showcase, and he does it."

—Howard Thompson in a review of King Creole in the New York Times, 1958

YOU CAN GO HOME AGAIN

Gladys Presley relished returning to Tupelo to visit old friends, especially after Elvis's popularity soared. Her Sunday visits made her feel truly loved for being herself and not for the fact she was Elvis Presley's mother.

Today in

8 February

(1967) While on a horse-shopping trip in Mississippi with Priscilla and several of the boys, Elvis notices a 65-foot lighted cross towering over a 160-acre cattle ranch named Twinkletown Farm near Walls, Mississippi, about 10 miles south of Graceland. Perhaps upon impulse, Elvis immediately decides to purchase the ranch and makes a down payment of $5000 toward the $250,000 price. By the time Elvis gets the ranch to his liking, he's spent $437,000 on everything from trailers to be used as living quarters for the entourage to pickup trucks to a stocked pond for fishing and fifty head of cattle. Elvis immediately renames the spread the "Circle G Ranch" (for Graceland). He later changes it to the "Flying Circle G" because a Texas ranch already owns the Circle G brand.

quote of the day

"There is something magical about watching a man who has lost himself find his way back home.... He sang with the kind of power people no longer expect from rock 'n' roll singers."

—John Landau, review of Elvis

PAY THE PRICE, TAKE THE RIDE

Elvis's favorite ride at the fairgrounds was the "Zippin' Pippin'" roller coaster. Each ride on the wooden coaster cost 50 cents, and Elvis liked to take 15 or 20 trips in a row!

History

(1974) Elvis closes out a successful two-week engagement at Las Vegas's Hilton Hotel. Originally scheduled for a four-week run, the number of shows has been cut in half at Dr. Nick's recommendation. The performances are generally well received, with Elvis being described as "in a good humor" and "at the top of his form." At the same time, Elvis continues showing signs of irrational behavior, having shot out a chandelier and several television sets during this engagement alone.

9 February

quote of the day

"Mama would see the girls mobbing me, and she'd get upset—but I told her they just like me."

—Elvis Presley

TAKIN' A RIDE

Harley Enthusiast magazine featured Elvis on the cover of their May 1956 issue. The small, 23-page magazine was a forerunner for America's Harley enthusiasm.

Today in

10 February

(1955) Tom Diskin, Colonel Tom Parker's brother-in-law and one of his assistants, writes a letter at the Colonel's request to RCA Company country and western record division head Steve Sholes. Diskin and the Colonel are apparently trying to up the ante by playing hard to get, suggesting Elvis "is pretty securely tied up" at Sun Records. Diskin adds to the story by recommending another performer, Tommy Sands, as a suitable substitute. Sholes responded, "The last I heard from the Colonel seemed quite favorable toward our signing Elvis Presley, so naturally your comments with respect to Presley were a little surprising."

quote of the day

"I'm trying to make it in acting, you know. And it takes a long time, a lot of work, and a lot of experience. But I'm trying to make it that way, and if I can get established that way, I'm okay. But I don't know how long the music end of it will last. I don't know how long I'll last. I've got no idea really."

—Elvis Presley

FASHION QUIZ

Q: After finding fame, Elvis swore he would never wear a certain type of fabric again. What was the fabric?

A: Denim. He hated blue jeans, as they were the only thing he wore during his school days.

History

(1960) Wrapping up his stint in the United States army, Elvis is promoted to full sergeant. He was previously given command of a three-man reconnaissance unit assigned to the third Armored Division's 32nd Scout Platoon. He receives a standard pay increase to $122.31 per month. During an interview with Armed Forces Radio around the time of his promotion Elvis reflects, "People were expecting me to mess up, to goof up. They thought I couldn't take it, and I was determined to go to any limits to prove otherwise."

11 February

quote of the day

"I think it would be a bad mistake if I had somebody else telling me what to record and how to record it, because I work strictly on instinct and impulse.... I choose songs with the public in mind. I try to visualize it as though I'm buying the record myself."

—*Elvis Presley, 1960, in an interview with Armed Forces Radio regarding his return to civilian life as an entertainer.*

SAM'S MILLIONS

When Sam Phillips sold Sun Recording Studios, it was reported he had earned two million dollars from the songs and artists he worked with in the '50s.

12 February

Today in

(1977) Although Elvis is now in the company of Ginger Alden, who now claims to be Elvis's fiancée and is accompanying him on a concert tour through the South, some jealousy over the departure of Linda Thompson apparently remains. Thompson had lived with Elvis at Graceland since 1972 but left the singer in 1976 claiming she was "tired of seeing him self-destruct on drugs." After leaving Elvis, Thompson began a relationship with Elvis's tour band member piano and organ player, David Briggs. Briggs has joined this most recent tour at Elvis's insistence. He does not know whether or how much Elvis knows about him and Linda. He finds out when Elvis pulls the plug on Biggs's electronic keyboard during the tour.

quote of the day

"She [Priscilla] has everything a man could want in a wife. If she's not the right girl, then there just isn't one."

—*Elvis Presley*

HE'S GOT THE SKINNY

In 1955, Elvis weighed a mere 160 pounds. Gladys forced him to gain weight because she felt he was too skinny and unhealthy looking.

History

13
February

(1967) Elvis spends so much time riding his horses at the Flying Circle G Ranch in Mississippi that he develops saddle sores. Elvis's regular doctor is unavailable, but George Klein, a long-time friend of Elvis's from high school, has a solution. Klein's girlfriend, Barbara Little, works for a Memphis medical office, so Elvis asks her to bring one of the doctors to the ranch. Little summons Dr. George Nichopoulos to treat Elvis. This is the beginning of a long relationship between Elvis and his soon-to-be physician, later to be called "Dr. Nick."

quote of the day

"He was ahead of his time because he had such deep feelings. He had the privilege of deep feelings because he was deeply loved by his mother, Gladys. He was able to appreciate profound beauty in sounds. And he started a musical revolution. They say all revolutions start from love."

—Imelda Marcos, first lady of the Philippines

WHAT DO YOU KNOW?

Shortly after meeting JD Sumner, Elvis auditioned for the gospel singing group The Songfellows. Sumner told Elvis he did not have a good voice and should forget about a career in the music business. Lucky for JD, Elvis didn't hold a grudge. In the 1970s, Elvis hired the baritone singer as part of his backup group.

―――― Today in ――――

14 February

(1968) After becoming parents for the first time two weeks earlier, Elvis and Priscilla visit Gladys Presley's grave at Forest Hills Cemetery in Memphis. The couple leave a wreath of flowers with a card signed, "Elvis – Priscilla – Lisa Marie." Elvis also leaves special orders that the card is to be burned along with the flowers when they wilt. Upon his death, Elvis too is interred at Forest Hill in a crypt a couple hundred yards from his mother's grave. Months later the bodies of both Elvis and Gladys Presley are moved to the Meditation Garden behind Graceland.

quote of the day

"He's amazing. He's so unspoiled and fresh, everybody is crazy about him. In fact, he's more fun than a barrel full of monkeys. And, he is a gentleman."

—Debra Paget, Love Me Tender *costar, 1956*

SMOKIN' MAN

Elvis began smoking cigars in 1953. He tried to hide this as much as he could. After he found fame, Elvis refused to allow photographs of him while he was enjoying a cigar.

History

15 February

(1973) During his eighth engagement at the Las Vegas Hilton, Elvis walks off stage during the early show. Upon returning, he announces, "I'm sorry, ladies and gentlemen, but I have a touch of the flu, and my voice suddenly disappeared." Elvis finishes the performance, but the midnight show is canceled. The Hilton's owner, Barron Hilton, informs Colonel Parker Elvis will receive full payment despite the cancellation. The Colonel sends a written reply to Mr. Hilton that the missed shows will be made up. The Colonel asserts, "This letter is not intended to match your generosity and understanding, but it is intended to show that we think the same way along these lines. We will never, and never have intended to, shuck our obligations."

quote of the day

"I don't know anything about music. In my line, you don't have to."

–Elvis Presley

SHOW US THE MONEY

RCA Victor Records gave vice president Steve Sholes one condition regarding signing Elvis to the RCA label: Sholes had to personally guarantee that the advance cash would be paid back within the first year. Sholes agreed to the term and hoped for the best. It all worked out as RCA recouped their advance and a whopping profit.

16 February

(1957) Elvis is in Hollywood filming *Loving You*. Seizing the opportunity for a vacation, Gladys, Vernon, and three of their friends take a train trip from Memphis to Southern California. On-set, Elvis is able to arrange for them to appear as extras as members of the audience during the final, climactic concert scene. While in Los Angeles, Gladys and Vernon attend Tennessee Ernie Ford's television show. "Uncle Ern" introduces the Presleys from the audience and later meets them backstage.

quote of the day

"Pastor, I am the most miserable young man you have ever seen. I have got more money than I can ever spend. I have thousands of fans out there, and I have a lot of people who call themselves my friends, but I am miserable. I am not doing a lot of things you taught me, and I'm doing some of the things you taught me not to do."

—Elvis, to the Reverend James Hamill,
First Assembly of God Church, Memphis

"HEY ELVY!"

In his youth, Elvis had been nicknamed "Elvy," which he hated. His classmates also called him "Mama's Boy" because his mother would walk him to school each day.

History

(1962) Being stuck in Hollywood to complete the filming of *Kid Galahad,* Elvis had the rare occasion of missing Christmas at Graceland. Upon completion of the movie Elvis returned to Memphis for a much-deserved vacation. He and the entourage traveled across the country in a converted bus. With bus horn blaring, the boys swept up Graceland's driveway illuminated by hundreds of still-hanging blue Christmas lights left up until Elvis could return home for the holidays. A late snowfall in Memphis this year provides Elvis the opportunity to go sledding on the hills of the estate.

17 February

quote of the day

"I don't make no dirty movements."

–Elvis Presley

CONFIDENTIAL INFORMATION

The contract that Colonel Tom and Elvis signed with RCA Victor lacked an audit clause, effectively denying them access to accounting and sales reports.

Today in

18 February

(1973) Elvis is performing at the midnight show during an engagement at the Las Vegas Hilton. Toward the end of the show, four men jump onstage apparently trying to get to Elvis. The first is met and subdued by Red West, who appears from behind the curtain. The remaining three men are confronted onstage by Sonny West, Jerry Schilling, Jerry Scheff, Colonel Parker's assistant Tom Diskin, and Vernon Presley. In the ensuing melee, Elvis knocks one of the trespassers off the stage and into the audience, where he falls on and smashes a table. After the fight Elvis tells the crowd, "I'm sorry ladies and gentlemen.... I'm sorry I didn't break his goddamned neck is what I'm sorry about!... If he wants to shake my hand, that's fine. If he wants to get tough, I'll whoop his ass!" Elvis receives a seven-minute standing ovation for the declaration.

quote of the day

"Everyone in rock'n'roll, including myself, was touched by his spirit. I was, and always will be, a fan."

–Bryan Ferry

ONLY IN A JEEP

Stationed in the army in Germany, Elvis drove a BMV 507. When he wasn't driving that, he was in an olive-drab Willy's Jeep with "U.S. Army" and the numbers 20976607 painted on the hood.

19 February

(1973) It is now apparent the four stage crashers from last evening's performance at the Las Vegas Hilton were nothing more than overly enthusiastic fans. But Elvis is convinced otherwise, later coming to believe the four were sent by Priscilla's boyfriend, Mike Stone, whom Elvis blames for stealing away Priscilla and trying to take away Lisa Marie. This emotion is apparently triggered by Priscilla's refusal to allow Lisa Marie to visit Elvis in Las Vegas for the end of this stand. Enraged, Elvis insists to members of his entourage that Mike Stone needs to be killed. Elvis finally needs to be sedated, and abandons the notion several days later after calming down.

quote of the day

"Every time I think that I'm getting old, and gradually going to the grave, something else happens."

—Elvis Presley

ONE STOP IN SCOTLAND

A plaque commemorates the site of a refueling stop where Elvis's army plane landed on his trip back to America at Prestwick Airforce Base in Scotland. It was the only time Elvis set foot on the British Isles.

—— Today in ——

February

(1955) Elvis is on tour in Arkansas with the *WSM Grand Ole Opry Show*. He rates third on the bill behind the Duke of Paducah and Mother Mabel and the Carter Sisters. Also on the bill are Jimmie Rodgers Snow, Charley Stewart, the Singing Hardens, Sammy Barnhard, Bob Neal, and "Uncle Dudley" (the radio name for DJ Ernest Hackworth of KTWN in Texarkana). Tickets cost seventy five cents in advance, a dollar at the door and fifty cents for kids. Vernon and Gladys Presley attend the show not only to see Elvis perform, but because Elvis wants to introduce them to Colonel Parker. As an incentive for the trip, Elvis promises his mother she will have the opportunity to meet Whitey Ford (the Duke of Paducah). The Duke is a favorite of hers from his many appearances on the *Grand Ole Opry*.

quote of the day

"I love going out on dates, especially with a girl that likes to have fun. The kind of fun I mean is just going out, looking around at places and things, wondering about people. Trying to win prizes at the amusement park. And generally having a good time."

—Elvis Presley

WHAT'S IN A NAME?

Elvis's love interests always seemed to have cute little nicknames for the man. Among those: *Priscilla's: "Fire Eyes"; Ann-Margret's: "Scoobie"; Linda Thompson's: "Bunting" or "Button."*

History

21 February

(1966) While filming *Spinout*, Elvis grants an interview with journalist May Mann, a former Miss Utah and writer of the syndicated column "Going Hollywood with May Mann." Elvis tells Ms. Mann he will always keep Graceland as his home because of his mother. He also speaks of working on songs for a new religious album that will be his first non-soundtrack record in two and a half years. Finding a renewed interest in music, Elvis is exploring a diverse assortment of songs and instrument sounds. This is evidenced by his purchase today of an amplifier, twelve string guitar, and harmonica. His listening interests are also affected as he is now favoring everything from his staple gospel to "folk" artists like Peter, Paul & Mary and Bob Dylan.

quote of the day

"A lot of people have accused Elvis of stealing the black man's music, when in fact, almost every black solo entertainer copied his stage mannerisms from Elvis."

–Jackie Wilson

SOME FOLKS'RE HARD TO PLEASE

Someone wrote "Elvis Presley Go Home!" in chalk on the sidewalk near the Maxine Theater where Elvis taped a performance for *Ed Sullivan's Toast of the Town* in October of 1956.

Today in

February 22

(1966) Filming begins on *Spinout* at the Samuel Goldwyn Studios in Culver City. Although Shelley Fabares plays Cynthia Foxhugh, as Elvis's Mike McCoy's love interest in the film, another costar, actress Deborah Walley, is linked romantically to the star. This is Elvis's twenty-second film in ten years. To salute Elvis's tenth anniversary in films, MGM mounts a massive publicity campaign. Theaters receive a *Spinout* press kit that includes Elvis photos, posters, flyers, tabloid heralds, and booklets about his gold Cadillac. Also included is a twenty-page anniversary story about Elvis. More than 5,000 radio stations receive promo copies of the "Spinout" single release and MGM releases numerous movie and TV trailers.

quote of the day

"It's all great. I've been looking forward to this homecoming very much. I've been escorted out of these fairgrounds when I was a kid and snuck in over the fence. But this is the first time I've been escorted in."

—Elvis Presley, at a press conference at the Tupelo, Mississippi/Alabama State Fair on September 26, 1956

SPINNING FOR *SPINOUT*

Q: Actress Diane McBain portrays Diana St. Clair, author of *Ten Ways to Trap a Bachelor* and *The Mating Habits of the Single Male*, in the Elvis movie *Spinout*. What is the title of the book Ms. St. Clair is researching as a premise for the movie?

A: *The Perfect American Male*

23 February

(1967) Elvis becomes the legal owner of the 163-acre ranch on Horn Lake Road at State Highway 301 near Walls, Mississippi. The new name for the spread is the "Flying Circle G Ranch." Ralph Boucher, the prior ranch foreman, remains after Elvis moves in. For security reasons, other members of the entourage to make a permanent home of the ranch are Billy and Jo Smith, Alan and Jo Fortas, and Vernon's sister Nashval and her husband Earl Pritchett. Mike McGregor, a hostler from Oxford, Mississippi, takes care of the horses. McGregor is also a leather craftsman and will later design belts and other leather goods for Elvis.

quote of the day

"...At Sun Studio in Memphis Elvis Presley called to life what would soon be known as rock and roll with a voice that bore strains of the Grand Ole Opry and Beale Street, of country and the blues. At that moment, he ensured—instinctively, unknowingly—that pop music would never again be as simple as black and white."
—David Fricke in Rolling Stone, *1986*

TAILORED GOLD

Elvis's famous gold lamé suit, designed by Nudie Cohen, was made of leather imported from Switzerland. His silver shirt was made of thin kid skin and was lined with silk. Both pieces were custom painted and lined with rhinestones.

24 February

(1970) Around this time as Elvis is about to begin flying about the country for concerts Colonel Parker tries to put a rein on the expenses incurred by taking the whole entourage along. "It should be strongly considered to travel on your own steam," the Colonel writes in a memo to Elvis's number one aide, Joe Esposito, "so we will not be obliged to look after people when we get there, as we will not have time to do this. Also, from the undercurrent I've received, there is a great possibility that if there is any junket of that sort we would lose our complete privacy which we always guard so carefully for Elvis's sake." The memo brings limited success with all the usual guys making the trip, albeit without their wives.

quote of the day

"Am I a rock'n'roller and a balladeer or a movie actor? I feel I can do both and not let one interfere with the other. I stop thinking of my guitar when I step on the movie stage."

–Elvis Presley

KEEP OFF GRASS

When the Presleys resided on Audubon Drive in Memphis, Gladys became upset by souvenir-seeking fans who clipped grass from the lawn, collected water from the swimming pool, or stole milk bottles left for the milkman. Elvis eventually had a wall and gate installed around the property. This apparently appeased Gladys who was known to take a lawn chair down to the gates to sit and mingle with fans.

--- History ---

(1961) Tennessee Governor Buford Ellington and Memphis Mayor Loeb declare February 25 "Elvis Presley Day" in Tennessee and Elvis's hometown. The proclamation also grants Elvis the title of "Colonel, Aide de Camp on the Governor's Staff." The proclamation is followed by a charity hundred-dollar-a-plate luncheon in Elvis's honor at the Claridge Hotel in Memphis. RCA Victor is hosting the event to present Elvis with a diamond-studded watch and a commemorative plaque to honor sales of seventy-six million records. In addition, Elvis receives awards for record sales around the globe including Australia, Belgium, Brazil, Denmark, England, France, Germany, Japan, the Netherlands, Norway, Sweden, and the Soviet Union. Elvis is also recognized at the event with the award of "The Best Male Vocalist for 1960" by Dick Clark's *American Bandstand* television show.

25 February

quote of the day

"A live concert for me is exciting because of all the electricity that is generated in the crowd and onstage. It's my favorite part of the business, live concerts."

–Elvis Presley

TALK TO ME, MAN

Colonel Parker hated Elvis's southern drawl, as he felt it made it hard to understand him. Elvis also stuttered a lot. In late 1955, the Colonel forced Elvis to take speech classes with a certified therapist to help with his diction.

― Today in ―

26 February

(1954) Elvis and his girlfriend, fourteen-year-old Dixie Locke, whom he had met earlier in the year at the Rainbow Rollerdrome, attend an all-night gospel singing event at Ellis Auditorium in Memphis. Elvis, Gladys, and Vernon are regular patrons of this monthly event, an all-star gospel show put on by the Blackwood Brothers, a gospel quartet who moved to Memphis in 1950 from Mississippi. The Blackwoods are Gladys's favorite group, but Elvis prefers the more animated Statesmen, a Memphis gospel group founded in 1948. It is the Statesmen who later provide some of the inspirational music at Elvis's funeral service in 1977 singing "Sweet, Sweet Spirit" and "Known Only to Him."

quote of the day

"I don't want to read about some of these actresses who are around today. They sound like my niece in Scarsdale. I love my niece in Scarsdale, but I won't buy tickets to see her act."

—Elvis Presley

DEWEY PLAYED IT!

Memphis disc jockey Dewey Phillips was the first to play Elvis's first record, "That's All Right," on the air. In 1954 Phillips used it as background music for a commercial.

History

27 February

(1958) Elvis and several other cast and crew members who are filming *King Creole* travel by train from Los Angeles to New Orleans for location scenes. Elvis is accompanied by his usual entourage and Hollywood friend Nick Adams, an actor best known as Johnny Yuma on *The Rebel* TV series and also close friend to James Dean. In New Orleans, Elvis reserved the entire tenth floor of the Roosevelt Hotel for himself and the boys. Locations used by the film crew in New Orleans included several spots along Royal Street in the French Quarter (most clearly seen is the balcony located at 1018 Royal from which Elvis sang "Crawfish"). Other locations were the Andrew Jackson Memorial Park (Jackson Square) and the St. Louis Cathedral across the street, the Vieux Carre nightclub, and a lakefront stilt-house on Lake Pontchartrain.

quote of the day

"I eat health foods and just try to use a little will power. Don't stuff, you know? In this business, especially in the movies and everything, weight can be very bad for you."

—Elvis Presley

DICK, ARMED

When he went to the White House to visit Richard Nixon in 1970, Elvis the gun collector thought the president might like an antique gun. When the Secret Service refused to let him take the gun into the Oval Office, Elvis opted for signed photos instead.

— Today in —

February 28

(1956) Elvis has work done on his 1955 Cadillac including new upholstery and a paint job changing the black roof to white. Not long after, Elvis presents the refurbished pink-and-white Cadillac to his mother, who will always point to it as "her" car, even though she does not and never has driven a car. Shortly after, the band is seen riding in what appears to be an all-pink Cadillac limousine with a bolted-on metal roof rack, which they use for a few months before moving up to a black 1957 Cadillac limousine. Gladys Presley's pink-and-white Cadillac is currently on display at Graceland.

quote of the day

"I see [Elvis impersonators] as the functional equivalent of priests, because the role of a priest is to continue the tradition, to bring believers together and to act in the place of the messiah, the founder, or the guru."

–Professor Joseph Kotarba, University of Houston

ELVIS REMEMBERED

When Elvis heard that there was difficulty raising enough money to erect a memorial for the *U.S.S. Arizona*, he took on the cause. In a 1961 benefit concert he gave in Hawaii, Elvis raised awareness for the cause and $62,000 to kick off the fundraising campaign.

History

(1968) The National Academy of Recording Arts and Sciences announces the Grammy Awards and Elvis is a winner! Elvis doesn't win in the best pop single or album categories. He takes home a Grammy for "Best Sacred Performance" for the album *How Great Thou Art*. The awards are presented at simultaneous dinners in New York, Los Angeles, and other NARAS chapter cities. No venue finds Elvis in attendance.

29 February

quote of the day

"A lot has been written and said about why he was so great, but I think the best way to appreciate his greatness is just to go back and play some old records.... Time has a way of being very unkind to old records, but Elvis keeps getting better and better."

—Huey Lewis

HAIL TO THE KING!

Elvis was reportedly referred to as "The King of Rock 'n' Roll" for the first time in 1956 in a column in the *Waco News-Tribune* in which reporter Bea Ramirez wrote: "Shortly before he was to go onstage at the Heart O' Texas Coliseum, Elvis Presley, the new 21-year-old 'King of Rock 'n' roll' sat in a darkened Cadillac limousine for an interview—well hidden from the sight of 4,000 screaming, squealing teenagers, who were on hand to welcome him on Tuesday night. All the hep cats were there and not enough fuzz [police]!"

March

History

1 March

(1960) In anticipation of his pending discharge, the army holds a press conference just before Elvis's departure from Germany. There are over a hundred reporters and photographers in attendance at the enlisted men's club in Friedberg, just north of Frankfurt, West Germany, where Elvis is stationed. Elvis's commanding officer presents him with a certificate of merit citing his "cheerfulness and drive and continually outstanding leadership ability." Also present is Marion Keisker whom Elvis knows as the influential secretary at Sun Records. Ms. Keisker is now Captain Marion MacInness (her married name) who is serving out her army enlistment in Europe. When Elvis, who has not seen her since she enlisted in 1957, spots her, his enthusiasm prompts him to declare, "I don't know whether to kiss you or salute." "In that order," she replies.

quote of the day

"Did you see that show? This Debra Paget is on the same show. She wore a tight thing with feathers on the behind where they wiggle the most. And I never saw anything like it! Sex? Man, she bumped and pooshed out all over the place. I'm like a Little Boy Blue and who do they say is obscene? ME! It's because I make more money than Debra. Them critics don't like to see nobody win, doing any kind of music they don't know nothing about!"

—Elvis Presley, responding to criticism of his onstage "wiggling" on The Milton Berle Show in 1956.

DOES MR. WEATHERBEE KNOW?

When traveling by train in the 1950s, Elvis always took along and enjoyed reading *Archie*, *Jughead*, and *Veronica* comic books.

Today in

2 March

(1956) Colonel Parker informs his attorney that Elvis's "current" manager, Bob Neal, has no more business interests with Elvis. In truth, Elvis is still under contract to Neal who is collecting 15 percent of Elvis's earnings off the top. Even after Elvis signed his first contract with Parker he, in essence, agreed to pay Neal his 15 percent in addition to 25 percent for the Colonel. This isn't the only glitch the Colonel must find his way out of. Parker partnered with country singer Hank Snow in 1955 when the first Elvis contracts were signed. Snow expects to reap great financial rewards from his and Colonel Parker's mutual involvement in Elvis's career. The Colonel eventually forces Hank Snow out of the picture by unrealistically suggesting he and Snow pool all of their money to buy Elvis's contract from Bob Neal. Neither case ever comes to successful legal remedy, but both are the cause of controversy and recrimination for the next forty years.

quote of the day

"I don't know, it's hard to explain. It's like your whole body gets goose bumps, but it's not goose bumps. It's not a chill either. It's like a surge of electricity going through you. It's almost like making love, but it's even stronger than that."

—Elvis Presley, on his stage style

THE ELVIS CONFESSIONAL

In 1956, Cardinal Spellman of Buffalo, New York, made an official public statement regarding Elvis and rock 'n' roll music saying, "A new creed has been patterned by a segment of the young people in America...a creed of dishonesty, violence, lust, and degeneration."

History

(1959) While stationed in the U.S. army in Germany, Elvis is granted leave and travels to Munich with entourage members Lamar Fike and Red West who are staying in Germany during Elvis's time there. The three are traveling to visit Vera Tschechowa, an 18-year-old German actress whom Elvis met in January while doing publicity shots for the March of Dimes. Elvis buys up all the tickets to the play in which Vera is performing in a small theater. He and the guys sit through a German-language production none of them understands. That evening, Elvis and the boys go out to dinner with Vera and several of her theatrical friends. Afterward, they go to a show at the Moulin Rouge, a striptease club.

3 March

quote of the day

"Oh, no sir, not at all. I kinda expected it because even out in civilian life I get harassed a little bit by a few people, you know, and I expected it in there. But when those guys looked around, they saw me pulling KP and marching with a pack on my back and everything. Then they figured, 'Well he's just like we are.' So I got along very well with them. And they're a good bunch of guys."

—Elvis, responding to the question of whether he was tormented by fellow servicemen because of his notoriety

DRESSED FOR SUCCESS

It's been said that Elvis never wore the same outfit twice. His family and friends say he had more clothes in his closet than were in Lansky's department store.

Today in

4 March

(1956) The entertainment magazine *Billboard* publishes an article entitled "Presley as Hot as $1 Pistol on Victor." The article begins, "The hottest artist on the RCA Label this week has been none other than the amazin', young, country warbler, Elvis Presley." The complimentary article reveals Elvis is responsible for six out of the company's top twenty-five selling singles: "Heartbreak Hotel / I Was the One," number 2; "Mystery Train / I Forgot to Remember to Forget," number 9; "Good Rockin' Tonight," number 14; "Baby Let's Play House," number 15; "That's All Right," number 21; and "Milk Cow Blues Boogie," number 23.

quote of the day

When I first heard Elvis's voice I just knew that I wasn't going to work for anybody; and nobody was going to be my boss.... Hearing him for the first time was like busting out of jail."

—Bob Dylan

NIP & TUCK

In 1975, Elvis began taking comments about his "age" to heart. He decided to get a facelift and eye job from a plastic surgery specialist. His regular doctors told him it was completely unnecessary and tried to talk him out of it. But he had the job done, albeit with virtually no noticeable difference.

History

(1969) Elvis begins work on his thirty-first, and what will be his last, feature film, *Change of Habit*. This is the movie element of a contract signed with NBC which also included the TV special *Elvis,* often called "the '68 Comeback Special." *Change of Habit* is a fictionalized account of Sister Mary Olivia Gibson's work with handicapped children. Sister Mary was head of the speech clinic at Maria Regina College in Syracuse, New York. In working with children who had speech problems, she used variations of theatrical techniques. During filming, singer Mahalia Jackson visited Elvis on the set. A press release later said that Elvis patterned his vocal style after Ms. Jackson and the Ward Gospel Singers. Upon release, *Change of Habit* eventually reaches as high as #17 on *Variety's* weekly list of top-grossing films.

March

quote of the day

"Singers come and go, but if you're a good actor, you can last a long time."

—*Elvis Presley*

NO CHANGE OF HABIT

Q: In the 1969 film *Change of Habit*, Elvis plays the part of physician Dr. John Carpenter. From what locale did the good doctor come?

A: Shelby County, Tennessee, the same as Elvis.

Today in

6 March

(1963) Elvis satisfies his penchant for cars by purchasing a Rolls-Royce Phantom V Touring Limousine. Before being sent to the United States, the British dealer sees to it the vehicle is customized to meet Elvis's expectations. The Rolls is 12 feet in length and powered by an enormous 6.2-liter V-8 engine with a four-speed automatic transmission. The exterior is midnight blue with gray cloth interior. The vehicle comes with an engraved sterling silver ice thermos with two cut-glass decanters and five crystal glasses. This is Elvis's "car of choice" until 1968 when he donates it to a charity auction.

quote of the day

"Money's meant to be spread around. The more happiness it helps create, the more it's worth. It's worthless as old paper if it just lies in a bank and grows there without having been used to help anybody."

—Elvis Presley

WHO'S YOUR DADDY?

The former Phillip Stanic, age 43, claims his mother met Elvis Presley when she was an extra for the film *Blue Hawaii*. The duo, according to Stanic, had an intimate liaison which resulted in, well, Phil. Taking his paternity claim to federal court, Phil had his name legally changed to Elvis Presley, Jr. Today Junior travels the world as an entertainer performing (what else?) Elvis songs.

History

(1967) Production begins for Elvis's twenty-fifth film *Clambake*. The film's original title, *Too Big for Texas,* is only one indicator of geography incongruities as the movie's script has the location as Miami Beach, Florida, while Elvis did all of his scenes (including outdoors) in Hollywood (all of Elvis's Florida beach scenes used a double). One of the glaring examples of "mixed-up" geography occurs when Elvis and costar Shelley Fabares sit around a fire on the beach as the sun sets over the ocean, presumably on Florida's East-coast Miami Beach. Along with Ms. Fabares (whom Elvis doesn't kiss until the final scene), Tom (Sugarfoot) Brewster and TV's Flipper appear in the movie.

7 March

quote of the day

"I want to become a good actor because you can't build a whole career just on singing. Look at Frank Sinatra, until he added acting to singing, he found himself slipping downhill."

—Elvis Presley

GRACELAND OUTLANDISH

Elvis did his own decorating at Graceland, coming up with some great ideas to suit his own tastes. He had a carpeted ceiling and doors, a 9′ x 9′ king-size bed with two televisions in a recessed ceiling above, and a closet with a refrigerator-type light that came on when the door opened.

Today in

8 March

(1970) Elvis and Priscilla are vacationing in Palm Springs and house shopping while there. The couple choose a mid-size estate at 845 Chino Canyon Road that once belonged to Marjorie McDonald of the hamburger fortune McDonald's. The Spanish-style home has a terra-cotta tile roof, vaulted ceilings, and sits on 1.75 acres of prime desert land, complete with lava rocks, palm trees, and yucca plants. They purchase the three-bedroom home for $85,000 and immediately begin renovations that cost an additional $80,000. When the Presleys are ready to move in, they've added four bedrooms, seven baths, maid's quarters, two saunas, a swimming pool, and a twelve-person Jacuzzi, enlarging the place to 5,029 square feet.

quote of the day

"I only really feel at home in Memphis, at my own Graceland Mansion.... A man gets lonesome for the things that are familiar to him—my friends and acquaintances."

—Elvis Presley

COST OF DOING BUSINESS

In 1955 a lot of entities were interested in buying Elvis's contract from Sun Records. Dot Records offered $7,500, Columbia offered $15,000, and Atlantic Records $25,000. RCA Victor won out that year with a bid of $35,000.

History

(1967) While in California for the filming of *Clambake*, Elvis takes a spill in the bathroom of his Rocca Place home in Bel Air. Reportedly tripping over an electric cord and striking his head on the edge of the bathtub, Elvis laid unconscious on the bathroom floor for several hours before being discovered. A doctor is called and X-rays taken. It's determined Elvis suffers from a slight concussion, and the doctor advises rest as the remedy. This is apparently the opening Colonel Parker is looking for to gain some control over "the guys." The Colonel is concerned over Elvis's deep interest in matters of religion and the paranormal. Larry Gellar, Elvis's hairdresser and the person credited with introducing Elvis to "spiritualism," is promptly fired. Marty Lacker is removed as entourage "foreman" and replaced by Joe Esposito, who is told to take his orders from the Colonel. The Colonel completes the "cleanup" by ordering all of Elvis's books on mysticism and spiritualism destroyed.

9 March

quote of the day

"You know, when some people get down and out, they go out and get drunk and forget it all. Me, I just go out and buy another car. I've got money and I could buy anything there is to buy, but I still can't get out and mix with people like I'd like to."

—Elvis Presley

HOUND DOGS BEWARE!

In 1941, at the age of 32, Thomas Parker worked as a dogcatcher in Tampa, Florida.

Today in

10 March

(1964) Production is beginning for Elvis's sixteenth film, *Roustabout*. The film is a Hal Wallis production and puts Elvis in the role of a traveling carnival worker. Because the film and the accompanying LP contain the song "Little Egypt," a professional dancer of the same name sues Paramount Pictures, RCA Victor, and Elvis Presley Music, Inc., for 2.5 million dollars and an injunction restraining exhibitions of either the movie or its soundtrack. Little Egypt contends that the use of the name in the film was done without her authorization, causing her irreparable harm and holding her up to public ridicule. Little Egypt loses the case. Although actress Sue Ane Langdon and Elvis provide the movie's sex appeal, another "symbol" makes her debut in *Roustabout*. Twenty-four-year-old Raquel Welch is seen in the first few minutes of the film as one of the two college girls who drive up to "Mother's Tea House" with their boyfriends and go in and sit down at a table. Raquel's first screen line: "Uh, how come they call this place a tea house, dear?"

quote of the day

"I've got an awfully long way to go yet. I don't have any method. I've never been to dramatic classes or any coach, and I still have my southern accent."
—Elvis Presley, early in his filmmaking career

TOO HOT TO HANDLE!

In 1956, *Confidential* magazine ran a story claiming Elvis had been discovered in bed with three girls at the same time. After reading the piece, Elvis laughed and told the boys the report was only partially correct—the actual number was six.

History

11 March

(1968) Production begins on MGM's *Live a Little, Love a Little* at the Goldwyn Studios in Culver City, California. This is Elvis's twenty-eighth film and the final time he will work with director Norman Taurog, who has previously directed nine Elvis films starting with *G.I. Blues* in 1960. *Live a Little, Love a Little* finds many of Elvis's entourage doing acting work. Sonny and Red West are seen early in the film teaming up against Elvis in a fight scene. Charlie Hodge appears in the film talking to the band in the background of a poolside party scene. Vernon Presley has a small part in the movie as a photographer's model. Even Elvis's Great Dane Brutus gets into the film cast as "Albert." Although Elvis has been married less than a year, and is a father of only six weeks, he is often spotted on the set kissing his costar, Michele Carrey.

quote of the day

"More than anything else, I want the folks back home to think right of me. Just because I managed to do a little something, I don't want anyone back home to think I got a big head."

–Elvis Presley

FURNISH YOUR HOME WITH ELVIS

The Hungerford Furniture Company had plans to release a line of Elvis Presley furniture in the spring of 1957 that never materialized beyond an Elvis photo appearing in one of the company's ads. Had it come to fruition, the set would have included forty pieces, from record cabinets to dining room tables, with prices ranging from $39 to $340.

Today in

12 March

(1977) This month's issue of *Ladies' Home Journal* publishes an article entitled "Arthritis Update," reporting Elvis has long suffered with the malady. A portion of the article reads: "Elvis Presley has been hospitalized repeatedly in the past few years because of arthritis. He is said to suffer from Reiter's Syndrome, an ailment characterized by inflammation of the urinary tract, eye irritation, and severe joint pain."

quote of the day

"Elvis Presley is morally insane! The spirit of 'Presleyism' has taken down all the bars and standards. We're living in a jellyfish morality!"

—Reverend Carl E. Elgena, from a statement made in Des Moines, Iowa, 1956

DUDS GOOD ENOUGH FOR A FUNERAL

In 1957 Elvis hired Hollywood designer Nudie Cohen to create what would become signature clothing for the entertainer. Nudie was also responsible for stage costumes worn by many other popular performers, including the suit in which country legend Hank Williams was buried in 1953.

History

13 March

(1958) From New Orleans for location filming of *King Creole*, Elvis is back in Hollywood and attends a cast party thrown by producer Hal Wallis. Elvis's induction into the army is imminent, but he tells columnist Vernon Scott, "The army can't be any worse than the merry-go-round I've been on for the past two years." Elvis and entourage depart for Graceland and upon arrival Elvis speaks to reporters at the front gate. When asked how his parents feel about his going into the service, Elvis concedes his mother is very upset—but that she is no different from any other mother. To the query of whether his popularity will fade during his army absence Elvis responds, "That's the sixty-four-dollar question. I wish I knew."

quote of the day

"Isn't it only right the draft should apply to everybody alike? Rich or poor, there should be no exceptions."

–Elvis Presley

PINNED UP

Modern Screen magazine published the first-ever Elvis color pinup in a 1956 issue. Debbie Reynolds appeared on the cover.

Today in

14 March

(1955) Elvis, his second manager Bob Neal, and the band arrive in New York City to audition for the CBS TV show *Arthur Godfrey's Talent Scouts*. The group came to New York to try out as "walk-in's," the least likely way to get on the program. The number of "walk-in" hopefuls wind around the block on audition days, often waiting six hours before receiving the opportunity to perform for five minutes. Those granted the opportunity to appear on the show receive round-trip flights on American Airlines and accommodations at the Victoria Hotel. Elvis apparently fails to impress the producer(s) and he, Scotty and Bill and Bob Neal remain in New York only one day.

quote of the day

"Elvis is a shouter...who yells a song and seems to have some sort of St. Vitus dance...a candidate for a spastic hospital."

—John Crosby, 1950s syndicated TV critic based in New York

OH, THAT HENNY YOUNGMAN!

Comedian Henny Youngman was the guest emcee who introduced Elvis during his fifth appearance on the Dorsey Brothers' television program *Stage Show*.

History

15 March

(1965) During the filming of *Harum Scarum*, Elvis becomes involved with the Self-Realization Fellowship. Founded in 1920 by Paramahansa Yogananda, an Indian holy man who came to America in 1920 at the invitation of the International Congress of Religious Liberals, the fellowship is an ecumenical movement teaching broad-based religious principles by which the seeker of any orientation can find spiritual solace. Elvis begins to spend a great deal of time at the fellowship's Lake Shrine Retreat in Pacific Palisades. Elvis also meets Sri Daya Mata, a disciple of Yogananda and the group's spiritual leader at fellowship headquarters in Pasadena. Elvis's relationship with Daya Mata affects Elvis spiritually for the rest of his life.

quote of the day

"Don't criticize what you don't understand, son. You never walked in that man's shoes."

—Elvis Presley

HUNGRY MAN

Elvis's love for food was legendary from the beginning of his career. Then-girlfriend Dixie Locke once told a Memphis newspaper reporter that " recently at one sitting he ate eight deluxe cheeseburgers, two bacon-lettuce-tomato sandwiches, and topped it off with three chocolate milkshakes."

16 March

(1957) Because of constant visits and interruptions from zealous fans, Vernon and Gladys Presley scour Memphis for a larger and more secluded home. They find a suitable mansion on the outskirts of Memphis on Highway 51 South just north of the Mississippi border. The estate, set well back from the highway "in a grove of towering oaks," encompasses fourteen acres. The place is called Graceland, named after the great aunt of the woman who built it in 1941. The Presley family purchases Graceland for $102,500. They receive $55,000 for the sale of their house on Audubon Drive, pay $10,000 in cash, and obtain a twenty-five-year mortgage for the balance. Days after the purchase, Elvis hires local decorator George Golden, who has just completed a "space-age" renovation of Sam Phillips's new ultramodern ranch house, to begin interior "modern" design.

quote of the day

"He's not at all conceited. He doesn't like to go out often. We spend evenings listening to pop records or he would play the piano and sing folk songs. I was surprised he could play the piano so well. He plays the guitar and says as little as possible about his success as a singer."

—Margit Buergin, a seventeen-year-old German girl Elvis dated while he was stationed overseas

ROCKIN' FOR A BUCK!

An automatic Elvis Presley 45 rpm Victrola (model 7EP45) sold for $44.95 in 1956. It came complete with an RCA Victor triple pocket EP, "Elvis Presley" (SPD-23). The phonograph sold on a "special easy payment plan" of a dollar down and a dollar each week.

History

(1962) "Good Luck Charm" enters *Billboard's* "Hot 100" at number 51. It eventually reaches number one and stays on the charts for thirteen weeks. Elvis is the subject of at least three front-page stories in *Billboard*. "New Presley Record Hypos Singles Market," reads one headline adding, "that this disc ("Good Luck Charm") shapes up as one of the biggest—indicating that the chanter has lost none of his sales appeal, despite earlier reports to the contrary." Other headlines read, "Presley Leads Charmed Life," and "'Charm' and 'Jam' Get N.Y.C. Action." The latter article reads, "'Good Luck Charm' was starting to move in the New York area but not with the impact the dealers had expected." ("The Jam" mentioned is a two-part instrumental single by Bobby Gregg, another Memphis musician.)

17 March

quote of the day

"I know that I get carried away with the music and the beat sometimes. And I don't quite know what I'm doing. But it's all rhythm and the beat—it's full of life. I enjoy it. The kids understand it. It's the newness. I think older people will grow to understand. It's being young—you know—this generation."

—Elvis Presley

GRANDMA'S FAVORITE?

Minnie Mae Presley's bedroom at Graceland displayed photos of Elvis, Gladys, and one of Elvis's ex-girlfriends, Anita Wood.

Today in

18 March

(1965) Production begins on Elvis's nineteenth film, *Harum Scarum* at MGM studios in California. Producer Sam Katzman, known for making movies in a hurry, completes filming in only eighteen days. Elvis is often overheard complaining about his dislike of the overall concept of the movie. At one point Colonel Parker even insists a "speaking camel" be written into the script, an idea Katzman quickly dismisses. Despite the movie's exotic theme, it is shot entirely on soundstages and back lots at MGM studio. One of the sets, an ornate temple, was originally built for Cecil B. De Mille's silent classic *King of Kings* forty years earlier. Costumes are also recycled from 1944's *Kismet*. Elvis's salary for *Harum Scarum* balloons to a cool million dollars plus fifty percent of the profits, leaving only $200,000 to pay the rest of the cast.

quote of the day

"Oh, my God! I shook hands with Marlon Brando!"

—*Elvis Presley, after meeting Brando in Paramount's commissary*

THERE GOES THE NEIGHBORHOOD

As Elvis's star rose, the Presley home on Audubon Drive became increasingly overrun with fans and visitors. There were even popcorn vendors on the street. Elvis's neighbors resented the disruptions, including Gladys's hanging laundry in the yard and the constant stream of "hillbilly relatives," so much they eventually offered to buy the house. Elvis shot back an offer to buy their homes instead.

History

19 March

(1955) Elvis, Scotty, and Bill return to Memphis after their first appearance outside the South in Cleveland, Ohio. Scotty Moore's Chevrolet, which had registered an enduring 300,000 miles on its odometer, finally gave up the ghost after the trip. Needing transportation for future bookings, Elvis buys a 1951 Lincoln touring car. He has a rack installed on the top to transport Bill Black's bass fiddle, and on the outside of the front doors he has painted: "Elvis Presley on Tour."

quote of the day

"There have been a lot of tough guys. There have been pretenders. And there have been contenders. But there is only one king."

—Bruce Springsteen

SAINTS PRESERVE US!

In Great Britain, South Wales, just twenty miles from the Prescelley Mountains, is a town called St. Elvis.

— Today in —

20 March

(1974) Elvis performs at an added fifth show at Mid-South Coliseum in Memphis at the end of a southern tour. The first four sold-out shows around Memphis prompted Colonel Parker to add a fifth. This tour is Elvis's first concert appearance in his home town since 1961. The Colonel hears Elvis tell the crowds, "Hello, Memphis. It's good to be home," and figures it's a good time to record a live homecoming album and a way to circumvent having to coax Elvis back into the recording studio. Without apparent preparations for either repertoire or plans for backup recording, RCA has its mobile recording truck in Memphis to record this final show of the tour. All of the shows on this stand can be summed up in the *Memphis Press Scimitar*'s final review of the show's opening number when at the end of the overture, "...like a streak of white lightning, Presley darts on stage. He is dramatically clad in all-white which sparkles with jewels and nail heads." This and the unfurling of the American flag for the "American Trilogy" finale are reviewed as high points of the show.

quote of the day

"The only time I feel alive...is when I'm in front of my audience, my people. That's the only time I really feel like a human being."

—Elvis Presley

WHAT'S IN A NAME, MAN?

On Elvis's birth certificate, attending physician Dr. William Hunt spelled Elvis's name "Ailvis Aaron Presley."

History

21 March

(1961) This week, Elvis records some of the classics from *Blue Hawaii*: "Can't Help Falling in Love," "Beach Boy Blues," and "Rock-a-Hula Baby." According to the RCA Victor matrix numbering system, another three songs could have been recorded during this session, but there is no record of what they might be. Completely different versions of "Can't Help Falling in Love" are used in the movie and on the record. It won't be until 1997 when the master recording will be released on the *Elvis Presley Platinum* box set.

quote of the day

"Okay, I've done those movies, I've had a smash TV special.... I'm ready to cut some hit records."

–Elvis Presley

"COOL CAT, KITTEN!"

In a 1959 issue of *Teen* magazine, the "Cool Cat Comic," by artist Jack O'Brien, features the Cool Cat at a jukebox with a record flying out of it. A kitten, sitting on a couch sipping a soda watches as Cool Cat exclaims: "That Elvis was really a 'way out' kitten!"

Today in

22 March

(1957) Elvis is in downtown Memphis signing autographs for a group of young women when a young soldier, eighteen year-old P.F.C. Hershell Nixon literally bumps into him. Nixon confronts Elvis and accuses the entertainer of "bumping into his wife" several months earlier. Elvis tells Nixon he knows nothing about any such incident, and besides, he was in Hollywood at the time of the alleged "bump." Elvis turned to leave with a persistent Nixon following him down the street. Elvis responds by pulling a gun (actually a movie prop) saying, "You don't want to start trouble with me, do you? I'll blow your damn brains out, you punk!" Nixon backs off and the situation eventually cools with he and Elvis shaking hands. The press, however, gets wind of the event, which is essentially over. Nixon later tells reporters he will not consider charges as there was no harm done, "except to my ego."

quote of the day

"He was an instinctive actor.... He was quite bright...he was very intelligent...he was not a punk. He was very elegant, sedate, and refined, and sophisticated."

—Walter Matthau, from a 1987 interview

MIDDLE-EAST CONNECTION

In 1958, Elvis Presley won popularity polls as the number one singer in Cairo, Egypt, and Iraq.

History

23 March

(1966) This week Elvis's twentieth film, *Frankie and Johnny*, opens across the United States. Although a United Artists release, the film was shot at MGM. Based on a folk song of the same name, the origins of Frankie and Johnny vary with a popular version occurring in St. Louis in 1888. Frankie (a young lady) guns down her boyfriend, Johnny, with a Derringer she had hidden in her garter after she learns Johnny has "done her wrong." This is the first major film appearance for former Miss New Orleans Donna Douglas (who later portrayed Ellie Mae on *The Beverly Hillbillies* television sit-com. The film was directed by *Bedtime for Bonzo* veteran Fred de Cordova who later also found fame on television as director of *The Tonight Show Starring Johnny Carson*.

quote of the day

"If I were a good actor, I think I would like it [being in films] a little better. Although if I ever break into acting completely, I'll still continue singing. I'll still continue to make records."

—Elvis Presley

SCHOLARLY OPTIONS

In 1958, a London newspaper reported that Elvis fans received lower marks in school than Pat Boone fans, Perry Como fans, and Frank Sinatra fans.

―――――― Today in ――――――

24 March

(1958) At 6:35 A.M. Elvis and his then-girlfriend, Memphis radio personality Anita Wood (also a reputed one-time fiancée), accompanied by Vernon and Gladys Presley, reports to his local draft board at 198 South Main Street, where he and twelve other recruits board a bus for Kennedy Veterans Memorial Hospital. Elvis is assigned serial number 53 310 761 and after his physical he is placed in charge of the group who will be taking an army bus to Fort Chaffee, Arkansas. In the meantime, Elvis's parents wait anxiously outside to say good-bye. Colonel Parker is on hand passing out *King Creole* balloons to a growing crowd. During the trip Elvis meets Dresden, Tennessee, native Rex Mansfield, who will become one of his closest army friends.

quote of the day

"I don't know if I'll be doing any singing in the army, haven't so far.... I guess the army knows best."

—*Elvis Presley*

HOSPITAL BREAK

Ed Sullivan was in a car accident in Connecticut in 1956 and was hospitalized at the time of one of Elvis's appearances on his show. Actor Charles Laughton served as his replacement host.

History

(1958) Elvis's first day in the army begins with reveille at 0510 hours. He is the first man out of bed in his group. As he walks out of the barracks he encounters Colonel Tom Parker flanked by seventy photographers and reporters who showed up to record the event. Parker tells the press he came to Fort Chaffee "to look after the boy...and see he gets everything he needs." In the morning, Elvis takes a five-hour aptitude test which is followed by his first GI haircut. The haircut costs 65 cents which Elvis forgets to pay out of the seven dollar advance he received that morning on his monthly $83.20 military paycheck. The reason for Elvis's oversight is apparently some confusion caused by eager members of the press scrambling to get a clipping of Elvis's hair as a souvenir.

25 March

quote of the day

"My hair is my trademark. I never meant to offend anyone with it. But people have been making such a big to-do with keeping my hair. I don't want any partiality. I don't want to go into the service and have the rest of the boys in short hair and me in long hair. All GIs get crew cuts."

—*Elvis Presley*

I CARRY A BADGE, OR FIFTY

Elvis was a hard-core cop buff his whole life. When he was on army leave shortly after the death of his mother, the Tennessee Highway Patrol sent a police helicopter to Graceland to give him flying lessons to try to cheer him up.

26 March

(1968) Elvis's uncle, Travis Smith, who works as Graceland's gatekeeper and lives in a three-bedroom wooden house on the estate, becomes ill. This prompts Travis's son Billy to submit his resignation as Elvis's valet in Los Angeles. Billy is Elvis's cousin and one of the people closest to the entertainer. Elvis keeps Billy on the payroll until he finds a steady job in Memphis working on the railroad. Billy and his wife, Jo, continue to live in a trailer at the Flying Circle G ranch in nearby Mississippi.

quote of the day

"I just take every day as it comes. I don't plan too far ahead. There'll be record albums, of course, and movies too. Don't know anymore, maybe I'll go back to driving a truck."

—Elvis Presley

WHOLE LOTTA LOVIN' GOIN' ON

There are over 600 Elvis fan clubs worldwide. The largest official membership is the Elvis Presley Fan Club of Great Britain with over 20,000 members. Second is the "Elvis My Happiness Club" in France.

History

(1961) Elvis is in Hollywood at Paramount Studios to begin production of *Blue Hawaii*, his eighth film and the first from a five-year contract he's just signed with producer Hal Wallis. Originally, Juliet Prowse, Elvis's love interest in *GI Blues*, is asked to portray a similar role in *Blue Hawaii*. Ms. Prowse, however, makes several demands of Hal Wallis the producer is unwilling to meet, including equal billing with Elvis, a request which Colonel Parker finds laughable. Consequently, the role is given to lesser-known actress Joan Blackmon who will work with Elvis again in *Kid Galahad* later in the year. Elvis and Ms. Blackman dated briefly in 1956, but romantic notions, if there were any, had mellowed into friendship. Elvis did, however, have a romantic interest in *Blue Hawaii*'s cast-in blond starlet Pam Akert, who portrays one of four teenage tourists in the movie. Ms. Akert changes her last name to Austin by the time she costars with Elvis in *Kissin' Cousins*.

March

quote of the day

"The first concert I attended was an Elvis concert when I was eleven. Even at that age he made me realize the tremendous effect a performer could have on an audience."

—Cher

MISTER NUMBER ONE

In 1958, *Teen* magazine ran a poll asking readers who was "Mister Number One." Elvis finished first by acclaim, beating #2: Ricky Nelson, #3: Johnny Mathis, #4: Pat Boone, and #5: Perry Como.

Today in

March

(1975) Elvis is performing his now-annual stage show at the Las Vegas Hilton. After the midnight show he receives backstage visitors Barbra Streisand and her hairdresser boyfriend, Jon Peters. Ms. Streisand is visiting Elvis to offer him the costarring role in her upcoming remake of the Hollywood classic about the rise to and descent from stardom, *A Star Is Born*. Elvis displays great enthusiasm for the idea. Colonel Parker has serious reservations, however, with "business" concerns such as who will control publishing, what payment will be, and what effect Jon Peters, as the scheduled yet completely inexperienced director, would have on Elvis's image.

quote of the day

"I look at my old movies, and I can pick up on my mistakes. There's a lot I'd like to change."

—*Elvis Presley*

NUMBER TWO TURKEY

For his portrayal as American Indian Joe Lightcloud in his twenty-sixth film *Stay Away, Joe*, Elvis won a nomination for a "Golden Turkey Award" in the "Most Ludicrous Racial Impersonation in Hollywood History" category. He finished "Number Two Turkey" to Marlon Brando's part as an Okinawan islander in *The Teahouse of the August Moon*.

History

(1974) Elvis learns of the death of rhythm and blues artist Arthur "Big Boy" Crudup, the writer and original performer of Elvis's first Sun record "That's All Right." Elvis credits Crudup with being a major influence in his music style once saying in a 1956 interview, "Down in Tupelo, Mississippi, I used to hear old Arthur Crudup bang his box the way I do now, and I said if I ever got to the place where I could feel how old Arthur felt, I'd be a music man like nobody ever saw." Big Boy is 68 years of age when he dies of a stroke in Nassawadox, Virginia. He is also the author of the Elvis RCA recordings "My Baby Left Me" and "So Glad You're Mine." Though the two never met in person, Elvis financed several of Crudup's recording sessions at New York-based Fire Records in the 1960s.

29 March

quote of the day

"The colored folks been singing it and playing it just like I'm doin' now, man, for more years than I know. They played it like that in the shanties and in their juke joints, and nobody paid it no mind 'til I goosed it up. I got it from them."

—Elvis Presley, on his music in 1956

THE KING ON THE AIR IN MEMPHIS

Memphis's first radio station with an all-black format was WDIA. B.B. King began his entertaining career as an announcer there. The station, an Elvis favorite, played gospel and R&B music. In 1956, Elvis told everyone how much the music had inspired him at a WDIA charity event.

— Today in —

30 March

(1972) Filming for *Elvis on Tour*, his thirty-third film and second documentary, begins with a simulated recording session at the RCA Studios in Los Angeles. The film focuses primarily on Elvis's fifteen-city tour in April 1972. Producers Pierre Aldridge and Robert Able are fresh off of another critically acclaimed music documentary, *Mad Dogs and Englishmen*, about the 1970 Joe Cocker all-star and all-experience tour. *Elvis on Tour* is voted "Best Documentary of 1972" by the Hollywood Foreign Press Association. This is the only time an Elvis Presley film receives such a high honor. Prior to winning national acclaim for his directing, Martin Scorcese works on *Elvis on Tour* as montage supervisor. He has previous documentary experience as co-supervising editor of the popular film *Woodstock*. *Elvis on Tour* eventually tops out at #13 on *Variety*'s weekly list of top grossing films.

quote of the day

"No one, but no one, is his equal or ever will be. He was, and is, supreme."

—Mick Jagger, commenting on Elvis

HILLBILLY HEAVEN

The Roanoke Times named Elvis "The Hillbilly Frank Sinatra" in 1956 and 1957.

History

31 March

(1959) Colonel Parker reputedly engineers an effort to have Elvis send a telegram to his own office regarding his nearing discharge from the army and return to civilian life in Tennessee. Elvis's telegram reads: "Please convey my thanks to the various groups in Memphis who have suggested a special homecoming for me when I return to Memphis. However, I wish to return to Memphis the same way that any other serviceman returns to his hometown, without ceremony or fanfare. I served as they served and was proud to do it. Seeing the city of Memphis, my family, friends, and fans, will be the most welcome sight in the world to me. I appreciate their kind gesture. I know they will understand and I am glad you are in agreement with me on this. Best wishes to you and Mrs. Parker. From Dad, Grandma and myself."

quote of the day

"I've learned a lot about people in the army. There was all different types. I never lived with other people before and had a chance to find out how they think. It sure changed me, but I can't tell offhand just how."

–Elvis Presley, upon discharge from the army

"AND WE ALL SHINE ON..."

When Beatle John Lennon was told that Elvis had died, he replied, "Elvis died the day he went into the army."

April

History

1 April

(1960) It is only two weeks since Elvis's first post-army record studio work and again he boards a chartered bus this week from Memphis to Nashville for a second recording session. Boots Randolph, the noted saxophonist, joins the usual band members this time. The plan is to record ten songs over the next couple nights, but Elvis makes twelve of his most diverse and ambitious tracks in one marathon session lasting from 7:30 P.M. to 7:00 A.M. Some of the songs he records are "It's Now or Never," a song based on the Tony Martin standard "There's No Tomorrow" (which in turn is based on "O Sole Mio"), a Peggy Lee-influenced version of Little Willie John's "Fever," and "Are You Lonesome Tonight?" which Elvis records at Colonel Parker's request because it's his wife Marie's favorite song. This may be the only time in his career Elvis records a song his manager explicitly requests.

quote of the day

"It's all a big hoax.... I get one-third of the credit for recording it. It makes me look smarter than I am."

—*Elvis Presley, on recording music*

MILLIONS SERVED

Elvis's biggest selling single of all time is "It's Now or Never," which has sold over 1,210,000 copies in the U.K. alone.

Today in

2 April

(1956) Today Elvis is at Paramount Studios in Hollywood to appear in screen tests for producer Hal Wallis. The tests last three days and are overseen by veteran director Frank Tashlin. Elvis performs two scenes from *The Rainmaker*, which is scheduled to start shooting in two months with Burt Lancaster and Katherine Hepburn in the starring roles. Elvis also lip-synchs and does his patented stage act to his recording of "Blue Suede Shoes." Screenwriter Allen Weiss later comments in the straight scenes Elvis "came across like the lead in a high school play." Weiss adds that with the music added, however, "the transformation was incredible...electricity bounced off the walls of the soundstage, it was like an earthquake in progress, only without the implicit threat."

quote of the day

"I knew my script. They sent it to me before I came to Hollywood...and I got out there and just tried to put myself in the place of the character I was playing, just trying to act as naturally as I could."

—Elvis Presley, commenting on his screen test for The Rainmaker

TWO-TRICK PONIES

In the film *One Trick Pony,* Paul Simon plays the part of a failing folk singer whose wife tells him, "You have wanted to be Elvis Presley since you were thirteen. Now that's a goal you're not likely to achieve. He didn't do so well with it himself."

History

(1972) Just in time for Easter, this week RCA Victor releases the single of "He Touched Me"/Bosom of Abraham." The first pressing of "He Touched Me" goes entirely wrong when it is produced at 33-1/3 speed instead of 45 rpm. The single is immediately recalled and re-issued. The record fails to sell in large enough quantities to chart on *Billboard*.

3 April

quote of the day

"My first love is spiritual music—some of the old colored spirituals from way back. I know practically every religious song that's ever been written."

–Elvis Presley

GOD'S HAND AT WORK

Completely devastated by Gladys Presley's death, Elvis later saw the army as a blessing in disguise. "It was a time of grief for me," he said, "My mother had just died and I had to leave my home and go to Germany. It came at a time when I sorely needed a change. God's hand at work. The army took me away from myself and gave me something different."

Today in

4 April

(1968) Martin Luther King, Jr., is assassinated in Memphis, an event that Elvis takes hard. Elvis is reminded of the assassination five years earlier of President John F. Kennedy, but this has occurred in his hometown. Dr. King's "I Have a Dream" speech is one of Elvis's favorite rhetorical pieces, one that he recites often over the years. Elvis is in California when he receives the news.

quote of the day

"Elvis was the perfect one for the 'transition' that I wanted to make to help the black person to get a reception and help the white person feel that hey, we got a kinship, especially in the South."

—Sam Phillips

SWEET INSPIRATION

Myrna Smith, a member of the Sweet Inspirations vocal group who provided backup for Elvis, recalls that when Elvis performed at the Houston Astrodome, certain parties suggested he "leave the black girls." Elvis responded by seeing to it the ladies received the "star treatment," including a trip around the Astrodome in an open-top limo.

History

(1936) At 8:17 P.M. one-year-old Elvis Presley and mother Gladys take refuge in the home of Elvis's great-uncle, Noah Presley, as a tornado blows through the Tupelo valley obliterating fifteen residential town blocks and leaving a path of destruction four miles long and a mile wide. The tornado reportedly kills 213 people and as many as a thousand are injured. The Tupelo City Hospital is devastated, leaving the town with little in the way of medical aid. Two of the sections of town, Park Lane and Commerce Street, are leveled and bodies float to the surface of the bog along Commerce Street for days. The ensuing rain manages to contain various fires in town. After leaving Tupelo, the line of tornadoes progresses eastward across the South, killing people in a number of towns, including Gainesville, Georgia. Weeks later, canceled checks from the destroyed Bank of Tupelo are found littering the ground as far north as Nashville.

5 April

quote of the day

"Adversity is sometimes hard upon a man; but for one man who can stand prosperity, there are a hundred that will stand adversity."

–Elvis Presley

"GIRLS, I'LL SEE YOU..."

After a show in Jacksonville, Florida, Elvis joked, "Girls, I'll see you backstage!" Thousands in the audience took the invitation literally, storming the dressing room area. Police eventually managed entry and rescued Elvis, who was found clinging to the top of one of the showers, stripped of his shoes and most of his clothing.

Today in

6 April

(1956) Elvis is in Hollywood and participates in a press conference with film producer Hal Wallis to announce the signing of a contract between Elvis, Wallis, and Paramount Pictures. Reports have indicated that Wallis wanted to sign Elvis to a seven-year contract at a starting salary of $15,000 for his first film. This was normal for a new actor coming into the movie business. Colonel Parker intercedes, however, negotiating a final contract that allows Elvis to remain a virtual "free agent." The terms of the contract commit Elvis to three pictures in seven years for Wallis. Elvis's salary escalates from $100,000 for the first film to $150,000 for the second and $200,000 for the third. Because Wallis does not have a suitable picture for Elvis at the time, he almost immediately "loans" him to Twentieth Century Fox for what ultimately becomes *Love Me Tender*. In return for the "loan," Wallis reportedly receives nearly $100,000 from Twentieth Century Fox.

quote of the day

"It's something I didn't ever think would happen to me, of all people. It just shows you can never tell what's going to happen to you in life."

—Elvis Presley, upon receiving his first movie contract

ONLY A MOVIE?

Q: In a scene from the film *Men in Black*, Tommy Lee Jones puts Elvis on the car stereo. Will Smith asks, "You know Elvis is dead, right?" What does Jones reply?

A: "No, Elvis is not dead—he just went home."

History

(1962) Elvis arrives in Hawaii to begin shooting his eleventh film, *Girls! Girls! Girls!* Upon arrival at the airport Elvis is mobbed by several thousand fans. In the melee he loses his diamond ring, a tie clip, and his watch. Location filming for *Girls! Girls! Girls!* include the restaurant at Ala Wai Yacht Harbor and the Bumble Bee Tuna Company's canning plant at Kewalo Basin, both near Waikiki Beach on Oahu, the Mariner's Restaurant overlooking Honolulu harbor, and the picturesque village of Miloli (renamed "Paradise Cove" in the film) on Hawaii's Kona Coast. Noted actress and January 1960 Playboy Playmate of the Month Stella Stephens appears in *Girls! Girls! Girls!* in her singing role debut.

7 April

quote of the day

"When this day is over, an unhealthy chunk of Miami's teenage girls will have unashamedly screamed their lungs out to frank adoration of the biggest freak in modern show-business history. Elvis is a no-talent performer riding the crest of a wave of mass hysteria."

—Miami Herald, 1956

SILVER TONGUED

Elvis briefly dated Hollywood actress Joan Blackman. The two met by Elvis driving up to the starlet on the Paramount lot and yelling, "Hey, you, c'mere!"

—— Today in ——

8 April

(1973) Elvis is in California attending the state karate championships at the San Francisco Civic Auditorium. The event's producer is Ed Parker, Elvis's karate instructor and a bodyguard for several months. Advance publicity advertises Elvis will perform a demonstration of brick-breaking prior to the championship matches. The venue's marquee even displays Elvis's name in large letters. However, the Sahara Tahoe Hotel, which has Elvis under contract forbidding "personal appearances" within a radius of three hundred miles within thirty days of a Lake Tahoe appearance, learns of the event, eventually quashing Elvis's appearance. Elvis attends the matches only as a member of the audience, reportedly disappointing 3,500 fans who showed up to see the performer.

quote of the day

"Baby, you should have been there. Every time D.J. [Fontana] did his thing on the drums, I wiggled my finger and the girls went wild. I never heard screams like that in my life. I showed them sons of bitches calling me vulgar."

—*Elvis Presley, responding to a juvenile court judge's injunction that Elvis restrain his "vulgar" movements*

MAGIC FINGERS

Q: In 1968 Elvis did a reprise of his "dancing pinky" routine. On what show did he demonstrate the digit dance?

A: The TV special *Elvis*

History

(1953) It's time for the annual Humes High School "Annual Minstrel Show," and Mrs. Scrivener, one of Elvis's teachers who is in charge of the show, talks Elvis into entering the 8:00 PM entertainment in the Humes Auditorium. Elvis is mistakenly billed in the program as "Elvis Prestley, guitarist." He is listed sixteenth out of the twenty-two acts, and he sings "Take Them Cold Icy Fingers Off of Me," a 1950 country record by recording artist Pee Wee King. The performance brings an enthusiastic response and Elvis is allowed the only encore in the show. He sings "Till I Waltz Again with You." According to Mrs. Scrivener, 1500 students, faculty, and parents are treated to the very early performance.

9 April

quote of the day

"I wasn't popular in high school. I wasn't dating anybody there. I failed music—only thing I ever failed. And then they entered me in this talent show and I came out and did my first number, "'Til I Waltz Again with You," by Teresa Brewer. And when I came on stage I heard people kinda' rumblin' and whisperin' and so forth, 'cause nobody knew I even sang. It was amazing how popular I became after that."

—Elvis Presley

HAI-KARATE PEACEKEEPING

Legend has it Elvis was driving past a gas station one afternoon when he noticed two men fighting in the lot. Elvis jumped from his car, telling the fighters, "If you want trouble, give it to me." He proceeded to karate-kick a pack of cigarettes out of one of the guy's pockets, got back in his car, and drove off.

10 April

(1957) This month, Yvonne Lime arrives in Memphis to spend some time with Elvis, whom she had met on the set of his second film, *Loving You*. Miss Lime is a perky blond and aspiring actress who earlier appeared in *I Was a Teenage Werewolf*, which starred a young actor named Michael Landon. Yvonne will later go on to make regular appearances on three TV series, *Father Knows Best*, *The Many Loves of Dobie Gillis*, and *Happy*. Yvonne and Elvis had dated occasionally in Hollywood the past year. During this visit, Elvis is suffering from a recurring skin rash, so their first evening's date is confined to the patio of the Presley's home on Audubon Drive, where Elvis continues to reside while Graceland is remodeled.

quote of the day

"I'm as horny as a billy goat in a pepper patch. I'll race you to the bed."

—Elvis Presley, to renowned stripper Tempest Storm who he dated briefly while on vacation in Las Vegas

GET THEE TO A NUNNERY

Dolores Hart was Elvis's costar in the films *Loving You* and *King Creole*. He called her "Hot Lips" after an on-scene stage kiss in New Orleans. Delores described Elvis as "charming but unrefined, like a young animal." Shortly afterwards, Ms. Hart entered a convent.

History

11 April

(1962) *Follow That Dream* premieres in Ocala, Florida, the site of much of the location filming. This is Elvis's ninth film. *Follow That Dream* is based on the 1957 novel *Pioneer, Go Home*, by Richard Powell. The novel previously appeared in *Reader's Digest* in condensed form. Joanna Moore, who portrays Alicia Claypool in the movie, is the mother of Tatum O'Neal, the 1973 Academy Award winner for Best Supporting Actress. Another future star has a tie to the film, Tom Petty. Location shots are made near the eleven-year-old's home. Fourteen years later, Petty goes on to form the rock and roll group Tom Petty and the Heartbreakers.

quote of the day

"If people just knew me. I get sick and feel bad and I get depressed, you know, just like everybody else from time to time."

—Elvis Presley

MAD FOR ELVIS

Mad Magazine once predicted that the most popular names for the future would be Elvis and Frankenstein.

12 April

(1961) On the Hollywood social scene, it is reported that Elvis is dating seventeen-year-old Tuesday Weld, his costar in *Wild in the Country*. While dating Miss Weld, Elvis is introduced to aspiring Louisiana blues singer Lance LeGault. LeGault invites Elvis to come to a club where he is playing and Elvis surprises him by showing up that evening. LeGault quickly becomes a member of Elvis's inner circle and eventually works as Elvis's double in several films including 1963's *Kissin' Cousins* where LeGault appears as "the other Elvis" in scenes requiring another actor for Elvis's dual role.

quote of the day

"For the teenagers, he's a whiz. For the average Vegas spender, he's a fizz."

—Variety, *in reviewing Elvis's first Las Vegas appearance*

GET YER FEET OUTTA MY SOUP!

Elvis concerts in Las Vegas were not performed in a traditional theater or arena environment where people sat in assigned rows, but rather allowed the audience to sit at tables eating dinner and enjoying drinks. Consequently, over-enthused female fans would climb over the tables, stepping in meals and knocking over glasses of wine, to get to Elvis. Viva Las Vegas!

History

13 April

(1963) *Billboard*, in reviewing the album *It Happened at the World's Fair,* said it ""should be a blockbuster." All ten songs from the movie appear on the soundtrack album. *It Happened at the World's Fair* reaches number 4 on *Billboard's* top LPs chart, staying on the chart for 26 weeks. On the stereo LPs chart, it has a seventeen-week stay, peaking at 15. The film *It Happened at the World's Fair,* which includes scenes shot at the Seattle World's Fair, reaches a ranking of 55 on *Variety*'s list of top-grossing films for 1963, grossing $2.25 million for the year.

quote of the day

"It was getting harder and harder singing to the camera all day long. Let's face it, when you have ten different songs for each movie, they can't all be good. Eventually, I got tired of singing to turtles and guys I'd just beaten up."

—Elvis Presley

ELVIS ACROSS AMERICA!

Q: Elvis performed in all but nine of the United States: Alaska, Idaho, Montana, Wyoming, North Dakota, Delaware, New Jersey, New Hampshire, and Vermont. In what state did he play the most towns?

A: Texas

Today in

14 April

(1956) Elvis is in Amarillo, Texas, for two shows at the city's Municipal Auditorium. Shortly after midnight, Elvis and the band charter a twin-engine plane to fly from Amarillo to Nashville for a recording session. En route, the pilot loses his way and the plane becomes low on fuel. The pilot makes an emergency stop at the airstrip in El Dorado, Arkansas, for more gas. On leaving, their takeoff is almost a disaster because the pilot forgets to switch the plane's fuel system over from the empty tank to the full one. Afterward, Elvis displays a fear of flying for many years, traveling only by train or motor home as part of a promise he makes to his mother. In fact, while he often takes the train on long trips, as most Americans do in the '50s, later, in the 1960s, he will prefer to travel by motor home as a way of escaping the boredom of being cooped up on a train.

quote of the day

"Elvis is the greatest blues singer in the world today."

—Joe Cocker

PLAY ME, BABY, PLAY ME

Q: In the 1950s, Bob Smith, a disc jockey from radio station XERF in Mexico, played Elvis records frequently on his show. In Las Vegas in 1969, Elvis talked about his memories of listening to Smith, and then introduced him from the audience. When Elvis died in 1977, Bob Smith proclaimed, "Two thousand years from now they'll still be hearing about Elvis Presley." Do you know the name of Bob Smith's on-air persona?

A: Wolfman Jack

History

15 April

(1965) During this week, *Girl Happy*, Elvis's seventeenth film, opens at five hundred theaters and drive-ins nationwide, breaking box-office records in many locations. Over the Easter weekend, the film grosses $178,500 in Detroit. In Los Angeles, the movie is shown simultaneously in fifty-eight theaters. The following year, *Variety* reported the movie brought in $3.65 million during its first ten days of release. In reviewing *Girl Happy* the *Hollywood Reporter* said the film "should do the customary brisk Presley business." *The Motion Picture Daily* agreed, "With a product like this, Presley's status…can't go anyway but up…he seems to enjoy it as much as his audiences will." *Variety* added: "…another winner…the type of pleasant fare which Presley's fans have come to expect."

quote of the day

"We shot Kissin' Cousins *in seventeen days, and I think that was the turning point in Presley films. Up until then, certain standards were maintained, but that was when we noticed that there was no rehearsal for all the numbers."*

—Lance LeGault, an actor in several Elvis films

SHORT ON FANS

Tom Parker didn't believe in spending money on top-rate opening acts, so he used less popular acts who could endure the crowd's demand for Elvis during their whole performance. Once in Chicago, Parker regressed to his barking days and hired some dwarves at a local carnival to appear on-stage as the Elvis Presley Midget Fan Club.

Today in

16 April

(1955) In an effort to get Elvis exposure in the large Texas entertainment market, manager Bob Neal arranges four appearances on *The Big "D" Jamboree* show, a Dallas–based live Saturday-night show that, like *Louisiana Hayride* and the *Grand Ole Opry*, broadcasts over a prominent local radio station with a strong signal. Elvis tops the bill that includes rising country star Sonny James, veteran *Hayride* performer Hank Locklin, Charlene Arthur and many others. Around this time Elvis's repertoire of songs includes "That's Alright," "I Don't Care if the Sun Don't Shine," "Tweedle Dee," and "Blue Moon of Kentucky." Local newspapers report that during Elvis's performances "many of the young women swooned with his every appearance on stage." Conversely some men in the audience are quoted as saying: "I'd better not see any girlfriend of mine going up after an autograph from that singer."

quote of the day

"It was like an earthquake in my neighborhood. How can a person possess that kind of power that it even comes off the TV and grabs me in this ghetto neighborhood?"

—Bobby Womack

JACKIE WILSON SAID

Singer Jackie Wilson reputedly taught Elvis the secret of his profuse sweating on stage, which women apparently loved. Wilson said to take salt tablets and drink a lot of water. Elvis took up the process as a quick, and unhealthy, way to lose weight.

History

17 April

(1971) Elvis orders the first of the famed "TCB" ("Takin' Care of Business") necklaces as gifts for his close friends and associates. The insignia displays the three letters across the top with a diamond-studded lightning bolt descending from the "C." The slogan originated in a December 20, 1968, NBC-TV special, *T.C.B.-Taking Care of Business,* featuring Motown recording artists the Supremes and the Temptations. The necklaces were designed and will be manufactured by Schwartz & Arbitzer Jewelers in Beverly Hills, California. The "TCB" ring that Elvis wears was designed by Lowell G. Hayes and Sons in Memphis. Later in the year, members of Elvis's band and the Imperials and Sweet Inspirations are seen wearing the necklaces during performances in Las Vegas.

quote of the day

"I lose myself in my singing. Maybe it's my early training singing gospel hymns. I'm limp as a rag, worn out, when the show's over."

—Elvis Presley

BATHROOM READING

When Elvis died several books were found lying near his body. They included *The Scientific Search for the Face of Jesus,* about the Turin shroud mystery, and *Sex and Psychic Energy.*

18 April — Today in

(1972) Elvis travels to Albuquerque, New Mexico, where early the next day he is made an honorary "Colonel, Aide de Camp" to Governor Bruce King of New Mexico. Later the same day Elvis appears at Albuquerque's Tingley Coliseum for the final appearance on this particular tour. During intermission in the show, Elvis meets with Denise Sanchez, age eight, in a small trailer outside the coliseum. She is terminally ill, suffering from cancer. Elvis dedicates "You Gave Me a Mountain" to Denise during the concert. Elvis flies back to Memphis following the show.

quote of the day

"God Blessed America. He Gave Us Elvis!"

—motto for Denver's "Mile High Elvis Fan Club"

A KISS IS STILL A KISS

In the 1950s, a fan took his small daughter to meet Elvis at his Audubon Drive home. Elvis kissed the girl on the cheek, where she had a large birthmark. From then on, if others teased her about it, she'd simply say, "That's where Elvis kissed me."

19 April

(1916) Vernon Elvis Presley is born in Fulton, Mississippi. When Vernon turned seventeen years-old, he married twenty-one-year-old Gladys Love Smith. In 1935 the couple became parents to twin boys Elvis Aaron and Jesse Garon. Jesse was stillborn, leaving Elvis as the family's only child. Poorly educated (an eighth grade drop-out), Vernon took on menial jobs such as farmer, truck driver, and painter. In 1938 and 1939 Vernon spent nine months in the Parchman Penitentiary for forgery. In 1948, Vernon moved his family from Tupelo, Mississippi, to Memphis, Tennessee, where he found work with the United Paint Company. After Gladys's death in 1958, Vernon devoted himself to Elvis's flourishing career. In 1960, Vernon married Davada (Dee) Stanley, becoming the stepfather of her three sons. Vernon and Dee divorced in 1977. At the time of Elvis's death in 1977, he was paying his father $75,000 a year as his business manager, a job that seemed over Vernon's head as evidenced in later financial documents.

quote of the day

"It's American."

—*Elvis Presley, responding to a question about his ancestry*

"SHOTGUN SHACK"

Vernon built the two-room house where Elvis was born on Old Saltillo Road in Tupelo, Mississippi. The house was described as a "shotgun shack," meaning if you fired a shotgun from the front door through to the back, you'd hit every room in the house.

Today in

20 April

(1964) The *Las Vegas Desert News and Telegram* prints an article entitled "Elvis Helps in Success of Burton–O'Toole Movie." The piece centers on an interview with Hollywood producer Hal Wallis and suggests the profits from Elvis Presley movies enables Wallis to finance more "classy" films like *Becket*, starring Richard Burton and Peter O'Toole. "In order to do the artistic pictures," Wallis is quoted as saying, "it is necessary to make the commercially successful Presley pictures. But that doesn't mean a Presley picture can't have quality too." Elvis's ego is deeply injured by the remarks and he vaguely mentions them in private discussions about his film career for the rest of his life.

quote of the day

"I prefer to think of them as members of a little country club I run. Most of them are my friends from back home, they're not my bodyguards. One is my accountant, another my travel consultant. I need a valet, a security officer, and a wardrobe man with me nearly all the time."

—Elvis Presley, on members of the so-called "Memphis Mafia"

YOU WANT MUSTARD ON THAT?

In 1956, Memphis diners served special platters with hot dogs called "Hound Dogs" and hamburgers called "Hound Burgers." The platters sold for eighty-nine to ninety-eight cents.

History

21 April

(1976) Announcing "Elvis's first business venture outside the entertainment world," the *Memphis Press–Scimitar* runs a photograph of Elvis bodyguard and friend Joe Esposito, Dr. Nick, and Elvis business associate and Graceland racquetball partner Mike McMahon breaking ground on the site of one of two proposed racquetball facilities to be built by Presley Center Courts, Inc. Contrary to the auspicious beginning, Elvis later withdraws from the racquetball agreement. He wants his name taken off the project, he tells his lawyers, because, contrary to his initial understanding, he now realizes he is expected to contribute a considerable amount of money to the project. As relevant as the legal red tape that ensues, Elvis is enraged with Joe Esposito and Dr. Nick for getting him involved in the venture in the first place. He threatens to fire Joe and tells Dr. Nick over the phone that he is going to take another doctor on the next tour.

quote of the day

"I'd rather be angry than bored."
—Elvis Presley

IS THERE A DOCTOR IN THE HOUSE?

Elvis kept a copy of a medication catalog, *The Physician's Desk Reference,* by his bed. The superficial medical information was enough to convince him he knew what he was doing when it came to prescription drugs.

Today in

22 April

(1956) *Billboard* magazine reports Elvis's record sales are bringing in $75,000 a day in retail record shops across the country. In Canada, Elvis records are responsible for the first eight singles of RCA Victor's top ten best-sellers. Back in the United States, Elvis LPs and EPs are selling at a rate of 8,000 copies a day, while the number of Elvis singles selling in a day increases to 50,000. These numbers account for an astounding 50 percent of RCA Victor's total pop record business. Not surprisingly, *Billboard* ranks "Heartbreak Hotel" as number one in sales for the week.

quote of the day

"Colonel, you put a lump in my throat."
"Elvis, you put a lump in my wallet."

—Exchange between Elvis and his manager, Colonel Tom Parker

GET A NEW MANAGER, JACK

Early in Elvis's film career, Colonel Parker demanded $100,000 for Elvis to star in *Love Me Tender*. This was an absurd amount for the time, and the film's producer informed Parker that even Jack Lemmon didn't make that kind of money. The Colonel answered that maybe Lemmon should get a new manager.

―――― History ――――

23 April

(1956) Elvis opens a two-week engagement at the Venus Room in the New Frontier Hotel in Las Vegas. It is an older, "less hip" audience. Elvis later recalls, "After that first night I went outside and just walked around in the dark. It was awful.... I wasn't getting across to the audience." At the same time Elvis is thrilled with Las Vegas. He has the opportunity to meet such show business legends as Johnny Ray and Liberace, a favorite of his mother's. Liberace's flamboyant style seems to have an impact on the young performer as well. Elvis catches a number of other shows, including Freddie Bell and the Bellboys, whose performance of Big Mama Thornton's rhythm-and-blues hit "Hound Dog," impresses him as a show stopper.

quote of the day

"There are several unbelievable things about Elvis, but the most incredible is his staying power in a world where meteoric careers fade like shooting stars."

—Newsweek, *on Elvis's successful return to Las Vegas*

RUSSIAN ROULETTE?

Tom Parker's gambling habit became an addiction in the Las Vegas years. He moved into a luxury suite at the International Hotel, where he was given "high roller" privileges. He reputedly lost over $1,000,000 a year at the roulette tables.

24 April

(1957) Released earlier in the month, Elvis's gospel favorite, "Peace in the Valley" reaches number 39 on the record singles chart. With more than 400,000 copies of the four-track EP recording sold, the listening public's view of Elvis as an entertainer is clearly showing him in a new light. Past criticisms of "just another rock 'n' roll rabble rouser" begin to fade as Elvis's spiritual side begins to emerge. Elvis continues to perform and record gospel music throughout his life and career, often identifying it as his favorite form of musical expression.

quote of the day

"The Lord can give ... and the Lord can take away. I might be herding sheep next year."

–Elvis Presley

THROUGH THE EYES OF THE MASTER

Elvis owned a copy of the book *Through the Eyes of the Masters: Meditations and Portraits* which he carried with him often. In his edition he inscribed in pen, "God loves you but he loves you best when you sing."

History

(1912) Gladys Love Smith is born to Robert Lee Smith and Doll Mansell Smith in Pontotoc County, Mississippi. After marriage to Vernon Presley in 1933, Gladys gave birth to Elvis Aaron Presley in 1935. Gladys worked as a sewing machine operator in Tupelo, and later in Memphis worked as a nurse's aide and a seamstress. Elvis and his mother were very close. Upon success, Elvis bought her cars and houses and maintained a close relationship with her until her death. Unfortunately, as Elvis gained fame, Gladys became more and more unhappy. She began drinking, usually vodka in her later years. She always had the feeling she didn't fit into Elvis's new world. A country woman, Gladys enjoyed the simple things she was used to, like raising chickens, which she did at Graceland. Gladys Presley died at age 46 of a heart attack brought on by acute hepatitis.

25
April

quote of the day

"My mother, I suppose since I was an only child, we might have been a little closer, I mean everyone loves their mother, but I was an only child and mother was always right with me all my life. It wasn't only like losing a mother, it was like losing a friend, a companion, someone to talk to."

–Elvis Presley

DIFFICULT LABOR

Due to the hardship of labor, Gladys Presley suffered constant hemorrhaging after the birth of her sons. At the urging of her friend Mertice Finely she went to North Mississippi Medical Center for treatment. She remained in the hospital for two weeks.

Today in

26 April

(1970) *Let's Be Friends,* the first of the "Camden budget" releases, is put into distribution. Camden Records is a subsidiary of RCA Victor named after the RCA record-pressing plant in Camden, New Jersey, that makes records at budget-friendly prices. The Colonel agreed to the Camden contracts in December 1969, and his faith in the free-market system and buying public are not disappointed. *Let's Be Friends* consists mostly of previously unreleased movie and studio cuts. The record does not achieve a position on the charts because of its cost–album charts are based on dollar volume, not sales figures.

quote of the day

"Elvis is my religion. But for him, I'd be selling encyclopedias right now."

–Bruce Springsteen

ELVIS LA PELVIS

South America recently got its first Elvis store, the Elvis Shop Argentina in Buenos Aires. Argentinean fans can purchase a 1950s compilation album titled *Elvis La Pelvis.*

History

27 April

(1960) Elvis begins his first recording session at RCA Victor's new studios in Hollywood. Previously, all of his Hollywood recording sessions were at Radio Recorders. All of the songs are scheduled for the film *G.I. Blues*. The session proves to be a long one, with only seven of the fifteen tunes attempted deemed worthy of release. Declared worthy of going to print are: "Didja Ever," "Doin' the Best I Can," "G.I. Blues," "Tonight Is So Right for Love," "What's She Really Like," a new version of "Blue Suede Shoes," and "Wooden Heart." Of the other eight songs that are started but need to be redone, only "Whistling Blues" is never tried again. The other incomplete songs are "Shoppin' Around," a different version of "Tonight Is So Right for Love," "Frankfort Special," a second version of "Wooden Heart," fast and slow versions of "Big Boots," and "Pocket Full of Rainbows." The unusual number of unfinished songs are likely the result of this being Elvis's first time recording in RCA's new studio.

quote of the day

"He epitomized America, and for that we shall be eternally grateful. There will never be anyone else like him. Let's all rejoice in his music."

—Ronald Reagan

CRAZY FOR ELVIS

In 1956, a doctor at the Iowa Mental Health Institute claimed Elvis's music actually soothed the mental patients in his hospital.

Today in

28 April

(1976) Today finds Elvis performing at the Summit in Houston, Texas. *Houston Post* reporter Bob Claypool writes a review the following day that sends a shockwave through Colonel Parker. Claypool's column reads: "Elvis Presley has been breaking hearts for more than twenty years now, and Saturday afternoon in the Summit–in a completely new and unexpected way–he broke mine." He describes Elvis's performance as, "a depressingly incoherent, amateurish mess served up by a bloated, stumbling, and mumbling figure who didn't act like 'The King' of anything, least of all rock 'n' roll." Parker is mortified when he realizes the off-duty Houston police officers, who augment the security force, are talking about it too. The Colonel's attempt at a "quick fix" is to call for the return of the recently fired Dr. Nick. Dr. Nick returns despite still smarting from Elvis's blame for the failed racquetball facility ordeal for which he was terminated.

quote of the day

"Since his return to live performing, Elvis has apparently lost interest. He's not just a little out of shape, not just a bit chubbier than usual, the living legend is fat and ludicrously aping his former self."

—The Hollywood Reporter

BEGINNING OF THE END

In 1973, Elvis was treated by a California doctor for a strained back. The doctor gave him multiple injections of Demerol. By the time Elvis returned to Memphis, he was physically addicted to Demerol. By the end, he would be injecting it into himself between his toes.

History

(1977) A story breaks in the *Nashville Banner* that Colonel Tom Parker is in the process of selling Elvis's contract. "Authoritative sources" in Los Angeles, Memphis, and Nashville are cited. The reason given is mounting gambling debts incurred by the Colonel. The Colonel's response says otherwise: "I'm here," he says, "I'm working with Elvis, I'm in good health, and I don't have any debts, at least none I can't pay." Suspicion and conjecture surface surmising the early leak of the Colonel's plan had as much to do with the lack of follow-through as any change-of-heart on the Colonel's part.

29 April

quote of the day

"That'll be just fine for me, but how much are you going to give the boy?"

—*Colonel Tom Parker's response to a TV executive's offer of $50,000 for a single Elvis television appearance*

GOOD WORK IF YOU CAN GET IT

Q: As a side earner, Colonel Tom Parker insisted on getting a credit in all of Elvis's films—as an "advisor," "consultant," or "technical director"—and an accompanying salary. What did these positions require him to do?

A: Absolutely nothing

Today in

30 April

(1964) Hairdresser Larry Gellar arrives at Elvis's Hollywood Perugia Way home as a replacement for regular hairdresser Sal Orifice. During an ensuing conversation, Gellar speaks of his dedication to spiritual studies. Elvis responds that he too has a long-standing fascination with the subject. "What you're talking about," Elvis tells Gellar, "is what I think about all the time.... I've always known that there had to be a purpose for my life. I mean, there's got to be a reason...why I was chosen to be Elvis Presley." At conversation's end, Elvis convinces Gellar to quit his job and go to work for him. Elvis also asks Gellar to bring some of the books they were talking about to the recording studio the next day. This marks the beginning of one of Elvis's most significant long-term relationships outside his immediate circle of Memphis and show-business acquaintances.

quote of the day

"No, Jesus Christ is King!"

—Elvis Presley, *responding to fans holding a sign that read "Elvis, You're the King" at a concert at Notre Dame University*

BROTHER ELVIS

Once, in 1965, while Elvis was driving through the desert, he said he saw a cloud formation first resembling the face of Joseph Stalin, then that of Jesus Christ. Elvis told Larry Gellar the sight gave him a feeling of serenity and that he wanted to become a monk. The fact that he had been awake for two days at the time may or may not have had something to do with it.

May

1 May

(1967) Today is Elvis's and Priscilla's wedding day! At 3:30 AM, Elvis and Priscilla obtain a marriage license from the Clark County, Nevada, clerk's office for fifteen dollars. From there, a limousine takes the couple to a Las Vegas hotel where they walk through the lobby and out the back door to a second limousine waiting to take them to the Aladdin. At 5:30 AM, guests who had arrived in Las Vegas the previous evening are awakened and told to come to the lobby of the Aladdin. Once there, they are sequestered in a private suite. At 9:41 AM, in a second floor private suite belonging to Aladdin Hotel owner Milton Prell, Elvis and Priscilla are married in an eight-minute, double-ring ceremony performed by Judge David Zenoff, a member of the Nevada Supreme Court. Joe Esposito and Marty Lacker are best men.

quote of the day

"Elvis, yesterday I realized how much I love you, so I broke off my engagement."

—graffiti on the walls of Graceland

OH BABY!

Almost immediately after marrying Elvis, Priscilla became pregnant. By eating one meal a day and snacking on hard-boiled eggs, Priscilla gained only a few pounds during her pregnancy and never needed maternity clothes. Pricilla's baby shower was organized by Nancy Sinatra.

History

2 May

(1960) Elvis is at Paramount Studios in Hollywood to begin production of his fifth movie, *G.I. Blues*. All of Elvis's scenes are shot on the Paramount lot, the outside shots of Germany having been filmed in 1959 without Elvis's participation. Elvis's costar in *G.I. Blues* is South African actress Juliet Prowse. She and Elvis date while working on the film and continue for a short time afterward. Occasionally they can be seen at Hollywood nightclubs like the Cloister, where Elvis and Juliet attend a Bobby Darin show. Miss Prowse is currently considered to be Frank Sinatra's girlfriend. This causes some awkward moments when Sinatra visits the set. While Elvis is sneaking dates with Juliet Prowse, he's also dating another *G.I. Blues* costar, Judy Rawlins. Miss Rawlins later marries singer Vic Damone. Yet another date is local teenager Sandra Ferra. Miss Ferra later marries game-show host Wink Martindale who, ironically, works at a local radio station in Memphis at the time.

quote of the day

"I really don't like parties.... I don't like loud noise, and I don't smoke or drink."

—Elvis Presley, 1959, on why he didn't go to Hollywood parties

DON'T DRINK, DON'T SMOKE, WHAT DO YA DO?

Q: Elvis didn't like alcohol much, and he hated beer. When he did drink, what was his favorite cocktail?

A: Margaritas

Today in

3 May

(1969) Elvis's recording of "In The Ghetto" begins climbing *Billboard*'s "Hot 100" at number 79. It remains on the charts for thirteen weeks, finally topping out at number three. This is Elvis's first Top 10 single since "Crying in the Chapel" in the spring of 1965. "In The Ghetto" was written by Mac Davis and first offered to Bill Medley of the Righteous Brothers and then to Sammy Davis, Jr., neither of whom decided to record it. The full title of the song is "In The Ghetto (the Vicious Cycle)," but RCA sought permission to release it without the subtitle. "In The Ghetto" peaked at a disappointing number 60 on the country charts, but when Dolly Parton covers Elvis's recording later the same year, her version reaches number 50 on the country charts.

quote of the day

"I don't see how any type of music would have any bad influence on people. When it's only music... I mean how would rock 'n' roll music make people rebel against their parents?"

—*Elvis Presley*

BROTHER MELVIN

In 1956, Elvis appeared on *The Milton Berle Show*. The show was broadcast from the deck of the aircraft carrier USS Hancock, in port in San Diego. Elvis was paid $3000 for the appearance, and endured a comedy skit with Berle dressed up as Elvis's hillbilly brother, Melvin.

History

4 May

(1973) Elvis opens a seventeen-day engagement at the High-Sierra Theater in Del Webb's Sahara Tahoe Hotel in Stateline, Nevada. Linda Thompson is accompanying Elvis on this trip. The Sahara Tahoe overlooks the showroom for some of the performances, and there are reports of near riots as hundreds of fans who made advance reservations are not admitted to the show. Despite the enthusiastic sell-out crowds, *Variety* finds Elvis's performances disappointing, reporting Elvis is "some thirty pounds overweight, puffy, white-faced, and blinking against the light. His voice is weak, delivery is flabby."

quote of the day

"You can...love someone and be wrong for them."

–Elvis Presley

BEAUTY QUEEN BLUES

Elvis met the then-Miss Tennessee Linda Thompson in 1972 when friend George Klein invited her to one of Elvis's private movie screenings in Memphis. The two became a couple and, for a year, Linda stayed with Elvis 24/7. In 1976, unable to cope, Linda left Elvis even though she loved him and had cared for him during the worst of times.

Today in

5 May

(1956) The album *Elvis Presley* is number one on *Billboard*'s LP chart, and stays at number one for the next ten weeks. The single "Heartbreak Hotel" also reaches number one on the "Top 100," where it stays for six weeks. Among other successes, *Billboard* notes: Elvis is voted the top new and favorite c&w artist in a poll conducted as part of *Billboard*'s annual review of the Music Operators of America (jukebox owners). *Billboard* reports in an article titled "E.P. Is V.I.P. For Victor" that "I Want You, I Need You, I Love You" has the largest advance order of any RCA Victor release. Elvis is also the first RCA Victor artist to have two million-sellers in a row. By now, sales of "Heartbreak Hotel" have topped 1,350,000, and the LP *Elvis Presley* is now the best-selling album in RCA's history.

quote of the day

"I don't know how long it will last. When it's gone I'll switch to something else. I would like to sing ballads the way Eddie Fisher does and the way Perry Como does. But the way I'm singing now is what makes the money. Would you change if you were me?"

—*Elvis Presley*

SING IT, NIPPER

Q: At a concert in Los Angeles, Elvis made some suggestive overtures toward a toy version of RCA's Nipper dog. The audience went into a frenzy, leading the theater manager, in an attempt to quiet the crowd, to say what immortal statement?

A: "Elvis has left the building."

History

(1974) News sources throughout the world reported to disappointed fans that Elvis was turning down offers to perform anywhere outside the United States. This time, it's mentioned that Elvis refused $500,000 to perform in Japan and a similar amount in Singapore. The official explanation is that Elvis is completely booked through 1976, but fans know better as all previous concerts are announced only six weeks, or less, in advance.

6 May

quote of the day

"He will read it and he will be hopping mad at us because he will know that every word is the truth, but maybe, just maybe, it will do him some good."

—Sonny West on how he thought Elvis would react to reading his book, Elvis: What Happened?

ELVIS'S LAST STAND

In 1996, the City of Indianapolis decided to demolish the local concert venue, Market Square Arena, with the proposal to build a more modern facility. The city was deluged with emotional protests as Market Square Arena was the location of Elvis's final live concert. One fan claimed it was equal to tearing down Graceland. But the city prevailed, and the location became history.

Today in

7 May

(1966) Soul artist James Brown is appearing at the Memphis Coliseum and, after getting Elvis's number from local DJ and Elvis high school friend George Klein, tries to reach Elvis by telephone during the day. Every time Brown calls, however, he's told, no doubt truthfully, that Elvis is asleep. George Klein finally introduces James Brown and Elvis later at a Jackie Wilson concert in Los Angeles. After the usual exchange of compliments, Brown says, "Man, Elvis, you sure do sleep a lot." According to Klein, "Elvis almost fell on the floor laughing. He said, 'Aw, James, you know how it is, being a night person...' And James said, 'I know, brother,' and slapped Elvis's hand."

quote of the day

"Elvis was a God-given, there's no other explanation. A Messiah comes around every few thousand years, and Elvis was it this time."
—Little Richard

A COOL MIL

Elvis banked at the National Bank of Commerce in Memphis. He liked to have a balance of at least $1,000,000 in his account at all times. Beyond that, he took no interest in his finances whatsoever.

History

(1957) Elvis is in Hollywood doing pre-production work on *Jailhouse Rock,* at MGM Studios. Meanwhile, back in Memphis, the Presleys are busy moving into Graceland. Elvis receives the master bedroom upstairs. Vernon and Gladys take the second upstairs bedroom. On the second floor the family also have a third bedroom that is used as an office, two large bathrooms, two large closets, and a dressing room off Elvis's bathroom. Grandma Minnie also moves into Graceland, taking a first-floor apartment behind the living room, with an entrance off the main hallway.

8 May

quote of the day

"Please read and observe. No loafing in office. Strictly for employees only! If you have business here, please take care of it and leave. Vernon Presley."

—Statement on wooden sign posted on the door of Vernon Presley's office at Graceland

GREYSLUN HISTORY

Graceland was built in 1939 in the Southern colonial style by Dr. and Mrs. Thomas D. Moore. The house is named after Mrs. Moore's great-aunt Grace. The rooms were designed for musical enjoyment in terms of space and acoustics. This was for the benefit of the Moore's daughter Ruth Marie, who later joined the Memphis Symphony Orchestra. Graceland sits in fourteen acres of hilly woodland south of Memphis. Graceland opened to the public in 1982 and attracted over half a million visitors its first year. Visitors now stand at around 650,000 annually. It's the second most visited home in the U.S., after the White House.

Today in

9 May

(1972) Elvis is in New York for his first performance there since the 1956 and 1957 appearances on the Dorsey Brothers, Steve Allen, and Ed Sullivan television shows. It has been suggested the absence of New York City appearances were part of Colonel Parker's plan to protect Elvis from the intense condescending media scrutiny Elvis received there at the beginning of his career. The Colonel now believes it is time for an older, wiser Elvis to win over that same media. Elvis, poised and confident, proves himself up to the task at an early press conference. Asked about his image as a shy, humble country boy, Elvis answers, "I don't know what makes them say that," then stands to show reporters the jeweled International Hotel gold belt under his jacket.

quote of the day

"I just wanted to show you all this because you paid for it."

—*Elvis Presley, showing his expensive jewelry to a concert audience*

RAVE REVIEWS!

Reviews of Elvis's record-breaking sell-out Madison Square Garden concerts proved the events were career highlights. The *New York Times* said when Elvis came on-stage, "he looked like a prince from another planet." *Billboard* said, "Elvis has transcended the exasperating constrictions of time and place."

History

(1977) It is around this time that *The Sun*, a supermarket tabloid, blasts the headline: "Presley is Fat, Forty and Fading." The accompanying article is the first public disclosure that Elvis is "heavy into pills." The article is based on interviews with Elvis's former bodyguards Red and Sonny West and Dave Hebler. The three have just finished dictating a book-length exposé of their years with Elvis to Steve Dunleavy, a gossip columnist for *The Sun*.

quote of the day

"Elvis had the arteries of an eighty-year-old man. His body was just worn out, and his arteries and veins were terribly corroded."

—A spokesman at Memphis Baptist Memorial Hospital where Elvis was taken the day he died

WAY TOO MUCH

Dr. Nick prescribed for Elvis a total of 4,097 pills in 1975, 6,111 pills in 1976, and 8,805 pills up until August 1977. This didn't include drugs Elvis received from other doctors. The lab results from Elvis's autopsy reported he had fourteen different drugs in his system when he died, leaving no doubt the cause of death was poly-pharmacy, or having too many drugs in the system at once.

Today in

11 May

(1973) After tonight's midnight show, Elvis gives a special 3:00 AM Mother's Day performance at the Sahara Tahoe Hotel. Elvis donates his check for the concert to the Barton Memorial Hospital at Lake Tahoe in Gladys Presley's name as a tribute to his late mother. The auxiliary of Barton Memorial Hospital is running the souvenir stand at the hotel throughout this seventeen-day engagement. All of the merchandise for sale is donated by Elvis and Colonel Parker, with all the proceeds going to the hospital's cardiac and intensive care wing.

quote of the day

"My mother always taught me to behave, to have good manners, to help people, not harm them, to work hard and never give up, and to make it on my own."

—Elvis Presley

MOVIN' ON UP

Q: When Elvis signed his contract with RCA Victor, he was living at a Memphis address that seems fitting and almost prophetic of his future. What was the Presley family address in 1955 when Elvis signed?

A: 1414 Getwell Road

History

(1960) From 9:30 to 10:30 PM EST on ABC, Elvis makes his first television appearance since his discharge from the army on Frank Sinatra's Timex TV Special titled *Welcome Home, Elvis*. The duo commands 41.5 percent of the television viewing audience. Elvis was paid $125,000 for his six-minute appearance. The audience consists of seven hundred fans (400 of the Elvis Presley fan-club members) crowded into the ballroom for the taping. Elvis sings "Fame and Fortune" and "Stuck on You." In a duet with Sinatra, Elvis sings "Witchcraft" (Sinatra's hit), and Sinatra sings "Love Me Tender." To start the show, the entire cast, including Elvis, sings "It's Nice to Go Traveling."

12 May

quotes of the day

"His kind of music is deplorable, a rancid smelling aphrodisiac...it fosters almost totally negative and destructive reactions in young people."

—Frank Sinatra (early on)

"I'm just a singer, Elvis was the embodiment of the whole American culture."

—Frank Sinatra (sometime later)

"There have been many accolades uttered about Elvis's talent and performances through the years, all of which I agree with wholeheartedly. I shall miss him dearly as a friend. He was a warm, considerate and generous man."

—Frank Sinatra (at the end)

HAVE YOU SEEN ME LATELY?

Q: What U.S. city is the Elvis-sighting capitol of the world?

A: Kalamazoo, Michigan

13 May

(1972) In an attempt to patch up their deteriorating marriage, Elvis and Priscilla vacation in Hawaii. The couple, along with Lisa Marie and twelve of Elvis's friends, stay at the Rainbow Towers, part of the Hilton Hawaiian Village, the same hotel Elvis will return to next year for production of the *Elvis: Aloha From Hawaii* television special. While in Honolulu, Elvis attends a karate demonstration. He also reportedly purchases $5,000 worth of opals from one of the hotel shops.

quote of the day

"We are the best of friends and always have been. Our divorce came about not because of another man, but because of circumstances involving my career, nothing else, regardless of what you have read or have been led to believe. I don't think it was fair on Priscilla, with me gone so often and traveling so much."

—Elvis Presley

TRUANT, MAN!

In 1956, the *Tupelo Daily Journal* ran a story entitled: "Judge Upholds School's Right To Expel Boy For Wearing Elvis Presley Haircut: Mother May Appeal."

History

14 May

(1957) In a letter to Elvis, Colonel Parker writes that he has "been bombarded, befuddled, befogged, bewildered, and snowed under" with requests for Elvis to appear on RCA-sponsored NBC television specials. "They have told me everything under the sun how good this will be for you for exposure [and have] come up with pretty good offers several times, but I turned them all down with respect to our motion picture reasons I know are best for us. I told them that our next TV show for any sponsor we do would be $50,000, as I want to do one or two TV shows this year, and with a set-up like we would blast the whole country with.... They say we will never get it from no one. Well, maybe we won't [but] at least you won't be overexposed like some of the top stars that are now working for nothing as they are worn out on TV." The Colonel explains he is writing so that Elvis will "know what is going on. Please indicate by marking yess [sic] if you think you should work cheaper, or nuts if you think I should keep snowing for the $50,000. I will guide myself either way you want to go."

quote of the day

"No matter what you do, you can not, not, not, not mess up for Elvis, or change anything, because you'll change history. Big time."

—Holograph Al to Sam (as Elvis) in the TV show Quantum Leap

FOR LOVE AND MONEY, MOSTLY MONEY

Colonel Parker once admitted he didn't read the script for any of Elvis's movies. His formula was simple—three films a year, with plenty of singing. "All we want is songs for an album," he added.

15 May

(1956) Elvis is headlining in his hometown at Memphis's Ellis Auditorium. He is billed over Hank Snow and the Jordanaires for Bob Neal's Cotton Pickin' Jamboree, which is part of Memphis's twenty-second annual Cotton Festival. Prior to the performance, then-manager Bob Neal announces Elvis will be playing a charity benefit show in Memphis on July 4. The announcement brings "a wild roar of approval" and "Elvis will have plenty of company" at the show according to the *Memphis Press-Scimitar*. The audience gives Elvis an equally enthusiastic welcome as he appears on-stage dressed in black pants, a white shirt, and a Kelly-green jacket. Elvis sings "Heartbreak Hotel," then introduces Little Richard's "Long Tall Sally" as a beautiful song "recorded by a friend of mine....I never met him, but here's the song." He closes with the soon-to-be famous, "Hound Dog."

quote of the day

"I'm not kidding myself—my voice alone is just an ordinary voice. What people come to see is how I use it."

— *Elvis Presley*

HANGING AT THE GREEN OWL

Growing up in Memphis, Elvis sometimes went to a neighborhood bar called the Green Owl, a beer joint with a primarily black clientele. He enjoyed the music and tried to learn from the musicians. He particularly liked the musician whose instrument was constructed from a bucket, a piece of rope, and a broom handle.

―――― History ――――

16
May

(1954) Two years before becoming a headliner at the event, Elvis is in the audience at the annual Cotton Festival in Memphis. One of the featured acts is Eddy Arnold, who has coincidentally been previously managed by Colonel Tom Parker. At Arnold's performance at the Cotton Festival, he is backed by the Jordanaires, who Elvis knows from prior gospel shows. Elvis manages to make his way backstage to meet the Jordanaires and reportedly tells them, "If I ever cut a record, I want you guys singing background with me."

quote of the day

"Boy this is my favorite music. When I'm out there [on stage] I do what they want to hear. When I'm back here I can do what I want to do."

—Elvis Presley, referring to gospel music in 1954

BROKEN HEART ―――――――――――――

In the spring of 1954, Elvis went to audition as a singer at Memphis's Hi Hat Club. After hearing a couple of songs, bandleader Eddie Bond told Elvis he was better off as a truck driver. Elvis later told a friend, "That son of a bitch broke my heart."

Today in

17 May

(1957) Elvis is resting at the Beverly Wilshire Hotel after a brief hospital stay at Southern California's Cedar of Lebanon Hospital. Elvis had dislodged a cap from one of his teeth while filming the dance scene for *Jailhouse Rock*. The cap had become lodged in one of Elvis's lungs and required a doctor to remove it with a forceps. Elvis's three-hundred-pound friend, Lamar Fike, shows up at the Wilshire unannounced. A year earlier, the Presleys noticed Lamar hanging around their house on Audubon Drive in Memphis. Fike tells Elvis he was in Jacksonville, Florida, when he heard of his hospitalization. Without hesitation, Lamar drove directly to Hollywood. Once at Elvis's side, Lamar Fike never left, becoming the earliest person outside of Elvis's relatives and Memphis pals allowed into the inner circle. Fike remained with Elvis to the end.

quote of the day

"It was like the world went from black and white to Technicolor."

—Rolling Stone Keith Richards, on Elvis's music contribution to the world

PULP ELVIS

Film director Quentin Taratino occasionally makes Elvis references in his movies. In *Pulp Fiction*, Uma Thurman's character opines that "you're either an Elvis person or a Beatles person," and some of the film's fans are convinced that Marsellus's suitcase really contains Elvis's gold lame suit. Also, Buck, the degenerate nurse from *Kill Bill*, likes to wear Elvis sunglasses.

History

18 May

(1973) Elvis is nearing the end of a seventeen-day engagement at the Sahara Tahoe hotel when he is taken to a local hospital for chest x-rays. Fans are lined up at the High Sierra Theater when they are told that tonight's and the weekend shows will have to be canceled. Elvis flies home to Memphis, and the Colonel returns his $100,000 payment to the hotel. Considering the recent events in Tahoe, there is, for the first time, open discussion among family and friends about Elvis's prescription drug abuse. Prompted by their concerns, particularly those of Colonel Parker and Vernon Presley, a Los Angeles attorney is hired to determine who is providing Elvis with his seemingly unlimited supply of drugs. Over the next several months, an investigator determines there are three physicians and one dentist who seem to be the main suppliers. Attempts to talk to the doctors and interdict the drugs are unsuccessful, however, without Elvis's cooperation.

quote of the day

"When I got sick...I heard I was strung out on heroin...If I find the individual that has said that about me...I will pull your goddamn tongue out by the roots! Thank you very much!"

—Elvis Presley, from the stage of a live performance

THE LAST SONG

Q: What was Elvis's final single released just weeks prior to his death?

A: "Way Down"

Today in

19 May

(1965) Colonel Parker is actively and enthusiastically working to promote Elvis's eighteenth film, *Tickle Me*. The Colonel persuades RCA to purchase Elvis's gold Cadillac and ship it around the country as a kind of stand-in for the star himself at local *Tickle Me* premieres. The 1960 Cadillac limousine was customized for Elvis by North Hollywood's George Barris. Deemed the "Solid Gold Cadillac," it is equipped with two telephones, a complete entertainment console, a refreshment bar, and an electric shoe buffer, all gold-plated with a golden guitar insignia. The limo's exterior is finished in a white-gold Murano pearl with gold plated trim. The vehicle makes its way cross-country undoubtedly bringing out some fans, but the Colonel becomes increasingly concerned over what he sees as an inability to produce Elvis himself.

quote of the day

"Tell Elvis not to drive a Rolls Royce without a tie."

—Jerry Lee Lewis, to Colonel Parker upon Lewis's having seen Elvis driving around Beverly Hills

GRAND THEFT AUTO

Q: The first 1971 Pontiac Stutz Blackhawk to arrive in Los Angeles was earmarked for another famous buyer, but silver-tongued Elvis talked the dealer into selling it to him instead. What celebrity was left without the car?

A: Frank Sinatra

History

(1971) Elvis is in the middle of a week-long recording session at RCA Studios in Nashville. The sessions generally begin at 7:00 PM During the sessions, Elvis buddies Charlie Hodge and Joe Esposito play guitar on several tracks. This series of sessions is scheduled to produce a Christmas album, plus a few new singles for a future studio album. It is rumored Elvis is recording a cover of the Carpenter's popular Christmas song "Merry Christmas Darling," which, if he does, is never released. Elvis does record, however, his patently famous "Merry Christmas Baby" during the week. "Merry Christmas Baby" is also recorded as an extended studio jam for release on future albums in an edited version. There are a total of thirty songs recorded during this marathon session with overdubbing of background vocal from the Imperials and a violin section occurring later.

May

quote of the day

"I used to when I first started singing, but hardly anyone came to hear me. But when I latched onto rock 'n' roll I had it made."

–Elvis Presley, on why he went from singing ballads to rock 'n' roll

OPERA ELVIS

Elvis often stated he liked all kinds of music. This bears out the fact that he owned records by Italian singer Mario Lanza and the Metropolitan Opera.

Today in

21 May

(1971) In lieu of Elvis, who is in a recording session in Nashville, Vernon and Dee Presley attend the first annual Memphis Music Awards banquet at the Memphis Rivermont Holiday Inn. Elvis is nominated in ten categories and is voted winner of the "Founder's Award." "Suspicious Minds" also wins the "Outstanding Single Recorded In Memphis For 1970" award. Elvis's friend from Humes High School and "Memphis Mafia" member Marty Lacker is chairman of the board of Memphis Music and thus chairman of the event.

quote of the day

"I like the piano, though I guess I don't play it the way you're supposed to. I just hit whatever keys look good to me."

–Elvis Presley

HOLY GRACELAND!

A nearby church used the downstairs rooms of Graceland for meetings before the Presley's moved in. The same church later complained of the traffic problems brought on by their star-neighbor in residence.

---— History ———

May

(1968) During this week Elvis, Priscilla and Lisa Marie are vacationing in Hawaii at Honolulu's Ilikai Hotel. During the trip, Elvis takes his entourage to the Karate Tournament of Champions at the Honolulu International Center. The event is promoted by Ed Parker, who eventually becomes Elvis's body guard and personal karate instructor who Elvis will nickname "Kahuna" (Hawaiian for "High Priest"). Among those competing for the mainland against Hawaii is future movie star Chuck Norris. The tournament winner is one Mike Stone, karate's international grand champion since 1966. Afterward, Elvis and Priscilla meet Parker, Norris, and Stone. Mike Stone eventually becomes Pricilla's karate instructor and eventually good friend, lover, and live-in boyfriend. Reportedly, Elvis hated Stone so much he wouldn't even watch the ABC TV series *The Streets of San Francisco* because Karl Malden portrayed "Detective Mike Stone."

quote of the day

"And ye shall know the truth, and the truth will make you free."

—Holy Bible *John 8:32, favorite Elvis Bible Quote*

KANSAS CITY, HERE I COME

Q: What is the official term for someone who dresses up as Elvis but doesn't perform? Kansas City has an annual parade for such folk.

A: An Elvisoid

Today in

23 May

(1968) Today the Mexican newspaper *Ultimus Norticus* prepares to run a story reporting Elvis will marry Yvonne Lime in Acapulco sometime "next week." Ms. Lime is costar in *Loving You*. Elvis and Yvonne dated from time to time in Hollywood and she visited Graceland earlier in the year, even attending Easter church service with the Presley family. According to the newspaper's "source," "Elvis and Ms. Lime were to elope to Mexico, flying in the following Monday. The Associated Press picked up the story and published it in the United States. This story, like so many other rumors of nuptials for Elvis, was completely unfounded.

quote of the day

"My Daddy's got Presley's Used Car Lot out on Audubon Drive. I do have four Cadillacs. I haven't got any use for four, I just, ah, maybe someday I'll go broke and I can sell a couple of 'em."

–Elvis Presley

ZIGGY STARDUST HAS LEFT THE BUILDING—

At age eleven, David Bowie made his first live performance by imitating Elvis for some boy scouts in England. Years later, Bowie painted Elvis's "TCB" lightning bolt on his face for the cover of his *Aladdin Sane* album. Ziggy Stardust concerts often closed with the song "Rock 'n' Roll Suicide," for which Bowie changed into a sparkling jumpsuit before exiting the stage to the announcement, "David Bowie has left the building."

History

May 24

(1945) Priscilla Ann Wagner is born in Brooklyn, New York. Her father, James Wagner, is a navy pilot who, in October of this year, dies in an air crash while returning home on leave. In 1949, Priscilla's mother, Ann, will marry Joseph Paul Beaulieu, another air force officer. Lt. Beaulieu will adopt Priscilla and in the ensuing years the Beaulieus will be stationed at a number of air force stations. In 1959, now-Captain Beaulieu and his family are living at Wiesbaden Air Force base near Friedberg, Germany. At the same time army Private Elvis Presley is stationed nearby. Later that year, fourteen year-old Priscilla is introduced to Elvis at his Bad Nauheim home. By 1962, Priscilla moves to Graceland and finishes high school in Memphis. She and Elvis marry in 1967, they have their only child, Lisa Marie, nine months later. The couple will eventually divorce in 1973.

quote of the day

"I visited him night after night. We grew closer and closer. Our relationship remained chaste. He wanted his woman "pure," if indeed I was his woman."

—Priscilla Presley, on coming to know Elvis in Germany, from Elvis By The Presleys

EVERYTHING CHANGES

Elvis reportedly didn't make love to Priscilla for many months after their daughter's birth, and when he did, the passion seemed to be waning.

Today in

25 May

(1955) Today Elvis is just one of a list of performers at the third annual Jimmie Rodgers Memorial Celebration in Meridian, Mississippi. Rodgers, who was a Meridian native and is buried there, is considered one of the founding fathers of country music. During this two-day event, there are scheduled appearances by many country entertainers including Jimmie Davis, Slim Whitman, Ernest Tubb, Jimmy Newman, Jim Reeves, Johnny Horton, and even an appearance by ex-baseball all-star Dizzy Dean. Also on hand are two individuals representing companies who will play an important part in Elvis's business future, Charles Crumbacker of RCA Victor and Gerlun Landon of Hill & Range Publishers.

quote of the day

"Don't you move you big sonofabitch. I told the Colonel to stay off the stage!"

—Elvis's response to a stuffed gorilla that was thrown on-stage at a performance

THE X-FILES ON ELVIS

In the popular television series *The X-Files*, Agent Mulder refers to one of his closed-minded co-workers as "the type of person who thinks Elvis is dead." In one episode Mulder tells Scully he's taking vacation time to go on a spiritual "journey," leaving out the part about heading for Graceland.

History

(1973) Their relationship over, Pricilla has hired the law firm Tankell, Toll, and Leavitt who schedule a meeting with Vernon and Gregory Hookstratten, Elvis's lawyer. Vernon promises to supply Elvis's income tax returns for Priscilla's consideration. Days later, since Vernon has not fulfilled the promise, Priscilla files a motion in Santa Monica Superior Court to set aside the original agreement in which she was to receive a lump sum payment of $100,000, a few cars, and $1500 per month for spousal and child support. Instead, she now wants $20,000 a month in spousal support and $2500 a month in child support.

quote of the day

"Crazy world–hasn't been the same since Elvis and Priscilla broke up."

—Grandfather Huxtable in an episode of the popular TV series The Cosby Show

NO ASPIRIN NECESSARY

Reportedly Pricilla Presley believed that Elvis could cure her headaches by merely touching her temples.

—— Today in ——

27 May

(1966) Elvis is recording for the final day of a three-day session at RCA's Studio "B" in Nashville. This is Elvis's first non-movie session since January, 1964. The musicians and vocalists gather late each evening and stay until after daybreak. After a midday recess, they resume for the evening. During the session, "Run On" and "How Great Thou Art" are recorded for the *How Great Thou Art* album. Two songs are used as fillers for the *Spinout* soundtrack, "Down in the Alley" and "Tomorrow is a Long Time." Two non-religious songs are recorded to be released as singles, "Come What May" and "Fools Fall in Love." And tapes are made for "If the Lord Wasn't Walking By My Side" and "Where Could I Go But to the Lord."

quote of the day

"It more or less puts your mind at ease, it does mine."

—*Elvis on why he enjoys singing gospel songs after performances*

TECHNICALITIES

Elvis was Christian, but he wore the Hebrew symbol of life, the Chi, around his neck. He also changed his mother's headstone to contain a Holy Cross on one side and the Star of David on the other. When asked about the variety of symbols Elvis replied, "I don't want to miss out on heaven on a technicality."

History

(1955) Tonight Elvis appears for the second time on the "Big D Jamboree" radio show broadcast on Dallas station KRLD from the City Sportatorium. Other performers tonight include Onie Wheeler, Arlie Duff, and Texas Bill Strength. Elvis appears a total of four times on the "Big D," all of them this year. It is at the "Big D Jamboree" that Elvis's first manager, Bob Neal, met Colonel Tom Parker. Neal eventually loses management rights for Elvis because he "lacked the connections Colonel Parker could provide," but goes on to represent a host of other recording artists including Johnny Cash, Jerry Lee Lewis, Carl Perkins, Roy Orbison, Conway Twitty, Lynn Anderson, and others.

28 May

quote of the day

"In 1985 when it was Elvis's 50th birthday and Michael Jackson was at his 'peak,' a reporter wanted to put Elvis's popularity into perspective. She said, 'If Michael Jackson continues to sell 35,000,000 records a year, it would take him twenty-five years to equal Elvis's numbers. That is if Elvis doesn't sell another record until then."

—Julie Niachos, elviscoolist.com

BIG D JAMBOREE

Q: When Elvis was appearing on the "Big D Jamboree" radio show in Dallas, Texas, in 1955, one of the show's staff members was an up-and-coming rock 'n' roll artist in his own right and went on to become a legend. Can you name him?

A: Roy Orbison

Today in

29 May

(1977) Elvis is struggling with his live concert schedule. Today, during a performance in Baltimore, Maryland, at the city's Civic Center, Elvis walks off the stage for thirty minutes in the middle of the show while his back-up singers struggle but do their best to carry on with the show. A venue spokesman attributes Elvis's "murmuring, swearing, and unscheduled hiatus to the reported intestinal problems that had kayoed him" earlier in the tour. *Variety* is not so understanding, reporting, "...at the finale there was no ovation, and patrons exited shaking their heads and speculating what was wrong with him."

quote of the day

"I'm self-destructive. I recognize it, but there's not a lot I can do about it."

—Elvis's response to Linda Thompson when she asked him to cite his biggest character flaw

JUSTICE-NOT-SERVED?

In 1981, Dr. Nick went on trial for ten counts of over-prescribing medicines to patients, including Elvis Presley and Jerry Lee Lewis. Dr. Nick's defense was based on the assertion that he was doing what he had to do, both support addictions and try to get the dosage down. He was eventually cleared on all charges.

History

30 May

(1943) One of eight-year-old Elvis's favorite places to spend time is the WELO radio studio in Tupelo located on the second floor of the Black & White Store on Spring Street. WELO radio is Tupelo's first radio station and has the power to transmit signals all over north-east Mississippi. The station's most popular program is the *Saturday Jamboree,* which is broadcast live from the courthouse every Saturday afternoon. Elvis and his friends are regulars at the shows. On weekday afternoons, Elvis drops by the studio to hear programs put on by local entertainers, all of whom have a fifteen-minute show. The music varies from hillbilly to spiritual to pop. One of Elvis's favorites is Carvel Lee Ausborn, aka "Mississippi Slim." Slim and young Elvis become friends and Elvis enjoys listening to the entertainer's extensive record collection.

quote of the day

"Elvis had this charisma about him. I don't think anybody could ever put their finger on what he did or how he did it. You could just sit and talk to him for a few minutes and he would mesmerize you."

–D.J. Fontana, Elvis's original drummer

OUT OF THE MOUTHS OF BABES

Elvis's voice was high-pitched and off-key when he was young. Many of his friends and relatives stated that it hurt their ears to listen to him.

31 May

(1967) A second wedding reception is held at Graceland for a hundred and twenty-five of Elvis's and Priscilla's Memphis friends and relatives and the Graceland staff who could not attend the Las Vegas ceremony. The guests, most of whom are casually dressed, party around the patio, normally reserved for the race car set-up, overlooking the swimming pool. Music is provided by Elvis's jukebox and local accordionist Tony Brasso. Dinner, prepared by Monty's catering, is served in the trophy room. Decorations include a bridal arch made of carnations and a three-tiered wedding cake complete with bride and groom atop. Elvis and Priscilla wear their wedding attire for effect. The Presley's greet every guest, cut the cake, then have a dance to "Let Me Call You Sweetheart." Grandma Minnie is the esteemed guest of honor. After the reception, Elvis, Priscilla, and many of the guests head to the Memphian Theater for a showing of John Wayne in *The War Wagon,* costarring Ann-Margret.

quote of the day

"Take it off? Are you kidding? It took me two hours to get into it."

—Elvis's reply to audience members imploring him to "undress"

OATH FOR HIGH FIBER

While on a long plane trip in 1971, Elvis wrote himself a TCB oath. He resolved to sharpen his skills, achieve greater respect for others, and to seek "freedom from constipation."

June

Today in

1 June

(1938) Vernon Presley arrives at the Mississippi State Penitentiary at Parchman to begin serving his sentence for an earlier forgery conviction. Reportedly, Vernon and two other men altered a check to read "8" dollars as opposed to "3" dollars. Incarceration at Parchman is, indeed, filled with endless, backbreaking, dawn-to-dusk workdays in the prison cotton, corn, and sugarcane fields. Reportedly, guards use whips as a method of assuring productivity. Twice a month, Gladys and young Elvis make the five-hour bus ride a hundred miles from Tupelo to visit Vernon. Vernon is eventually granted early release upon a "petition of leniency from the citizens of Lee County and on a letter from Mr. O.S. Bean, the party on whom the checks were forged."

quote of the day

"I never took any singing lessons and the only practicing I ever did was on a broomstick before my dad gave me my first guitar."

–Elvis Presley

GOVERNMENT SERVICE

In 1940, Vernon Presley worked for the Works Progress Administration (WPA), which was part of Franklin D. Roosevelt's New Deal. By working for the WPA, Vernon became exempt from military service during World War II.

History

(1952) At the beginning of summer, Elvis frequents the monthly gospel concerts at Tupelo's Ellis Auditorium. For Elvis, these shows are a source of not only religious inspiration but of inexpensive entertainment. Elvis reportedly is granted backstage access because he is willing to sell soft drinks at the auditorium. In fact, he is friends with many of the performers. J.D. Sumner, who will sing bass behind Elvis in the seventies, is with the Sunshine Boys at this time. Sumner assists Elvis in getting backstage. So does Gordon Stoker of the Jordanaires, a group who will later back Elvis on records and tours. Elvis's close friend from Sunday School, Cecil Blackwood of the Blackwood Brothers Quartet, also introduces Elvis to many of the gospel stars. G.L. Coffey, building superintendent from the auditorium, sometimes notices Elvis walking on-stage after the shows to sing over the loudspeaker to the empty auditorium.

June

quote of the day

"Rock 'n' roll music, if you like it, if you feel it, you can't help but move to it. That's what's happening to me. I can't help it. I have to move around. I can't stand still. I've tried it and I can't do it."

—*Elvis Presley*

A YOUNG MAN'S PREFERENCES

In the early 1950's, Elvis's favorite colors were pink and black. He was also quoted as saying that his mother's bacon and eggs were his favorite meal.

3 June

(1953) At 8:00 PM, in a ceremony at Ellis Auditorium, Elvis Presley receives his high school diploma, the first member of his immediate family to do so. From then on, the diploma always occupies an honored place in the family home. The Humes High School newspaper, the *Herald*, prophesizes about the class of 1953: "We are reminded at this time to not forget to invite you all out to the 'Silver Horse' on Onion [sic] Ave to hear the singing hillbillies of the road. Elvis Presley, Albert Teague, Doris Wilburn, and Mary Ann Propst are doing a bit of picking and singing out that-away."

quote of the day

"First thing he came out and spat out a piece of gum. His diction was real coarse. I can't over-emphasize how shocking he looked and seemed that night."

—Roy Orbison on the first time he saw Elvis at a show in Odessa, Texas

THE ART OF EDUCATION

Elvis attended Milam Junior High School where he was considered to be a loner. But his sixth grade report card shows he received top marks for courtesy, reliability, cooperation, and industry. He scored A's in music, physical education, and spelling, but brought home D's in arithmetic and geography.

History

(1970) Elvis travels to Nashville for a recording session at RCA's studios. The sessions last for five days from 6:00 PM to 4:30 AM each day. Elvis records thirty-four songs during the series, more than any other sessions of recording dates. Songs recorded tonight are: "Twenty Days and Twenty Nights," "I've Lost You," "I Was Born About Ten Thousand Years Ago," "The Sound of Your Cry," "The Fool," "Little Cabin on the Hill, and "Cindy, Cindy."

4 June

quote of the day

"Elvis is alive–and she's beautiful!"

—Madonna upon meeting k.d. Lang backstage at a concert

ROOTS

Q: Elvis's great-great-great-grandmother on his mother's side was a Cherokee Indian named Morning Dove White. Which of his facial features did Elvis attribute to this ancestor?

A: His high cheekbones

Today in

5 June

(1956) Elvis is in Los Angeles making an appearance on NBC's *The Milton Berle Show*. Other guests on the show include twenty-one-year-old actress Debra Paget, Arnold Stang, and the star of the TV show *Sheena, Queen of the Jungle*, Irish McCalla. Berle presents Elvis with a *Billboard* award for reaching number one on the retail, disc jockey, and jukebox charts on both the pop and country-and-western charts for "Heartbreak Hotel." Elvis performs his new single, "I Want You, I Need You, I Love You," and "Hound Dog" on the show.

quote of the day

"People say I'm vulgar. They say I use my hips disgustingly. But that's my way of putting over a song. I have to move. When I have a lot of energy, I move more. I lose three to four pounds a performance. I've always done it that way."

—Elvis Presley

TAKE A WALK

As a child, Elvis was a habitual sleepwalker who once nearly fell out a window. For the rest of his life, Elvis feared sleepwalking. He seldom slept alone.

History

(1968) Presidential candidate Robert Kennedy dies after being shot the day before in San Francisco. Elvis is in Los Angeles in rehearsals at Binder-Howe Productions offices for the upcoming *Elvis* television special. Elvis's heartfelt reaction to the assassination, the third in recent memory, inspires *Elvis* director/producer Steve Binder to ask songwriter Earl Brown to compose a closing number for the program that will capture something of Elvis's sentiments. Binder later says of the request, "I wanted to let the world know that here was a guy who was not prejudiced, who was raised in the heart of prejudice, but who was really above all that." The result, which Binder persuades Elvis to sing at the show's closing, is "If I Can Dream."

6 June

quote of the day

"I call the Sweet Inspirations my analysts. If anything goes wrong I go to their dressing room and I close the door and I confess everything to 'em."

–Elvis Presley

BARRIER BREAKER

Elvis records regularly topped the charts in traditional African-American markets across the US. Black disc jockey Nat Williams attended an Elvis concert once and noted, "...a thousand black, brown, and beige girls [who] took off like scalded cats in the direction of Elvis."

Today in

7 June

(1957) Around this time, Elvis and his growing entourage are en route to Memphis from Hollywood by train. Along the way, Elvis tries to contact sometime-girlfriend June Juanico, only to discover she had gotten married on June 1 and was on her honeymoon. Upset by the news, Elvis leaves the train in Lafayette, Louisiana, and rents a Cadillac to complete the trip to Graceland. He arrives at Graceland around midnight where he's greeted by his parents. This is the first time he's been home since right after the estate's purchase. Elvis is cheered a bit by the renovations and transformation that had taken place at the mansion since his departure.

quote of the day

"I know what poverty is. I lived it for a long time....I am not ashamed of my background."

—Elvis Presley

MY STUFF, MAN

The items on display at Graceland make up just a fifth of all Elvis's possessions. The rest of the archive takes up four warehouses. Three are at undisclosed locations around Memphis and the fourth is an earthquake-proof, tornado-proof and fireproof building on the Graceland estate. The Graceland bunker is kept at a continual 66 degrees Fahrenheit to preserve acetates, papers, and clothing.

History

8 June

(1971) Recently the Memphis County Commission, supported by Memphis Mayor Henry Loeb, has passed an ordinance that will re-name a portion of Highway 51 South as "Elvis Presley Boulevard." The section of highway in southern Memphis was previously known as South Bellevue Avenue. The new Elvis Presley Boulevard stretches from the Memphis city limits at South Parkway to the Mississippi State line. This portion of the highway is Graceland's address. It had been suggested that all of Bellevue, from the northern city limits to the Mississippi state line, be renamed for Elvis, but opposition from the Bellevue Baptist Church, one of the South's largest, prevented it.

quote of the day

"MGM is doing a movie here, so don't let these cameras throw you, and try not to throw the cameras. Those of you who have never seen me before will realize tonight that I'm totally insane and have been for a number of years. They just haven't caught me yet."

–Elvis, while on-stage

SODA POP ROCK

Q: What soft drink did Elvis drink so heavily that it was delivered by the truckload directly from a Memphis distributor?

A: Pepsi

9 June

Today in

(1972) Elvis begins a new tour schedule with a 4:00 PM press conference in the Mercury Ballroom of the New York Hilton Hotel, where he is staying. Parts of the press conference air on the national news and can be seen in the film *Elvis on Tour*. Each date on this tour guarantees Elvis $70,000 against 70 percent of the gate. Over the next three days, Elvis makes entertainment history as he is the first performer to sell out New York's Madison Square Garden for four consecutive concerts. RCA records portions of the show, later released on the LP *Elvis as Recorded at Madison Square Garden*. Among the fans in the audience, some celebrities are spotted including: John Lennon, George Harrison, Bob Dylan, David Bowie, and Art Garfunkel.

quote of the day

"The darkest, meanest, most dangerous white man ever to be on television. It was one of the transcendent moments of my life, altered my destiny. OK, that's what I want, white guys can rock 'n' roll too."

—Ray Manzareck of The Doors commenting on the first time he saw Elvis on television

WHO'S HE?

Elvis thought it was humorous to introduce himself as other people. He often said, "Hello I'm: Wayne Newton/Johnny Cash/Glen Campbell, or (even on occasion), Bill Cosby."

―― History ――

(1965) The *New York Times* reports that "Crying in the Chapel" has reached number one on the British Hit Parade. This is the first time Elvis has ever topped the Beatles in Great Britain, and the first number one British hit for Elvis in three years.

10 June

quote of the day

"I'd like to do something someday where I feel that I've really done a good job.... But, in the meantime, if I can entertain people with the things I'm doing, well, I'd be a fool to tamper with it.... If you goof a few times, you don't get many more chances in this business. That's the sad part about it."

—Elvis Presley on being in films

BETTER TO BE SAFE

Once while performing in Las Vegas, Elvis received a tip a woman was planning to shoot him. On stage, Elvis packed a pistol in his boot and FBI agents mingled with the audience. There were no incidents, but from then on, Elvis took security matters very seriously while on tour, often entering venues through the kitchen, back elevators, or side doors. His entourage received photo ID cards and anybody without one was not permitted backstage.

Today in

11 June

(1957) RCA Victor officially releases the single "Loving You"/"Teddy Bear." Less than a week later the record sells over 1.25 million copies, making it Elvis's eighth single to pass the million mark in sales. *Billboard* does their "Review Spotlight On..." column on the single saying the "special sleeve, spotlighting Elvis and a teddy bear, is powerful display material. Weeks later, "Teddy Bear" and "Loving You" enter *Billboard*'s top 100 at number 47 and number 81 respectively. "Teddy Bear" stays on the charts for twenty-nine weeks and reaches number one. "Loving You" peaks at number 28 and remains on the charts for twenty-two weeks.

quote of the day

"That boy made his pull from the blues, if he's stopped, he's stopped, but he made his pull from there."

—Muddy Waters

RIDING A BEAR

Elvis loved horses. He once owned a black Tennessee walker named Bear. Sometimes Elvis would dress himself and Bear in full regalia to put on a high-stepping show for fans at the gate.

History

(1968) Elvis's twenty-seventh film, *Speedway*, premieres in Charlotte, North Carolina, home of the Charlotte 500 stock car race, which is the background for the movie. Reviews of *Speedway* reflect the apparent facts about recent Presley films. *Variety* says: "An Elvis Presley film is money in the bank, regardless of the story or who appears with him." The *Hollywood Reporter* also mentions the bottom line: "The plot is tissue-thin, but the film is bound to make money by merely adhering to the regular distribution schedule." The *Los Angeles Times* remarks that the film: "...has a script that ran out of gas before Elvis Presley was born."

June

quote of the day

"After my first picture for Hal Wallis, it's non-musicals for me."

–Elvis Presley

LOYAL TO THE KING

Q: Eventually, even hardcore Elvis fans grew tired of his films. In the late 1960's, some distributors in parts of the US and Europe were refusing to buy his films. Which country remained loyal to Elvis films the longest?

A: India

Today in

13 June

(1962) NBC-TV contributes $2500 to the town of Tupelo, Mississippi, toward the construction of a park next to the house that is Elvis's birthplace. There are reports that teenagers have already raised $7000 for the project. The plan is for the city of Tupelo to purchase the two-room birthplace house along with two adjoining houses (presumable including the former home of Elvis's grandfather, J.D. Presley) which will be torn down to make room for the park.

quote of the day

"Elvis had a whole nation in love with him. You may be here because of "Love Me Tender."

–Ice T.

THERE GOES THE NEIGHBORHOOD

When Elvis lived in a posh area of Memphis at 1034 Audubon Drive, his neighbors became so fed up with fans continually hanging around they brought a public nuisance suit against him. In court, the magistrate threw out the suit, saying the fans were not Elvis's responsibility, and in any case, Elvis's house was the only one on the street that was fully paid for.

History

14 June

(1963) Priscilla Ann Beaulieu graduates from Immaculate Conception High School in Memphis, Tennessee. Elvis feels his presence at the graduation will cause enough commotion to detract from the event so he defers from attending. For a graduation present, Elvis gives Priscilla a red rear-engine Chevrolet Corvair. Upon graduation, Priscilla enrolls at the Patricia Stevens finishing school on Madison Avenue in Memphis. She models dresses a few times down the street from Graceland at the Picadilly Cafeteria at 3968 Bellevue where she uses a pseudonym. Priscilla also takes dance lessons from the Jo Haynes School of Dance, where she also uses a false name. The Haynes School is located at 4769 Bellevue Avenue which will eventually become Elvis Presley Boulevard.

quote of the day

"Well, what have we here?"

—Elvis's first words to Priscilla when she visited his home at 14 Goethestrasse in the autumn of 1959

HIGH SCHOOL CONFIDENTIAL

At Graceland, late nights and partying played havoc on Priscilla's schoolwork. She managed to pass Algebra by persuading the student next to her to show exam answers in return for an invitation to Graceland.

Today in

15 June

(1961) *Wild in the Country*, Elvis's seventh film and a movie based on a novel by J.R. Salamanca, premieres in Memphis. Proceeds from the event are donated to local charities. Elvis does not attend the premiere about which Colonel Parker quips, "Unless we can do our show, we don't go." Elvis later takes a group of friends and relatives, including Uncle Travis and Aunt Loraine Smith, and their sons Billy and Bobby, for a viewing of *Wild in the Country*. The press is obviously unimpressed with Elvis's early effort: *Variety* says of *Wild in the Country*: "Dramatically, there isn't a lot of substance, novelty or spring to this somewhat wobbly and artificial tale." The *New York Times* is less kind: "Even with Mr. Presley in the cast it should have been, at least, an honest drama, if not a particularly brilliant one. It isn't. It is shamelessly dishonest. Indeed, it is down-right gross in its social distortion of human values and social realities." The *Hollywood Reporter* simply referred to the film as, "a Southern '*Peyton Place*.'"

quote of the day

"I got hung up in Hollywood making pictures, and I got away from the people."

–*Elvis Presley*

MORE O' SAME

When George Klein asked Elvis what his next movie, *Easy Come, Easy Go*, was about, Elvis answered, "Same film, different location."

History

16 June

(1976) It is becoming increasingly difficult for anyone to contact Elvis. Even Colonel Parker is unable to get in touch with the star. Apparently desperate, the Colonel authors a letter: "As I told Vernon today, I have not heard from anyone since I got back, neither from Sonny or from any other member of your staff. I just wanted to let you know in the event you feel they are in contact with me but they are not." By now, most of the "staff" and Elvis are estranged. Joe Esposito is living in California. Lamar Fike lives and works in Nashville. Jerry Schilling is gone. And Elvis's relationship with Sonny and Red West is strained, partly because of the bodyguards' actions resulting in lawsuits, but more because of a general air of suspicion and mistrust permeating Elvis and the group.

quote of the day

"It was like witnessing a chilling prophecy."

—*A review of a 1976 concert of Elvis singing the "My Way" verse, "and now the end is near."*

SOMEBODY CALL A NURSE!

Elvis's nurse, Tish Henley, lived with the entourage at Graceland and administered her employer's drugs at "safe intervals." By the end, Elvis's tolerance for drugs was so great he needed three packets to sleep.

Today in

17 June

(1933) Vernon Elvis Presley and Gladys Love Smith elope by hitchhiking twenty miles from Tupelo to Pontotoc, Mississippi, to be married. Seventeen-year-old Vernon adds four years to his marriage license application to appear of legal age to make the commitment. Gladys, in turn, deducts two years from her actual age to appear as a nineteen-year-old bride. License in hand, the couple is married by circuit court clerk J.M. Gates. Vernon and Gladys lived with various relatives until Gladys became pregnant with twins in 1934. That fall, Vernon borrowed a hundred-eighty dollars to build a two-room house on North Saltillo Road across from Vernon's father's house. The elder Presley owned the lots for both houses, which were about twelve feet apart and shared the same hand-operated water pump. Vernon and Gladys moved into their new home in time to celebrate Christmas 1934. They had already chosen names for the coming twins. The firstborn would be Jesse, after Vernon's father. The second would be given Vernon's middle name, Elvis.

quote of the day

"He's my Daddy, and I can't say nothing against him."

—*Elvis's response to questions about Vernon's relationship with Dee Stanley*

O' HOLY DAY

Both in Tupelo and in Memphis, the Presley family were members of the revivalist First Assembly of God church. Elvis found roots in its loud preaching and rousing gospel music.

History

18 June

(1964) *Viva Las Vegas* opens this week in theaters across the United States. The film's national release did not follow the normal pattern. The movie was first issued earlier in the year in the Orient, where it was a major hit with Elvis fans, setting box-office records in Tokyo, Manila, and other parts of the Far East. Then, it appeared in Europe. The film "premiered" in New York in April, press screenings were not held until mid-May, and it opened nationwide this month. This is Elvis's fifteenth film and his first opportunity to work with soon-to-become life-long friend Ann-Margret. *Viva Las Vegas* eventually reaches number 14 on *Variety*'s list of top-grossing films. For the year of 1964, it listed in the number 11 spot, having grossed $4,675,000.

quote of the day

"*Supernatural, his own resurrection.*"

—Rolling Stone *magazine review of Elvis's return to live performances in Las Vegas*

LUCKY IN VEGAS

Q: In the film *Viva Las Vegas*, Lucky (Elvis) works as a waiter at what Las Vegas hotel? For double points: What position does his love interest, Rusty (Ann-Margret), hold at the hotel?

A: The Flamingo Hotel; Rusty teaches swimming

19 June

(1959) This week Vernon leaves Elvis in Germany and returns home to Memphis to attend to family business matters such as renewing the license plates on Elvis's two Lincoln Continentals and two Cadillacs. Vernon creates quite a stir when he is spotted around Memphis with Dee Stanley on his arm. Stanley is unknown to anyone in Memphis and speculation is split as to whether the thirty-three year old "stylishly-dressed, blue-eyed blond" is the interest of Elvis or Vernon.

quote of the day

"What profiteth it to gain the world if you couldn't share your good fortune with your friends?"

—Elvis to friend Larry Gellar about taking thirty friends on a Hawaiian vacation in 1977

FRIENDS LIKE THESE

When singer and friend Jackie Wilson suffered a stroke, Elvis sent his wife a check for $30,000.

History

(1956) An African-American newspaper, *Memphis World*, reports Elvis has "cracked Memphis segregation laws by attending the Fairgrounds Memphis amusement park on East Parkway, during what is designated as 'colored night.'" Elvis is viewed in a favorable light by Memphis's large black community. He has often credited Arthur Crudup and other black artists as being strong influences on his music. Some, including Colonel Parker, see the reports as potentially negative publicity in Memphis in 1956. Larry Kanaga, vice president of RCA, writes the Colonel reassuring him that "any negative press" Elvis is receiving is of little consequence because of Elvis's tremendous talent and the Colonel's keen business sense.

20 June

quote of the day

"Presley makes no secret of his respect for the work of Negroes, nor of their influence on his own singing. Furthermore, he does not shun them, either in public or private."

—Tan Magazine, *1957*

HILLBILLY CAT

In the 1950's, some record companies still had separate "race" catalogues. Elvis rendered these obsolete as the first "crossover" entertainer.

Today in

21 June

(1961) This week Elvis begins a recording session at RCA's studios in Nashville. "Kiss Me Quick," " That's Someone You Never Forget," and "I'm Yours" are scheduled for release on the *Pot Luck* album. The studio musicians are Elvis's usual Nashville sidemen: Scotty Moore, Hank Garland, and Neal Matthews (of the Jordanaires) on guitar; D.J. Fontana and Buddy Harmon on drums; Bob Moore, bass; Floyd Cramer on piano and organ, Gordon Stoker (of the Jordanaires), piano; Boots Randolph, saxophone; and the Jordanaires and Millie Kirkham on back-up vocals.

quote of the day

"You have no idea how great he is, really you don't. You have no comprehension—it's absolutely impossible. I can't tell you why he's so great, but he is. He's sensational."

—Phil Spector

THERE WAS NOTHING

Q: To celebrate being named as European City of Culture for 2008, what British city has opened a permanent exhibition called "Fingerprints of Elvis?" (hint: John Lennon's words are inscribed at the site—"Before there was Elvis, there was nothing.")

A: Liverpool

History

(1955) The past two days Elvis has headlined a show in Beaumont, Texas, billed as "Stars of the *Grand Ole Opry, Louisiana Hayride,* and *Big D Jamboree.*" The features entertainers Marty Robbins, the Maddox Brothers with Rose and Rhetta, the Belew Twins, Sonny James, Charlene Arthur, LaFawn Paul of the *Hayride*, singer-songwriter-emcee Johnny Hicks and the Texas Stompers. Admission is one dollar. The show's popularity causes three extra shows to be added in Beaumont with the local newspaper dubbing it "The Season's Greatest Hillbilly Show." The shows are put on for the benefit of the local police department which raises a reported $10,000. The entertainers make, as a package, $225 per day.

June 22

quote of the day

"We flat changed the world of music."

–Sam Phillips

DRIVERS WANTED

In 1954 Elvis got a job driving a truck for the Crown Electric Company being paid $40 a week. His task was to deliver electrical goods to electricians in the field. Elvis drove for Crown Electric for six months.

— Today in —

June

(1963) Elvis feels a need for a special place at Graceland where he could be alone with his thoughts. Marty Lacker arranges for some of his relatives, his sister Anne and her husband Bernie Granadier, to design the Meditation Garden. The project comes out beautifully and quickly becomes a favorite place for Elvis. Eventually, the Meditation Garden becomes the resting place for Elvis and his mother Gladys. Vernon Presley and Elvis's grandmother, Minnie Mae Presley, are also laid to rest there upon their deaths. A plaque in memory of Jesse Garon Presley is also located in the Gardens.

quote of the day

"Help me, Lord, to know the right thing."

—Note in Elvis's hotel suite, Las Vegas, 1976

KING BELIEFS

Early in his career, Elvis was unsettled by the criticism he received from religious leaders. He believed his talent and success were inspired by God. In 1956 he told *True Story* magazine, "My voice is God's will, not mine."

(1972) Having been on a multi-city tour, Elvis returns to Memphis to spend some of the summer at Graceland. There are increasing rumors of an imminent divorce between Elvis and Priscilla. The *Los Angeles Express* reports sightings of Priscilla with Elvis acquaintance and Priscilla's karate instructor Mike Stone. Meanwhile, Elvis is spotted at the midnight movies at the Memphian Theater accompanied by actress and Memphis native Cybill Shephard, who is scheduled to start work on the film *The Last Picture Show*. Some reports claim Elvis and Ms. Shephard, a former Miss Teenage Memphis and Miss Tennessee, first dated in 1966 when he was thirty-one and she was seventeen.

24 June

quote of the day

"Elvis is my man."

–Janis Joplin

RETURN TO SENDER

When Elvis and Priscilla divorced in 1973 the proceedings were held at the Santa Monica Courthouse in California. They agreed to share custody of Lisa Marie and it was an amicable separation at first. Elvis never bothered to pick up his copies of the official documents.

Today in

25 June

(1977) Elvis arrives in Cincinnati, Ohio, in the early morning hours to perform what will become his second–last concert. During the day, he anonymously visits Bill Randle's University of Cincinnati class. As a DJ in 1955, Randle was instrumental in breaking Elvis's records into the Northern states. At 3:00 PM, disgusted with the broken air conditioner at his hotel, Elvis leaves and checks into a room at the Netherland Hotel down the street where he's stayed before. He gets a room for himself and one for his bodyguards. Elvis appears at Riverfront Coliseum at 8:30 PM with 17,140 fans in attendance (your author is one of them). Elvis appears disoriented and seems to lack concentration, to the point of reading the words to "My Way" from a piece of notebook paper. He explains he's been to the dentist and has been taking pain medication as a result.

quote of the day

"I was at a football game and a lady asked a friend of mine, 'I hear Elvis Presley is here.' My friend said, 'Yeah.' She said, 'I hear he's in the bathroom.' He said, 'Yeah?' The lady said, very seriously, 'I didn't think he did that.'"

—Elvis Presley, from the stage during a live performance

BROKEN HEART

Upon his death, Elvis's heart was found to be enlarged 50 percent more than normal. A classic symptom of heart failure, this may also explain the dizzy spells, shortness of breath, and elevated blood pressure that plagued him in his final years.

―――――― History ――――――

(1909) Andreas Cornelius van Kuijk is born in Breda, Holland. In 1929, taking the name Thomas Andrew Parker, the young Dutchman illegally immigrates to the United Sates and claims Huntington, West Virginia, as his place of birth. "Tom Parker" serves in the United States army from 1929 to 1932, having sworn allegiance to the United States, thus renouncing his Dutch citizenship. He meets and marries a young lady he meets in Tampa, Florida, Marie Mott Ross. Parker begins his hawking career in carnivals and fairs, pushing anything he thinks he can sell. He founds the Great Parker Pony Circus and, later, Colonel Tom Parker's Dancing Chickens, in which he places live chickens on a hot plate covered with sawdust and adds music to make the chickens appear to be dancing. In the 1950's Parker becomes the manager of country singers Eddy Arnold and Hank Snow. In 1956, Parker officially becomes Elvis Presley's manager, a job he keeps until Elvis's death, never taking on another client.

26 June

quote of the day

"The Colonel lived and breathed Elvis twenty-four hours a day."

—Trude Forsher, Tom Parker's assistant on why the Colonel didn't take on any other clients besides Elvis

THANKS, POP

Elvis signed with RCA in 1955. The next day he sent a telegram to the Colonel promising he'd stick with him through thick and thin. Elvis also wrote to Parker he "loved him like a father."

Today in

27 June

(1954) Elvis continues to visit Sun Records trying to be noticed by the Memphis Recording Service. This week it seems his prayers are answered when Marion Keisker, Sam Phillips' assistant, tells Phillips she thinks it's a good idea to have "the boy with the sideburns" try out a new song Sam received from Nashville song publisher Red Wortham. Keisker makes the telephone call and Elvis beats feet to the studio. Elvis works on "Without You" all afternoon but can't seem to come up with a successful version of the song. Sam Phillips doesn't give up on young Elvis, however, and shortly after finds what he is after when Elvis, somewhat on a lark at a later session, launches into his version of Arthur "Big Boy" Crudup's "That's All Right."

quote of the day

"Music tells me more than anything else I've ever known, how good, how great it is just to be alive."

—*Elvis Presley*

STYLE, BABY, STYLE

Q: Country music around Memphis was mostly bluegrass, and singer Bill Monroe was its icon. Early in his career, Elvis was nervous about meeting Monroe because he had dramatically changed one of Monroe's best known songs. What was the song?

A: "Blue Moon of Kentucky"

History

28 June

(1962) While home in Memphis for the summer, Elvis acquires his most famous pet, Scatter the chimpanzee. The chimp was a performer on Memphis TV along with his owner "Captain" Bill Kinnebrew. Once Elvis "adopts," Scatter spends a lot of time at Elvis's home in Hollywood, where he is the life of the party. Scatter's favorite "trick" is to look under ladies' dresses. Alan Fortas, whose job in the entourage is to take care of Elvis's fleet of vehicles, often takes Scatter for rides, allowing the chimp to sit in his lap wearing a chauffeur's cap. Arriving at a stop sign, Fortas liked to slide down in the seat leaving Scatter holding the steering wheel. Scatter's appeal eventually wanes when he "acquires a taste for liquor," becoming a nuisance, and he is eventually confined to a pen at Graceland.

quote of the day

"It is impossible to housebreak a wallaby since it does not have any natural sanitation instinct."

—Colonel Tom Parker in a note to Elvis recommending he donate two wallabies sent as gifts from Australian friends to the Memphis Zoo

WHO DOES YOUR HAIR?

Elvis once owned a dog whose hair stuck out all over in a rather peculiar manner. He named the canine "Spontaneous Combustion."

Today in

29 June

(1956) Elvis and his cousin Junior Smith arrive in New York in the morning and head right for the rehearsal hall in midtown Manhattan to work on Elvis's upcoming television performance on *The Steve Allen Show*. The Colonel and two reps from the William Morris Agency meet Elvis at the hall. Steve Allen arrives with the show's two costars, Andy Griffith and Imogene Coca. Elvis and Griffith know each other from Florida shows a year prior. Elvis eventually makes his only appearance on *The Steve Allen Show* singing "I Want You, I Love You, I Need You" and "Hound Dog" (in which Elvis appears in a tuxedo singing to a basset hound wearing a top hat). He also appears with the other cast members in a comedy skit entitled "Range Round Up."

quote of the day

"You Can't Do That To Elvis!"

—the title of a Billboard article in which teenagers objected to Elvis wearing a tuxedo on The Steve Allen Show

THE SHIRT OFF MY BACK

Early in his career, Elvis developed a technique for undoing his shirt and maneuvering out of it in one swift motion so that grabbing fans could get the shirt without drawing blood.

History

(1954) Barely two weeks after winning first place on the *Arthur Godfrey Talent Scouts Show*, two members of the gospel quartet "The Blackwood Brothers," R.W. Blackwood and Bill Lyles, are killed in a plane crash in Clanton, Alabama. Cecil Blackwood subsequently takes over as the quartet's lead singer, leaving a vacancy on the band's younger group, The Songfellows. The Songfellows offer Elvis the vacancy, but he is unable because he has begun recording for Sun Records. The Blackwood Brothers were Gladys Presley's favorite gospel group. Elvis flew the quartet to Memphis to sing at Gladys's 1958 funeral service.

30 June

quote of the day

"I don't know what all the fuss is about. I'm just a guy who makes music—no different from anybody else."

—*Elvis Presley*

VICTORY OR DEATH

Elvis's first assignment in the army was to Company D of the Medium Tank Battalion, 32nd Armor, whose motto was "Victory or Death." His last assignment was a "Wintershield" exercise in Wildflicken.

July

1 July

(1955) "Elvis Prestley," as he is billed in a newspaper ad, continues on a week-long tour, this time playing at the Casino Club in Plaquemine, a small Louisiana town southwest of Baton Rouge. Elvis does one show, which lasts from 8:30 PM to 1:00 AM. Admission is $1.50. Appearing with Elvis is the club's owner and his band, Lou Millet and his Melody Makers. Meanwhile, current manager Bob Neal flies to Nashville to meet with Colonel Parker at Parker's home-office in nearby Madison. During the meeting, Neal signs an exclusive contract with Hank Snow Attractions that allows the company to represent Elvis "in all phases of the entertainment field." But Neal continues to serve as Elvis's personal manager.

quote of the day

"We're the perfect combination. Colonel's an old carny, and me, I'm off the wall."

–Elvis Presley

SPECIAL ADVISOR

When Elvis and Tom Parker signed their contract in 1955, the Colonel was described as "special advisor... to negotiate and assist in any way possible the build-up of Elvis Presley as an artist and ... to negotiate all renewals on existing contracts."

Today in

July

(1963) Elvis goes to Hollywood to begin work on *Viva Las Vegas*, his fifteenth film. The MGM picture originally is titled *The Only Girl in Town*, and it is released in Europe as *Love in Las Vegas*. Costar Ann-Margret is a relative unknown in Hollywood, having only appeared in two films. Not surprisingly, Ann-Margret and Elvis develop a smoldering relationship during the production. The first to notice are "the guys" who don't really wonder why Elvis insists on seeing Ann-Margret alone, without even a driver. Fan magazines quickly catch wind of the affair. The last to know is Priscilla, but it doesn't take long before she reads in gossip columns that Elvis is, in all likelihood, cheating on her. Typical of the headlines that Priscilla surely notices is a piece in the *Memphis Press-Scimitar* declaring "It Looks Like Romance For Presley And Ann-Margret."

quote of the day

"...it was like he came along and whispered some dream in everybody's ear, and somehow we all dreamed it."

—Bruce Springsteen

BEDTIME FOR GOZO

Viva Las Vegas was banned in Gozo, the sister island of Malta. Showings at Gozo's Aurora Theater were cancelled after Catholic authorities protested the film. The Gozo College of Parish Priests condemned the film as indecent. During Mass, one priest asked his congregation to protest the movie and avoid seeing it. Gozo was the only place in the world that objected to the film.

History

(1951) Elvis and his cousin, Gene Smith, begin working at Precision Tool, a Memphis company located at 1132 Kansas Street. The company employs three of Elvis's uncles. It is Precision's policy not to hire anyone under the age of eighteen; apparently Elvis lies to get the job. It doesn't take long before his true age is discovered (he was reportedly turned in by a fellow employee) and he is immediately fired. But the foreman has taken a liking to young Elvis, and tells him he can have a job when he turns eighteen.

3
July

quote of the day

"I look forward to our marriage and a little Elvis. I have never and never again will love anyone like I love you."

—Elvis to Anita Wood

AFTER SCHOOL QUIZ

Q: What snack did Gladys Presley make for Elvis when he came home after school, a snack he enjoyed the rest of his life?

A: Peanut butter and banana sandwiches

Today in

4 July

(1974) Back home in Memphis, Elvis puts on a ninety-minute karate lecture and demonstration with his bodyguard and karate instructor Ed Parker. The demonstration is held at the Tennessee Karate Institute, which Elvis founded and is to be run by Red West and Elvis's cousin Bobbi Wren. National kumite (sparring/kickboxing) karate champion Bill "Sugarfoot" Wallace, who had run a school for Kang Rhee while getting his master's from Memphis State, is hired as the principal instructor. This is the beginning of Elvis's strongest and longest-lasting commitment to karate.

quote of the day

"I get such a thrill out of performing till I wear myself out. Sometimes we have three or four shows a day and it's the same thing as a fighter going into the ring three times in one night. And not many fighters will do it."

–Elvis Presley

GETTING A KICK OUT OF PERFORMING

In the 1970's Elvis included loads of karate moves in his performances. Drummer Ronnie Tutt actually took martial arts classes to help him anticipate Elvis's moves so he could hit his drum accordingly. Tutt had to keep his eye on Elvis all the time because of his unpredictability during shows.

History

(1954) Elvis has rehearsed numbers with Scotty Moore and Bill Black for a while now and today the trio heads to Sun Records to take a try at recording. They try one ballad after another, garnering no interest from Sam Phillips. Then, during a break in what has technically been termed a "rehearsal session," discouragement rising, Elvis launches into Big Boy Crudup's "That's All Right." Bill and Scotty join in, but remain skeptical. Phillips, however, feels the song is just right for Elvis's first single.

July

quote of the day

"I've never been accustomed to getting things real easy. I know it looks like I came up overnight. Not so! I can tell you that it was a lot of hard work. I've done plenty of it. I worked as a common laborer. I drove a truck for Crown Electrics in Memphis at the same time I was going to high school. I'd get up at 3:30 and be on the job at 6:30 for $12.50 a week. Luckily, I don't need much sleep. I've got plenty of nervous energy."

—Elvis Presley

IN THE NAVY

In the late 1940's, Scotty Moore enlisted in the navy where he received both a Chinese and a Korean service medal. While in the navy, Moore started a band known as The Happy Valley Boys.

Today in

6
July

(1960) Elvis visits his mother's grave, then gives a heartfelt interview to the *Memphis Press-Scimitar*, where he says of his new step-mother, whom Vernon recently married, "She seems pretty nice. I only had one mother and that's it. There'll never be another, as long as she understands that there won't be any trouble." Of his father, Elvis adds, "He's all I got left in the world. I'll never go against him or stand in his way. He stood by me all these years and sacrificed things he wanted so I could have clothes and lunch money to go to school." The article isn't published until later when Vernon and Dee's marriage is announced in the press.

quote of the day

"I was raised in a pretty decent home and everything. My folks always made me behave, whether I wanted to or not."

–Elvis Presley

DADDY, PLEASE

As a teen, Elvis considered his father to be a lazy person and had little respect for him. Elvis had to force himself to show respect for Vernon in public.

History

(1955) Guitarist Scotty Moore trades in his Gibson ES295 for a Gibson L5 guitar at O.K. Houck Piano Company. Scotty's new guitar goes with the new custom-built Echosonic amplifier he purchased a couple of months ago on a payment plan. Elvis, too, purchases a new guitar, a Martin D-28, which he'll use in pictures taken for publicity stills later this month. Elvis's new guitar has a tooled leather cover which, in addition to its decorative qualities, prevents the back from getting scratched by his belt buckle during performances.

7 July

quote of the day

"I always felt that someday, somehow, something would happen to change everything for me, and I'd daydream about how it would be."

–Elvis Presley

RUBEN CHERRY BLUES

One of Elvis's favorite hang-outs was the House of Blues record shop on Beale Street. Owner Ruben Cherry was a blues fanatic who stocked everything pertaining to the blues. Ruben was the first dealer to stock "That's All Right" and he even loaned Elvis money so he could travel to gigs. Years later, Elvis wrote a thank you note to Cherry for all his help. The letter was read at Cherry's funeral.

Today in

8 July

(1961) Elvis arrives in Hollywood to begin filming his ninth movie, *Follow that Dream,* at United Artists studios. At this time, the movie is titled *Pioneer, Go Home,* the title of Richard Powell's 1957 book upon which the movie is based. The film is directed by Gordon Douglas, who worked on the *Our Gang* comedies in the thirties. As is becoming custom, Joanna Moore, who plays the welfare worker in the movie, is Elvis's steady date for the first few days of filming.

quote of the day

"I wasn't exactly James Bond in that movie, but then no one ever asked Sean Connery to sing while dodging bullets."

—*Elvis Presley*

TRUE PROFESSIONAL

Q: Film technicians always seemed to expect the worse from Elvis, but many are on record saying they found him to be punctual, prepared, and professional. Costar Millie Perkins said she never noticed Elvis using his star power to get his way on a film set. In what movie did she work with Elvis?

A: Wild in the Country

9 July

(1965) *Tickle Me,* Elvis's eighteenth film, opens this week across the country to reviews that are similar to recent others in the "three money-making movies a year" scheme. *Box Office* magazine says, "While the story would hardly win an Oscar for originality, the great popularity of Presley will surmount that, as witness his trident success over the years." *Variety* says, "Presley takes his character in stride, giving a performance calculated to appeal particularly to his following." Finally, The *Los Angeles Times* comments the movie has "lousy color, cheap sets, hunks of stage footage, painted scenery, and unconvincing process work, but who's to quibble when the movie is so much fun."

quote of the day

"I'd like to have the ability of James Dean...but I'd never compare myself to James Dean."

—Elvis Presley

THAT TICKLES

Tickle Me, despite being declared "the silliest, feeblest and dullest vehicle for the Memphis Wonder in a long time" by the *New York Times,* still saved its producers and Allied Artists from bankruptcy. It was also the studio's third-highest grossing film ever.

Today in

10 July

(1954) On KWEM in West Memphis, DJ Uncle Richard is the first DJ to play an Elvis record on the air when he spotlights "Blue Moon of Kentucky" on his 9:00 PM show. Across town, DJ Dewey Phillips at WHBQ radio in downtown Memphis plays both "That's All Right" and "Blue Moon of Kentucky" at about 9:30 PM. Listeners like "That's All Right" so much Phillips decides to call Elvis down to the station for an on-the-air chat. Dewey calls the Presley home but Elvis has gone to the movies. Friends and relatives search for Elvis and take him to the WHBQ studios where he does an on-air interview with Phillips.

quote of the day

"I didn't have enough money to do the record over, so I decided to let it stand as it was. I figured if nobody else liked the thing, Mom would, anyway, and she did."

—Elvis, referring to the record he made for his mother that launched his career

SCARED HEP CAT

Elvis was so scared of being interviewed that Dewey Phillips didn't tell him the microphone was on. One of the questions asked was which high school Elvis went to—a polite way in 1950s Memphis of letting the audience know Elvis's race. At the end Elvis asked, "Aren't you going to interview me?" Phillips replied he already had.

History

(1956) Around this time in New York, Ed Sullivan, who has previously stated he wouldn't "touch Elvis Presley with a ten-foot pole," makes the announcement that he's booked Elvis to appear on his popular, high-rated variety show. The Colonel insists to Sullivan's producers that Elvis retain complete control over the presentations of his songs and act. The Colonel maintains that fan mail is running ten to one against any restriction of Elvis's movements.

11 July

quote of the day

"I don't think there is a musician today that hasn't been affected by Elvis's music. His definitive years—1954-57—can only be described as rock's cornerstone. He was the original cool."

—Brian Setzer

OKAY, BREAK IT UP

At an early Cleveland concert Elvis provoked mass hysteria when he broke one of his guitar strings then proceeded to smash the guitar on stage. Police had to be called to get him out of the hall.

Today in

July 12

(1954) Today Scotty Moore becomes both the manager and booking agent for his new group with Elvis and Bill Black. Scotty's contract with Elvis reads: "Whereas W.S. Moore, III, is a band leader and a booking agent, and Elvis Presley, a minor, age 19 years, is a singer of reputation and renown, and possesses bright promise of large success, it is the desire of both parties to enter into this personal management contract for the best interests of both parties." Elvis and his parents sign the contract, and the group agrees to split all earnings, 50 percent to Elvis and 25 percent each to Scotty and Bill.

quote of the day

"My daddy had seen a lot of people who played the guitar and stuff and didn't work, so he said: 'You should make up your mind either about being an electrician or playing a guitar. I never saw a guitar player worth a damn.'"

—Elvis, on Vernon's feelings toward his career choice

ENOUGH TO GO AROUND

At the time he signed Elvis in 1956, Colonel Parker also signed Scotty Moore, Bill Black, and DJ Fontana.

History

13 July

(1976) In the morning several phone calls go out from Vernon's Graceland office, first to Sonny West in Memphis, then to Red in California and karate expert Dave Hebler. Each man is fired with one week's pay because, as Vernon puts it, it's been a difficult year and now is the time for belt tightening. It seems the true reason for the terminations are on-going friction within the group and Vernon's lingering suspicion that somehow the Memphis Mafia are taking advantage of his son. All three men are deeply offended not just because of the "see ya' later" attitude, but because Elvis wouldn't even take the time to deliver the news himself. Red West is a high school friend of Elvis, and understandably takes the news rather hard.

quote of the day

"Those bastards." They're going to finish me."

—Elvis, *after seeing a copy of* Elvis: What Happened?
in the summer of 1977

TKO'ED

One of the reported "true" reasons Red and Sonny West and Dave Hebler were fired from Elvis's employ was their increasingly violent tendencies while "body-guarding." Prior to their termination, they knocked a man out when he tried to gain access to one of Elvis's parties which generated a law suit. Some say the sensational book *Elvis: What Happened?* was written by the three men in retaliation for their discharge.

Today in

14 July

(1969) In anticipation of an upcoming Las Vegas engagement, Elvis puts together a band he deems up to the task. First he hires, as band leader, James Burton, a blues guitarist who is a television veteran having portrayed the leader of Ricky Nelson's band on the *Ozzie and Harriet Show*. Burton is now a top L.A. session musician as well as a member of the TV series *Shindig!* band. Burton brings in Larry Muhoberac, whose band appeared with Elvis in his 1961 Memphis charity concert, as pianist. Together, Burton and Muhoberac bring in Ronnie Tutt on drums, studio bass player Jerry Scheff and rhythm guitarist John Wilkinson. Elvis brings the Imperials and the Sweet Inspirations on board and the stage is set for the launching of his second live performance run.

quote of the day

"This is my first live appearance in nine years. I've appeared dead a few times."
—Elvis during his first stage appearance in Las Vegas in 1969

BREAKING VEGAS

In Las Vegas, hotel entertainment facilities were budgeted to operate at a deficit, with the expectation money patrons would spend in the casinos would more than compensate. Elvis's 1969 show in Las Vegas was the city's first in history to turn a profit.

History

15 July

(1966) Production of *Double Trouble*, Elvis's twenty-fourth film, begins this week at MGM studios in Culver City. The film's working title in the beginning is "You're Killing Me." Although the movie is set in England and Belgium, all of Elvis's scenes are filmed using backdrops and rear projections on the sound stages of MGM. The scene in which Elvis is shown aboard the tramp steamer S.S. Democles in Antwerp is shot in Long Beach Harbor. *Double Trouble* reeks of inconsistencies. In one scene taking place in Elvis's London apartment, Annette Day is wearing a white apron, then, she isn't. In another, a scene from Elvis's hotel room in Bruges, a burglar turns over a bedside luggage rack, then hides on a window ledge as Elvis and Ms. Day enter the room. The only problem is when the pair comes into the room, the luggage rack is mystically back in place. Okay, one more interesting sidebar: Elvis's cousin Billy Smith is the stunt double for Annette Day in one scene from the movie.

quote of the day

"What can you do with a piece of shit like this?"

—Elvis, commenting on the *Double Trouble* soundtrack

NUMBER, PLEASE

Elvis's membership number in the Screen Actor's Guild was 42838.

16 July

(1972) Elvis is taking it easy in Memphis. Current-girlfriend Linda Thompson is on vacation, and Elvis is seen keeping frequent company with Sandra Zancan. Elvis first dated Ms. Zancan in Los Angeles, where she had a small role in the touring company of *No, No, Nanette* at the Ahamson Theater. At that time, Elvis and Sandra took a reprise in Palm Springs, where Elvis lavished her with a white Datsun sports car and a ruby ring. Ms. Zancan and Elvis are seen at various Memphis locales for about two weeks. Around this time, Priscilla is also seen around Memphis briefly.

quote of the day

"I don't like to be called Elvis the Pelvis, it's one of the most childish expressions I've ever heard. Elvis the Pelvis. But if they want to call me that, there's nothing I can do about it."

—Elvis Presley

GIRLS! GIRLS! GIRLS!

When the Beatles (no slouches themselves in the potential-date department) came to meet Elvis, they were astounded by the number of women around him.

History

(1958) Elvis is in army training at Ft. Hood, Texas. He spends time with his friend Eddie Fadal, a disc jockey from KRLD in Dallas who Elvis met in Waco in 1956. Elvis often visits Eddie and his wife, LaNelle, driving the forty-five minutes from Ft. Hood to their home. This weekend Elvis, the Fadals, and some friends drive to Dallas. The group tries to get a room at the Dallas Sheraton, but they are turned away because they "have no luggage." They wind up renting an entire floor of another hotel where a hairdresser's convention is being held. Elvis spends the day hanging around the pool with admiring young women. Two days later, Elvis and the entourage return to the Fadal's in Waco. Elvis is furious at the Sheraton and tells the Colonel of his problem. Colonel Parker, contacts the president of the Sheraton Hotel chain who offers an official apology and free lodging at any Sheraton Inn. Elvis refuses the offer and always avoids the Sheraton when touring in the Dallas area.

17 July

quote of the day

"I love the fans. I love the pretty girls. When they come running to me, I want to run to them, not away from them. I hope they don't blame me when army regulations force me to look straight ahead on duty. I want them to know I'm not ignoring them."

—Elvis Presley

DO YOUR DUTY!

On army leave in 1958, Elvis went to Studio B in Nashville for a recording session—his last of the 50s. He showed up in his army uniform.

Today in

18
July

(1953) It's Saturday morning and Elvis drops by the Memphis Recording Service, a division of Sun Records, in downtown Memphis. The company advertises three mottos: "We record anything-anywhere-anytime," "A complete service to fulfill every recording need," and "Combining the newest and best equipment with the latest and finest sonocoustic studios." Marion Keisker, a local radio DJ, and secretary to Sam Phillips, is in charge of the studio this morning. When she asks young Elvis who he sounds like, he replies quite truthfully, "I don't sound like nobody." Elvis, guitar in hand, pays the $3.98 fee to record two ballads "My Happiness" and "That's When Your Heartaches Begin." Elvis receives his ten-inch 78 rpm disc with a song on each side. He tells Marion he is recording a record for his mother's birthday. Considering Gladys's birthday is in April, the story may be Elvis's way of disguising the fact that the record is for himself.

quote of the day

"I'd really wanted to hear myself sing. I can't remember exactly what hit me that day, but I had to know what my voice sounded like."

—*Elvis on his first recording session*

THE BEAT GOES ON

In 1954, when Elvis was nineteen years old, he applied for a job as a Memphis police officer. He was rejected because of his age.

History

19 July

(1954) Elvis's first professional single 45, "That's Alright"/"Blue Moon of Kentucky," is released. Fifteen-year-old Eldene Beard buys a copy at Charlie's Blues Record Shop on Main Street in Memphis. This is probably the first ever sale of an Elvis record. *Billboard* magazine describes Elvis as "a potent new chanter, who comes thru with a solid performance." By month's end, "That's All Right" sells 6,300 copies in the Memphis area alone. By February of 1955, the *Memphis Press-Scimitar* reports the record's sales, which are concentrated almost totally in the South and Southwest, are over 250,000.

quote of the day

"All the yelling is good because it covers up all my mistakes—if I hit a sour note."

—Elvis Presley

FIRST PHOTO

The March 1955 issue of *Country and Western Magazine* was the first periodical to feature a photograph of Elvis and a story on his blossoming career.

Today in

July 20

(1971) Elvis opens his first engagement at the High Sierra Room in the Sahara Tahoe Hotel located in Stateline, Nevada. Elvis performs two shows a night at eight and midnight. There is a $15.00 minimum for each show, which is extravagant for the time. Previously, a $7.50 minimum was the highest any performer received for the dinner or cocktail show at Lake Tahoe. The show's opener is comedian Nipsy Russell. Elvis breaks all Tahoe showroom attendance records with 3,400 patrons seeing the first two shows. Fans attending the opening night receive a special tote bag containing Elvis's *C'mon Everybody* album, a hat, scarf, button, photo album, and a teddy bear.

quote of the day

"The audience was whooping and hollering like crazy, when the song was through. That's when it really started, that night, and it's happened ever since."

—Elvis talking about audience reaction starting at the Memphis Music Jamboree

UNHEARD GOLD

Q: Elvis is the first artist to have a record reach gold status on advance orders alone. Over 1,000,000 people wanted copies of it before it was available on the shelves. What famous Elvis single accomplished this feat in 1956?

A: "Love Me Tender"

History

(1973) Elvis, after just completing tour dates, is in Memphis. RCA is asking for recordings to satisfy a contract signed earlier in the year. As Elvis is not inclined to go far from Memphis, recording sessions are scheduled at Stax Studio, just a couple of minutes from Graceland. Elvis doesn't show up for the first session and arrives late for the second. The studio musicians, most of whom haven't seen Elvis in some time, are shocked by his attitude and appearance. Nashville drummer Jerry Carrigan later explained, "It was the first time I ever saw him fat. His speech was slurred. He just seemed like he was miserable." Little of value is accomplished, save for a stumbling karate exhibition Elvis performs with his instructor Kang Rhee in the studio.

July

quote of the day

"I never wanted to become like Elvis...I don't want to become a fat, rich, sick, reclusive rock star. I want to continue as I've always done."
—Johnny Rotten, who's last job may have been appearances with other D-list celebrities on the TV show I'm A Celebrity, Get Me Out of Here.

LET'S GO KROGERING

In the Elvis Hall of Fame in Gatlinburg, Tennessee, a Graceland shopping list is on display. The list contains items that had to be available to Elvis at all times. The list includes: pickles, Pepsi, banana pudding, shredded coconut, at least three bottles of milk, fudge cookies, ingredients for meat loaf, and three packs each of spearmint, double mint, and juicyfruit chewing gum.

Today in

July

(1955) In a conference call, Colonel Parker, then-manager Bob Neal, Parker's then-partner Hank Snow, and Parker's assistant Tom Diskin discuss moving Elvis from Sun to a major recording label as well as booking him on a proposed Hank Snow weekly television show. At this point, Parker and Snow agree to put up $10,000 in cash to buy Elvis's release from Sun Records. In exchange, they expect a 2 percent share of Elvis's record royalties, calculating that he will receive a standard 5 percent and will presumably be happy with the 3 percent Sun is paying him. Not coincidentally, RCA makes a lucrative offer later in the day.

quote of the day

"Colonel Parker is more or less like a daddy when I'm away from my own folks. He doesn't meddle in my affairs. Ain't nobody can tell me 'you do this or that.' Colonel Parker knows the business and I don't. He never butts into record sessions, I don't butt into business. Nobody can tell you how to run your life."

—Elvis Presley

COLONEL DUTCHMAN

In 1973, RCA bought the recording masters, and royalty rights, of all of Elvis's previous recordings for the sum of $5.4 million. Elvis Presley Enterprises representative Jack Soden describes the deal as " right up there with the Indians selling Manhattan for $24." Seven years later an attorney for Elvis's estate, Blanchard Tual, concluded that Colonel Parker and RCA were "probably guilty of collusion, conspiracy, fraud, and misrepresentation."

History

(1967) Around this time, long-time friend and Memphis Mafia member Jerry Schilling flies into town to tell Elvis he's resigning his employ to try his hand at film editing for Paramount. He only stays the weekend, just long enough to see Elvis and collect his belongings. One of the best men at Elvis's wedding also returns to Memphis from California. It is rumored that Marty Lacker, another Memphis Mafia member, is being "demoted" by Elvis to caretaker at the Circle G Ranch. Two other inner circle members, Charlie Hodge and Richard Davis, mention they too are thinking of taking up permanent residence in California.

23 July

quote of the day

"He was a restless soul. He'd get hooked on something and just wear it out. He'd beat it to death, and that's it. He'd never go back to it."

—Red West

YAWNZEE-YAHTZEE!

Elvis and his Memphis Mafia once played the board game Yahtzee for four days non-stop.

Today in

24 July

(1975) Elvis is on the last of a three-day performance schedule at the Civic Center in Asheville, North Carolina. He has acted erratically lately, even inadvertently shooting Dr. Nick over an attempt to limit his medication intake. Tonight's performance at the Civic Center finds an irritable Elvis, who is frustrated by what he deems a lack of response from the audience. Losing his temper, Elvis solicits requests from the crowd, gives away a $6,500 ring to a fan, and throws his guitar into the audience. Upon checking out of his Asheville hotel, Elvis receives an invoice for $367.68, the cost of the television he shot into, the bullet from which struck Dr. Nick, who was not seriously injured.

quote of the day

"I think it was easier for The Beatles than Elvis.... He was on his own and....as his life went on, he ended up more and more on his own."

—Ringo Starr

NOT HIMSELF

Elvis's addiction to pain medications inevitable altered his personality. He was, by nature, a typical creative type, used to both euphoria and despair. The drugs, as in many cases of abuse, magnified this mood swing and flared his temper as well. In his last years, Elvis suffered depression that often lasted for weeks where he seldom left his bedroom.

History

(1965) This week Elvis begins production for *Paradise—Hawaiian Style*, his twenty-first film and the last under a second contract with producer Hal Wallis. The film is shot on location in Honolulu, Kauai (Hanalei Plantation Resort), Maui (Maui Sheraton Hilton), and the Kona Coast as well as Paramount Studios in Hollywood and the Torrance, California, Airport. *Paradise—Hawaiian Style* includes a production number entitled "Drums of the Islands" for which Hal Wallis decides to use a war canoe for the scene. The only one available on the islands at the time is Samoan. Because "Drums of the Islands" is based on a Tongan chant and Tongan rowers are used for the scene, the Samoans take offense, leading to several on-site fist-fights.

25 July

quote of the day

"I wasn't ready for that town, and it wasn't ready for me."

—Elvis, on Hollywood

PARADISE TRIVIA

Q: In the film *Paradise—Hawaiian Style*, characters Rick and Danny fly Mr. Cubberson to the Maui Sheraton Hilton Hotel for a convention of alligator-show salesmen, but it turns out to be the wrong hotel and convention. What group was holding its convention at the Maui Sheraton?

A: The Society For The Prevention of Cruelty To Animals.

Today in

26 July

(1954) Today in Memphis, Sun Records' owner Sam Phillips persuades local WMPS disc jockey Bob Neal, whose noontime gospel and hillbilly show Elvis often attends, to add young Elvis to his upcoming *Hillbilly Hoedown*, a package show starring *Louisiana Hayride* performers Slim Whitman and Billy Walker. Elvis is finally scheduled to appear in the show only a couple of days away in Memphis's Overton Park Shell. But that's not all, today is also the day Elvis signs a formal contract with Sun Records for a minimum of eight sides over a two-year period, with the contract renewable for an additional two years at the record company's option. Elvis receives the royalty rate of 3 percent of the wholesale price.

quote of the day

"It was the filthiest and most harmful production ... Indications of the harm Presley did were the two high-school girls whose abdomen and thighs had Presley's personal autograph ... There is also gossip that the Presley Fan Clubs degenerate into sex orgies."

—Letter to the FBI from the publisher of the La Crosse Register *newspaper*

OH PLEASE, MR. POSTMAN

In 1954 and 1955, Elvis answered his own fan mail. He stopped only when the hectic touring began and the mail count hit over 500 letters per week, which the Colonel will eventually have to hire a full-time secretary to handle.

History

(1963) Location shooting for *Viva Las Vegas* at an end, most of the cast and crew return to Los Angeles. By now Elvis and Ann-Margret are the subject of on-set gossip, which soon finds its way into the tabloids and press. "They hold hands. They disappear into his dressing room between shots. They lunch together in seclusion," writes AP reporter Bob Thomas. When shooting resumes at MGM studios, the Colonel takes a different view of Elvis's relationship with Ann-Margret. Parker is worried the film's director, George Sidney, is focusing too much attention on the female costar. The Colonel remedies the situation by cutting Ann-Margret's on-screen duets with Elvis to just one song, "The Lady Loves Me."

27 July

quote of the day

"He was a wonderful man."

—Ann-Margret's continued only response to questions about her relationship with Elvis

"BUNNY SAYS YOU'RE GOOD FOR IT"

Priscilla lived at Graceland in 1963 and had read accounts of Elvis's alleged affair with Ann-Margret. Consequently, when Ann-Margret called Elvis at Graceland, she used the code name "Bunny" (later changed to "Thumper" after the rabbit in the Disney film *Bambi*) It has been reported Elvis broke off his relationship with Ann-Margret after she had announced to the press that she and Elvis were engaged to be married.

―――― Today in ――――

July 28

(1954) Today's *Memphis Press-Scimitar* publishes its "The Front Row" column, by reporter Edwin Howard, which contains an interview with Elvis. Howard reports Elvis's first single is "getting an amazing number of plays on all Memphis radio stations." The column also has an accompanying photo of Elvis sporting a longish flat-top haircut, sideburns and a ducktail. He is wearing a plaid western cut suit and a bow tie. The same *Press-Scimitar* issue also has the first published newspaper ad for an Elvis appearance as part of the Slim Whitman show to be held at Memphis's Overton Park Shell.

quote of the day

"Rather flashily dressed—'playboy' type."

—Interviewer's notation on Elvis's 1953 employment application filed with the Tennessee State Employment Security Office

FASHION QUIZ

Q: According to those in the know, what article of clothing did Elvis never wear?

A: Underpants

History

July 29

(1973) Today, Elvis receives his seventh-degree black belt (associate master) in karate. During his life, Elvis practices martial arts for over eighteen years. He first became interested in karate while serving in the army in Germany. Elvis, whose karate name, as previously mentioned, is "Tiger," eventually achieved an eighth-degree black belt (master of the art). He studied tae kwan do with instructor Kang Rhee and kempo with instructor/bodyguard Ed Parker. Elvis's live performances almost always included some karate demonstration during the act in the 1970's. He also used karate in a number of movies, including: *GI Blues (1960), Wild in the Country (1961), Blue Hawaii (1961), Follow that Dream (1962), Kid Galahad (1962), Roustabout (1964), and Harum Scarum (1965).*

quote of the day

"Don't be so rough on the people when they come down here. Don't treat 'em like they're going to jail, God-dammit."

—Elvis from the stage to security personnel at a live performance

NOT EXACTLY A LIGHT-WEIGHT

Priscilla Presley, whose karate instructor was Mike Stone, achieved a green belt.

―――― *Today in* ――――

30 July

(1954) With his parents, girlfriend Dixie, and Sam Phillips in the audience, Elvis performs "That's All Right" and "Blue Moon of Kentucky" in the Slim Whitman *Hillbilly Hoedown* at Memphis's Overton Park Shell. Elvis is so nervous, he later states, that his legs began shaking during the performance of "That's All Right" without him even realizing it. The crowd goes crazy. Elvis, Scotty, and Bill then encore with "Blue Moon of Kentucky," and, as Elvis later describes it, "The very first appearance after I started recording ... I came out and I was doing a fast-type tune and everybody was hollering and I didn't know what they were hollering at. Then I came off stage and my manager told me they was hollering because I was wiggling my legs. And I was unaware of what I was doing ... So I went back out for an encore and I did a little more. And the more I did, the wilder they went."

quote of the day

"What I do is, I wiggle my shoulders and I shake my legs and I walk up and down the stage and hop on one foot ... I'd never do anything that was vulgar before an audience. My mother would never allow it."

—Elvis Presley

A PENNY EARNED

In late 1954 Elvis received his first royalty check for his first record, "That's All Right," in the amount of $82.50. This represented over two weeks' pay from his previous employer, Crown Electric, where he earned one dollar an hour.

History

31 July

(1969) It's 8:15 PM at the International Hotel Showroom in Las Vegas where Elvis is about to give his first live performance in years. The Sweet Inspirations are on-stage opening the show. Elvis is backstage experiencing a near panic attack from stage fright. At 10:15 PM, Elvis steps onto the stage unceremoniously and seems to hesitate. The anxiety dissipates as he proceeds to rock the house with a rousing version of "Blue Suede Shoes." The invitation-only show finds many celebrities in the audience. The audience response is explosive, leaving fans on their feet the entire show. Elvis bursts with energy, falling to his knees, sliding across stage, even doing somersaults at one point. By show's end, rave reviews are already being dispatched across the country and the world. There is *NO* negative response as Elvis enjoys near-universal acclaim.

quote of the day

"He's all man, top cat, the true king of the musical jungle."

—Review of an Elvis performance in Fabulous Las Vegas Magazine

A FAN OF A FAN

Many Elvis fans were A-list celebrities in their own right. Famous audience members Elvis introduced at his Las Vegas shows include: Carey Grant, Carol Channing, Pat Boone, Fats Domino, Phil Ochs, Barbra Streisand, Buzz Aldrin, Neil Diamond, Telly Savalas, Brenda Lee, Shirley Bassey, Mama Cass, George Hamilton, Petula Clark, Liza Minnelli, Charlton Heston, Nancy Sinatra, the Righteous Brothers, Roy Orbison, Englebert Humperdinck, and Bob Hope.

August

History

(1957) *Jet*, a weekly magazine geared toward the African-American market, publishes an article entitled, "The 'Pelvis' Gives His Views on Vicious Anti-Negro Slur." The article addresses a growing rumor that Elvis made the statement that African-Americans are only fit "to buy my records and shine my shoes." *Jet* reporter Louie Robinson interviews Elvis on the subject on the set of *Jailhouse Rock*. In the interview, Elvis tells Robinson he's said no such thing, or anything even close to it. Robinson also interviews several African-Americans who personally know Elvis, including Dudley Brooks, a Hollywood session pianist. By all accounts, Robinson concludes that Elvis believes "that people are people, regardless of race, color or creed."

1 August

quote of the day

"He was an integrator. Elvis was a blessing. They wouldn't let black music through. He opened the door for black music."

—Little Richard

ELVIS LESSON PLAN

Professor Vernon Clark of the University of Mississippi claimed at the Elvis Conference of 1995, "If it weren't for Elvis, millions and millions would still be enslaved in the thinking patterns of the oppressed and culturally colonized."

Today in

August

(1970) Elvis arrives in Las Vegas for an engagement at the International Hotel. During rehearsals, an MGM crew films footage to be used in an upcoming documentary, *Elvis: That's the Way It Is*. Five songs from the rehearsal are included in the film: "Bridge Over Troubled Water," "You've Lost That Lovin' Feelin'," "Mary in the Morning," "Polk Salad Annie," and "Words." *Elvis—That's the Way It Is* is Elvis's thirty-second film. It peaks at number 22 on *Variety*'s weekly list of top-grossing films.

quote of the day

"He was perfect for Hollywood and a casualty of Hollywood. He was perfect for Hollywood in that they could put him in anything and he would draw, and he was victimized by Hollywood for the same reason."

–Mike Stoller

HAIRY SITUATION

Elvis's contract with MGM specifically stated he, "Can never cut his hair off without our permission." When filming *Jailhouse Rock*, Elvis needed to wear a short-hair wig. To make one, a plaster cast of his head had to be produced. When the make-up artist cut the cast to remove it, he accidentally cut some of Elvis's real hair. Elvis's reaction? "Man, there's Frankie Avalon fans everywhere!"

History

(1956) Elvis arrives via automobile in Miami, Florida, to begin a week-long tour of the state. Following Elvis and the band is another vehicle containing Elvis's current girlfriend, June Juanico, and two of her friends. Elvis first met the auburn-haired, blue-eyed receptionist from Biloxi, Mississippi, in 1955 after a concert there. The group checks into the Robert Clay Hotel. Sometime during the day, a reporter from the *Miami Daily News* finds June for an interview. "Right now, he's married to his career," Ms. Juanico tells the reporter. She does mention her love for Elvis and the promising prospect of marriage. The interview puts the Colonel in a spin about the public's speculation on Elvis's "morals," and Elvis is ultimately inclined to appear on several radio programs to deny the matrimony rumors.

3 August

quote of the day

"I haven't given marriage much thought. I like to date girls who are fun to be with."

–Elvis Presley

YOU LIVE WITH YOUR MOM?

By most accounts, Elvis and June Juanico had an incredibly innocent, 1950's relationship. On the one occasion they got close to full-blown sex, they were "saved" when Gladys Presley arrived.

4 August

(1972) It's opening night for an engagement at the Las Vegas Hilton Hotel. (The facility has dropped the "International" title although the main entertainment area is still known as the Internationale Showroom.) Customary for opening night, there is only one show, at 8:00 PM, with invited guests including Richard Harris, Paul Anka, and Sammy Davis, Jr. Elvis complains of a headache and is only on-stage for thirty minutes, during which he doesn't perform any rock songs.

quote of the day

"I've wanted to perform again in public for a long, long time. The International Hotel has given me a chance to play where people come from all over. I need a live audience. It was getting harder and harder for me to perform for a camera."

—Elvis on his 1970 opening in Vegas

SAME TIME NEXT YEAR

From 1970 on, Elvis performed two two-week engagements a year in Las Vegas, in January and February, and August and September.

History

(1974) Requests have gone out for help for cancer victim Ivory Joe Hunter, the rhythm and blues singer-songwriter best known for "Since I Met You Baby," and author of several Elvis songs including "My Wish Came True." Elvis sends a check for $1,000 to the Ivory Joe Hunter fund in Memphis along with a note in which he writes, "I am very sorry to hear of Joe's illness. I have been a long time admirer of Ivory Joe and his talent. Please tell Joe for me that I wish him a speedy recovery. Joe is a great talent and has been an inspiration to many artists that have come along. It hurts me deeply to hear of his condition. I sincerely hope that this check will be of some help. Thank you for letting me know about Joe. Sincerely, Elvis Presley."

5 August

quote of the day

"An image is one thing, a human being is another. It's very hard to live up to an image."

—Elvis Presley

TAXMEN AND MANAGERS

Q: For a large portion of his career, how much of every dollar he earned did Elvis pay to taxes and Colonel Tom Parker?

A: Eighty cents

Today in

6 August

(1973) Elvis opens his latest "Summer Festival" at the Las Vegas Hilton with the customary single dinner show. This opening night is not one of his best. The *Hollywood Reporter* publishes a scorching review: "It's Elvis at his most indifferent, uninterested and unappealing. The living legend was fat and ludicrously aping his former self. ... His personality was lost in one of the most ill-prepared, unsteady, and most disheartening performances of his Las Vegas career.... It is a tragedy, disheartening and absolutely depressing to see Elvis in such diminishing stature."

quote of the day

"I hate Las Vegas .... This is my living folks, my life."

—Elvis from the Las Vegas stage, 1976

THE COST OF A DINNER SHOW

An Elvis autograph on a Las Vegas menu commands a price of $1,000 and up.

History

(1962) Anita Wood finally calls it quits with Elvis after five years. Since Elvis returned to Graceland earlier in the year, their relationship has been slowly cooling. Anita is aware of Elvis's feelings for Priscilla and she's finally decided she doesn't want to share Elvis's attention. Elvis and Anita met in 1957 and became romantically involved shortly after. Ms. Wood was a Memphis disc jockey and television personality. The former beauty queen also had a recording contract with ABC/Paramount Records. While Elvis was in the army, stationed at Fort Hood, Anita was a frequent visitor. A Memphis newspaper reported that Elvis and Anita were to marry prior to Elvis's departure for Germany for army service. Reportedly, Elvis and Anita wanted to get married, but Colonel Parker insisted Elvis stay single for his career's sake.

7 August

quote of the day

"Love and marriage are the most important things in life. Even more important than one's career."

—Elvis Presley

SMELLS SO SWEET

Q: In the late 1950's, what perfume did Elvis like most on women?

A: White Shoulders

Today in

8 August

(1954) Around this time Elvis begins what will become a regular gig as the headline attraction at Sleepy-Eyed John's Eagle's Nest Club in Memphis. In the near future the Eagle's Nest will become an important launching pad for Elvis's career on the local level. The Eagle's Nest has a reputation as a high-spirited place where the motto is: "Don't wear a tie unless your wife makes you."

quote of the day

"He was wearing a pink suit, white shoes and a ducktail, and I thought my wife was going out of the back door!"

—Scotty Moore on the first time he saw Elvis

FRIEND WITH A BADGE

Elvis became friends with Memphis police officer Bob Ferguson after meeting him at the Eagle's Nest in 1954. Throughout his life, Elvis became friends with countless police officers, collected police paraphernalia and enjoying aspects of law enforcement.

History

(1971) The second annual "Elvis Summer Fair" opens at the Las Vegas Hilton. The *Hollywood Reporter* gives the opening night performance a poor review, a symptom of the "roller coaster" ride the summer and winter engagements in Las Vegas will bring as to "which Elvis" will appear. This time around the show is called, "sloppy, hurriedly rehearsed, mundanely lit, poorly amplified, occasionally monotonous, often silly, and haphazardly coordinated.... Elvis looked drawn, tired, and noticeably heavier." But the *Reporter* says the audience seems unaffected and, "couldn't care less.... They absolutely loved, honored, and obeyed his every whim."

9 August

quote of the day

"The audience is the other half of me."

—Elvis Presley

OIL & WATER

From 1969 to 1971 Elvis used the gospel group the Imperials as back-up singers for Las Vegas appearances. But hardcore gospel fans felt that by appearing in Vegas the Imperials had "gone to hell," and their gospel bookings began to suffer. They eventually quit Elvis and were replaced by J.D. Sumner and the Stamps, who remained with Elvis until the end.

Today in

10 August

(1970) It's time to open the 1970 summer engagement at Las Vegas's International Hotel. The show brings cool reviews this year. *Cashbox Magazine* comments, "Elvis's show lacked the excitement of previous years." Audience reaction, however, is still charged. Elvis appears to be confident as he spends much of the show talking, free associating, and pursuing practical jokes during the performance. He turns the habit of handing out scarves to fans into a central part of the show, ordering them by the dozen from suppliers in Los Angeles and Las Vegas.

quote of the day

"I do try hard to please my fans, not just for the money it brings me, but because I like show business. There's a great personal satisfaction in performing when fans appreciate you."

—Elvis Presley

NUMBER ONE FANS

Father and son Paul and Elvis Aaron Presley Macleod of Holly Springs, Mississippi, claim to be the world's No. 1 Elvis fans. Their house, which they call Graceland Too, is a self-styled museum with every room dedicated to Elvis. Paul says his wife once gave him an ultimatum—her or the Elvis collection. Paul still owns the Elvis collection.

History

(1975) Elvis is relaxing in Palm Springs, California. He decides to go shopping for jewelry and finds his way to Harvey Austin's jewelry store in the evening hours. He goes to the store with two of his friends and three young women. He picks out items and goes to pay the $3,026 receipt but realizes he doesn't have any money on him. A quick call to Colonel Parker for the Visa card number, and the transaction is complete.

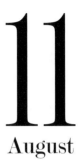

11 August

quote of the day

"I wonder how many of my friends that are here now would be here if it were five years ago. Not very many, because they're all looking for something from me."

—Elvis Presley

NO ROBIN HOOD

Elvis once gave Sammy Davis, Jr. a $30,000 ring. His reasoning? "Nobody ever thinks of giving a rich man anything."

― Today in ―

12 August

(1958) After one rejection, Elvis is finally granted emergency leave to visit his mother in Memphis because she has been admitted to Methodist Hospital. According to Elvis's friend Eddie Fadal, Elvis was visiting in Waco, Texas, when he received the leave authorization. Elvis and two friends drive from Waco to Dallas where they catch a Braniff jet for Memphis. Elvis arrives in Memphis in the afternoon and visits his mother at the hospital around 7:45 PM, staying several hours before returning to Graceland.

quote of the day

"Mama never could do enough for me. She took me to all those church meetings every Sunday to make sure I didn't ever go wrong."

—Elvis Presley

CHOIR PRACTICE

When Elvis was two years old, his mother regularly took him to the First Assembly of God church in Tupelo, just around the corner from their house. Gladys once said her toddler would climb off of her lap in an attempt to get up to the front and join the choir.

History

13 August

(1951) Reportedly, sixteen-year-old Elvis tries out for the Humes High School football team, the Tigers. Accounts vary on Elvis's actual participation. Red West, the team's fifteen-year-old center, says Elvis quit football after three weeks. Buzzy Forbess, a neighbor from Lauderdale Courts, remembers Elvis either staying on the team as a defensive end or just trying out in spring training. Alan Fortas, eventually a member of the Memphis Mafia, says Elvis didn't make the team. According to Rube Boyce, Humes High's football coach, Elvis kept bringing his guitar to the locker room. When he was told to either play football or sing, Elvis quit the team. In 1956, Elvis told a reporter in Little Rock, "I played end for two years. I never made real good of it, but, I mean, I enjoyed playing it."

quote of the day

"I'd like to have gone, but I never thought about it. We just didn't have the money."

—Elvis on why he never went to college

WORKING MAN

In 1952 Elvis got a job at Memphis's MARL Metal Manufacturing Company. He earned a dollar an hour in the fabrication division working the 3:15 PM to midnight shift. Gladys Presley made Elvis quit the job after only two months when she found out he was falling asleep in school.

14 August

(1958) Gladys Presley is in Methodist Hospital suffering from acute hepatitis and several other serious problems. Elvis visits his mother but returns to Graceland around 12:00 AM. Around 3:00 AM, Gladys suffers a heart attack. She dies at 3:15 AM with Vernon at her side. Vernon calls Graceland and talks to Elvis's cousin Billy Smith who must break the news to Gladys's only child. The boys drive to the hospital where Elvis stays with his mother's body until it is removed by orderlies. Gladys's body is brought to Graceland where she is laid to rest in the music room.

quote of the day

"One of the last things Mom said was that Daddy and I should always be together, so wherever they send me, Daddy will go too."

—Elvis on pending assignment in the army

"SHE WAS THE SUNSHINE OF OUR HOME"

Elvis brought Gladys's favorite gospel group, the Blackwoods, to Memphis to sing at her funeral. During the service, they sang Gladys's favorite song, "Precious Memories," and some of her other favorite hymns: "Rock of Ages," "In the Garden," and "I Am Redeemed."

History

15 August

(1955) Colonel Tom Parker, acting on behalf of himself "and/or" Hank Snow Attractions, a joint 50/50 partnership between Parker and Snow, signs Elvis to a one-year contract. The Colonel is to be Elvis's "special advisor" while Bob Neal remains as Elvis's manager. The contract allows Parker to pick up two additional one-year options. In his capacity as advisor, Parker receives $2,500 for his services, in addition to being reimbursed for any other expenses. The contract also stipulates, "As a special concession to Colonel Parker, ELVIS PRESLEY is to play 100 personal appearances within one year for the special sum of two hundred dollars including musicians."

quote of the day

"He's the only guy that really gave me the big breaks. I don't think I would have ever been very big with another man. Because he's—he's a very smart man."

—Elvis talking about Tom Parker in 1955

BUY A TICKET

Colonel Parker always held, "If you want to see Elvis Presley, buy a ticket." Parker refused to let Elvis give any performances to his fellow soldiers while he was in the army. He even turned down an invitation for Elvis to sing at the White House, saying that if the President doesn't pay, Elvis doesn't play. Similarly, Elvis never gave encores—always leaving the audience wanting more.

Today in

16 August

(1977) A little after midnight, Elvis and Ginger Alden return to Graceland from a dentist's appointment where Elvis had his teeth cleaned and several fillings done. At around 2:15 AM Elvis gets a prescription filled for six Dilaudid pills for dental pain. A couple of hours later, Elvis calls cousin Billy and his wife Jo to play racquetball. Shortly thereafter, Elvis heads for his bedroom where he takes the first of three packets of medication to make him sleep. When Ginger awakens around 1:30 PM, Elvis is not in bed. She discovers him shortly after lying face down on the bathroom floor in a pool of vomit. Elvis is rushed to Baptist Memorial Hospital where he is officially pronounced dead at 3:30 PM. The press is informed Elvis died of "cardiac arrhythmia due to undetermined heartbeat." Although autopsy results remain private, there is convincing evidence the cause of death was polypharmacy, with fourteen drugs detected in his system at the time of death, ten in significant quantity.

quote of the day

"Elvis was an extremist in all that he did."

—Jerry Schilling, Elvis's life-long friend and personal aide

WIDE AWAKE

In 1974, after collapsing in Louisiana, Elvis enrolled in a detox program at Memphis's Baptist Memorial Hospital. Doctors took him off of his sleeping medication assuming he would eventually go to sleep on his own. Elvis remained awake for four days.

History

17 August

(1964) According to hairdresser Larry Gellar's book, *"If I Can Dream": Elvis's Own Story*, Elvis, who is in Hollywood filming *Girl Happy*, meets privately with Colonel Parker on the MGM lot while Larry and the others wait so they can leave for a break in Memphis. Elvis emerges from the meeting enraged, saying the Colonel has just accused him of being on a "religious kick .... He doesn't know anything about me. My life is not a kick. It's real." This is just a symptom of the growing resentment almost all of the guys feel toward Larry's growing influence over Elvis's attention and religious/ spiritual views.

quote of the day

"And what do you do?"

—Elvis's serious question to Eric Clapton upon meeting him at Graceland

...LIKE A BOOK

Among Elvis's favorite books were *Autobiography Of A Yogi, Beyond the Himalayas,* and *The Impersonal Life,* which he gave copies of to all his friends. He also read *Leaves of Gold,* which contains various philosophies of life and death.

18 August

(1958) Still on leave from the army, and reeling over grief at his mother's passing, Elvis remains in seclusion at Graceland. There are many attempts to cheer him up. Musicians, including Johnny Cash, Jerry Lee Lewis, and Bill Black stop by to sing. The Tennessee Highway Patrol takes him on helicopter rides where he learns the basics of piloting. He visits the Rainbow Roller Rink and catches midnight movies. He and Rex Mansfield, an army buddy, practice karate. Other nights, Elvis rents Chenault's hamburger stand in Memphis and takes the entourage for all-night burgers and shakes. Elvis also buys a van and tours the Tennessee countryside and visits Tupelo.

quote of the day

"I've been kind of nervous all my life. They say you learn how to relax when you get older. I hope they're right."

—Elvis Presley, early in his career

ELVIS THE SOLDIER

In his 1983 book *Elvis the Soldier*, army friend Rex Mansfield claims that Elvis gave him amphetamine pills at Goethestrasse 14 (his home) in 1959. He also claims Elvis was buying pills from a soldier who worked in the dispensary.

History

19 August

(1974) It's this year's opening day for the annual Elvis Summer Festival at the Las Vegas Hilton Hotel. Elvis reinvents the show with an entirely new program. Gone is the 2001 introduction and medley of past hits. Blues like "Big Boss Man," "My Baby Left Me," and "Down in the Alley" replace some of the sentimental numbers. Elvis seems reinvigorated with the changes as evidenced in The *Hollywood Reporter's* opening night review: "...the best show...in at least three years. Presley looks great, is singing better than he has in years, and was so comfortable with his show—almost all new songs—the packed Hilton showroom gave him several standing ovations."

quote of the day

"We're gonna sing a lot of songs and try to make you happy. Make you forget about Watergate and all that jazz."

—*Elvis from the stage, 1974*

EVERYBODY'S A CRITIC

One night in Las Vegas Elvis was called backstage to meet singer Barbra Streisand. Streisand started making sarcastic remarks about Elvis's outfit, so he told her she was the ugliest star in Hollywood. They both laughed about the conversation and started a friendship.

20 August

(1962) Today Elvis purchases a previously unused 1959 Flixible VL 100 touring bus in Memphis prior to heading for the West Coast. Elvis likes the idea that the bus will allow freedom for the entourage to travel cross country without the limitations of rail travel. The land yacht is eventually customized by George "Customizer of the Stars" Barris of Hollywood to include special seats, a queen-sized bed for Elvis, tape players, a CB radio, a small kitchen, and a couch in the lounge that converts into a double bed. Almost immediately after making the purchase, Elvis and the guys make their inaugural trip from Memphis to Los Angeles.

quote of the day

"Goodbye, you long black sonofabitch."

—Elvis to his Cadillac as he boarded the bus for army basic training

SLOW IT DOWN, SON

Elvis was stopped for speeding seven times.

―――――――――――――――― History ――――――――――

21 August

(1975) Having decided to cancel the final performances of an engagement at the Las Vegas Hilton because he is sick, Elvis flies back to Memphis with Dr. Nick and is admitted to Baptist Memorial Hospital. The Hilton removes any and all of the signs, photographs, and publicity regarding the show. A small sign in the lobby reads: "The remainder of the Elvis Presley engagement has been canceled due to illness." The Hilton also releases a statement saying: "Mr. Elvis Presley was asked by his physician to cancel the remainder of his present engagement. This decision was prompted by a fatigue state that developed in recent weeks. Mr. Presley is to be hospitalized in Memphis for further tests and rest. His physicians do not believe there is any reason for alarm but are doing this for conservation reasons." The memo is signed by Dr. Elias Ghanem and Dr. George Nichopoulos.

quote of the day

"Retirement? Well, I'll put it like this. I'll never quit as long as I'm doing okay. As long as you're pleasing the public, you'd be foolish to quit."

—Elvis Presley

HEAVY THREADS, MAN

Early in his career, the suits Elvis wore to perform weighed about twenty-five pounds. But later ones, with the cape, weighed as much as seventy-five pounds. It was Elvis's idea to add the capes and heavy belts to his stage wardrobe, as he enjoyed wearing similar items off stage.

―― Today in ――

August 22

(1969) Well into his first live performance engagement in nine years, Elvis seems to have lost most of his stage fright during this performance at the International Hotel in Las Vegas. He indulges in informal banter with the audience and seems totally at ease. Colonel Parker feels Elvis may have become too relaxed in his performance and today's performance causes the Colonel to write Elvis, "Before I left I talked to Joe [Esposito], as the pressure is getting a little heavy regarding the off-color material. I am of course speaking mostly in regard to the dinner show when there are a great many children. I can only relate this to you. You are the only one who can change it."

quote of the day

"My first meeting with Colonel Parker was five hours after Mr. Hilton took over the hotel. I came in at noon and had a meeting with Colonel Parker at five. Tom Jones, Engelbert Humperdinck, and Barbra Streisand are all great stars, but there is only one who sells out the entire duration of an engagement as soon as his name is announced."

―*The vice-president of the Hilton Hotel, Las Vegas*

BIG BUCKS FOR BIG NAMES

Elvis was paid $400,000 for a four-week Las Vegas run, doing two shows nightly. Parker told Elvis before the first show, the Colonel could make everyone aware Elvis was in town, but only Elvis could make them buy a ticket. Opening night in 1969, as Elvis stepped on stage dressed in a black karate uniform, he was stopped by a roar from the audience. He received his first standing ovation of the engagement just for showing up.

History

23 August

(1956) Elvis reports to the 20th Century Fox studios to begin production on *Love Me Tender*, his first feature film. The film's producer is David Weisbart, who also produced 1954's *Rebel Without a Cause* starring James Dean, which is one of Elvis's favorite films. Through Weisbart, Elvis has the opportunity to meet Natalie Wood, Nick Adams and Sal Mineo. Elvis befriends Adams, and Natalie Wood, age eighteen at the time, becomes a frequent visitor to the *Love Me Tender* set. Natalie usually shows up in her white Thunderbird with red leather upholstery accompanied by Nick Adams. The three drive to P.C. Brown's ice cream parlor for hot-fudge sundaes or the Hamburger Hamlet. The three become best of friends.

quote of the day

"Is it a sausage? ... Is it a Walt Disney goldfish? ... Is it a corpse? ... A peculiar sound emerges. A rusty foghorn?"

—TIME *magazine review of* Love Me Tender

GIANT PROFITS

Q: *Love Me Tender* recovered its production costs in three days at the theater. It had the second-highest first-week earnings of 1956. What movie had the highest?

A: James Dean's *Giant*

Today in

24 August

(1956) Elvis is in California at the Fox Studio soundstage to record the three songs to be included in *The Reno Brothers* (the title was later changed to *Love Me Tender*). Scotty, Bill, and D.J. have driven to Hollywood, with Elvis's encouragement, in hopes of appearing in the film as well as recording for RCA. The musical director rejects the boys (they are told they're not "hillbilly" enough), and Elvis finds himself working with studio musicians in an uncomfortable situation, though the Colonel has arranged for Elvis to receive co-writing credit and for all of the songs to be assigned to his publishing company. In the end recording does not go badly. Elvis takes a special liking to one of the songs, "Love Me Tender," a reworking of the Civil War ballad "Aura Lee."

quote of the day

"People think all I can do is belt. I used to sing nothing but ballads before I went professional. I love ballads."
—Elvis to Hollywood reporter Army Archerd regarding his like for "Love Me Tender"

NEW YORK GIANT

Elvis's first film, *Love Me Tender*, opened at the Paramount Theater in New York City in 1956. A forty-foot cardboard cut-out of Elvis towered over the building. Since the film opened on a Thursday, truant officers were in attendance.

History

(1972) This week, Gregory Hookstratten, Elvis's attorney, files a petition for divorce in Elvis's behalf in Santa Monica superior court, Los Angeles County. The reason is listed as "irreconcilable differences." Priscilla does not contest the divorce and neither she nor Elvis appears in court. It is reported that the couple have reached an agreement on an undisclosed property settlement. Hookstratten tells reporters the reason for the divorce is "that Elvis has been spending six months a year on the road which put a tremendous strain on the marriage."

25 August

quote of the day

"I don't feel like I'm property. I can't get it out of my head that I'm property. People tell me 'you can't do this or that,' but I don't listen to them. I do what I want. I can't change and I won't change."

—Elvis Presley

PILL-OW TALK

At one time Priscilla took pills along with Elvis, but she quit when a pillow fight got out of hand and Elvis gave her a black eye by mistake. She dropped the pills but picked up the nickname "Toughie." Elvis declined to give up pills with her.

Today in

26 August

(1960) Elvis's army service proves to have not affected his popularity at all. This month alone, he has begun filming *Flaming Star*, his sixth film. A sneak preview of *G.I. Blues* is held at the Majestic Theater in Dallas, causing Raymond Willie, vice president and general manager of Circuit, Inc. to telegram Paramount, "We have never witnessed such marvelous reaction to any picture." Magazines are also ablaze with Elvis features. *Movie Stars TV Close-Ups Magazine* features Elvis on the cover with an article, "The Terrible Temptation In Elvis's Home." The temptation, it turns out, was for Elvis to tell Dee Stanley (who was not married to Vernon at the time the article was written) to start packing.

quote of the day

"I've learned one thing in this man's army. Man, coming home is the greatest."

—*Elvis Presley*

THE LAST "ONE" TRIVIA

Q: On this date in 1969 Elvis's last number-one hit was released. Name the popular ballad.

A: "Suspicious Minds"

History

(1965) The Beatles are in the States on their second U.S. tour. The Fab Four pay a visit to Elvis today at his Bel Air home on Perugia Way at 10:00 PM. They stay until 2:00 AM and spend the time telling stories, joking, and listening to records. Elvis drinks Seven-Up while the Beatles partake of either scotch or bourbon. The five entertainers even have an impromptu jam session with Elvis playing drums, piano, and showing Paul he can play the intro to "I Feel Fine" on bass guitar.

27 August

quote of the day

"Fantastic, he was like one of us, none of the old Hollywood show-off thing."
—Ringo Starr on being asked how it was to meet Elvis

"The only person we wanted to meet in the U.S.A. was Elvis Presley. We can't tell you what a thrill that was."
—John Lennon upon meeting Elvis

OFFICER OF THE CARNIVAL

During his carnival days, Tom Parker became friends with a singer named James Davis. When Davis was Governor of Louisiana in 1948 he bestowed an honorary Louisiana Colonel's commission on Parker, who was known as "Colonel" Tom Parker for the rest of his life.

Today in

August 28

(1970) Joe Esposito receives a phone call at his Los Angeles home in the early morning hours today demanding $50,000 to reveal the name of an individual who the caller claims plans to kill Elvis during his Saturday night show in Las Vegas. This is the second threat Elvis recently received. Ed Hookstratten, Elvis's attorney, notifies the FBI and calls in Elvis friend and private detective John O'Grady to oversee security in Las Vegas. Elvis places calls to Red West, Jerry Shilling, and Ed Parker to join him in Vegas to supplement the other bodyguards and security personnel who will surround the stage during the show. All of the security people are armed, as is Elvis, with a pistol stuck in each boot. No incidents occur during any of Elvis's shows.

quote of the day

"Sometimes my teeth get tired of smiling. It's dog-gone tiring. But it's worth it. After all, you just can't knock success."

—*Elvis Presley*

FLASHBACK!

One of Elvis's more unusual hobbies was to float flashbulbs in his swimming pool, then take out a gun and shoot them so they'd flash and sink to the bottom.

History

(1962) *Kid Galahad,* Elvis's tenth film, opens in theaters across the country to generally good reviews. *Daily Variety,* in its review, says, "Presley's acting resources are limited, but he has gradually established a character with which he doesn't have to strain too much for emotional nuance—the soft-spoken, unaffected, polite, unspoiled, forthright, and ultimately two-fisted country boy." The *Hollywood Reporter* calls the film "a good vehicle for the talents of Elvis Presley." But *The New York Times* thinks "Mr. Presley does not make a convincing pug."

29 August

quote of the day

"I never met Jimmy Dean, but how I wish I had."

—*Elvis Presley*

GEAR JAMMER

When Elvis wanted anonymity on the road, he drove his Chevy one-ton pick-up.

Today in

30 August

(1971) Elvis finally begins wearing the special belt presented to him by the International Hotel at this Las Vegas Engagement. Elvis refuses to wear the belt until all performances are guaranteed sell-outs. Elvis had done the same during his winter run in February at the International Hotel. The hotel presented Elvis with the silver belt featuring a large buckle at the end of the summer 1969 engagement for record-setting audience attendance. The belt's buckle was inscribed with the numbers: The total attendance for Elvis's month at the International Hotel in 1969 topped 101,509, breaking the previous Las Vegas record. The gross receipts had been $1,522,635, also a Las Vegas record.

quote of the day

"This belt says I set attendance records at the International Hotel, and these say I get to keep it."

—Elvis to apparent ne'er do wells eying his silver belt as he opened his jacket revealing two pistols in his waistband

SHOT INTO SPACE

In 1988 the US tabloid *The Sun* reported that a statue of Elvis had been found on Mars, and a radio receiver was picking up strains of "All Shook Up." UFOlogist Nikola Stanislaw concluded that aliens must have built it believing Elvis to be some sort of god. This was the only rational explanation.

31 August

(1957) Elvis is appearing at Vancouver, B.C.'s Empire Stadium. He enters the arena riding in a black Cadillac convertible and takes the stage at the Empire's north end. Elvis performs for thirty-five minutes when a crowd of Canadian teens breaks through the police barricade and heads for the stage. Elvis ends his show in mid-song, yelling, "I'm cutting out, man!" It takes over two hours to restore any semblance of order inside the stadium. Elvis, when he's finally able to leave the building, declares the show's over and heads for his hotel.

quote of the day

"I've been scratched and bitten and everything. I just accept it with a broad smile. They don't intend to hurt you. They just want a piece of you for a souvenir."

—Elvis Presley

A SISTER'S BROKEN VOW

Pupils at the Notre Dame Convent in Ottawa had to sign a pledge that they would not attend an Elvis concert. Eight girls were expelled for disobeying.

September

History

(1956) Elvis begins a three-day recording session at Hollywood's Radio Recorders Studio because RCA – West Coast offices don't have studio facilities at this time. Elvis's regular band, Scotty Moore on guitar, Bill Black on bass, and D.J. Fontana on drums, are in the sessions along with the Jordanaires singing back-up vocals. Piano is handled by musicians Dudley Brooks and Gordon Stokes of the Jordanaires. During these sessions, Elvis records "Playing for Keeps," "Love Me," "How Do You Think I Feel," "Long Tall Sally," "Old Shep," and "Too Much."

1 September

quote of the day

"I bet I could burp and make them squeal."

–Elvis Presley

TOP-RATE PRODUCER

Elvis took much longer than was normal at the time to record a song—he would do as many as forty takes then choose one from memory. Nothing was ever written out in the studios—the arrangements just happened as Elvis tried different things. He was effectively his own producer, from the very first session on.

Today in

2 September

(1975) After a cancelled engagement in Las Vegas, Elvis remains in Memphis's Baptist Memorial Hospital being treated for an "impacted colon and hypertension." Maurice Elliott, vice president in charge of public relations for the hospital, says Elvis is hospitalized "at Dr. Nichopoulos' request because Dr. Nick wants Elvis in a controlled environment where he can receive proper food and rest." Elvis's hospital stay is not without event. He gives a new Pontiac to eighteenth-floor nursing supervisor Marion Cocke and receives a "get well" call from former president Richard Nixon. Upon his release, two nurses, including Mrs. Cocke, leave the hospital to enter Elvis's employ.

quote of the day

"You can't fool yourself or the public for very long."

–Elvis Presley

BLAME IT ON THE PRESLEYS AND SMITHS

Elvis had an inherited medical condition, a ganglionic fold, which caused real problems. The disease limits the colon's function and efficiency. Elvis made matters worse by overusing laxatives, weakening his whole digestive system and causing a distended abdomen that caused considerable pain.

History

3 September

(1973) It's the final night of this year's Elvis Summer Fest at the Las Vegas Hilton. Elvis in a playful mood, entertains the audience with stage antics. He aggravates the Colonel, however, when he makes off-color remarks about the hotel for what he feels is poor treatment of a loyal employee. At show's end Elvis says, "I know we kid a lot and have fun and everything—but we really love to sing, play music, and entertain people. As long as I can do that, I'll be a happy old sonofabitch." After the show, the Colonel storms into Elvis's dressing room berating him for his "unprofessional" behavior. A shouting match ensues in front of shocked entourage members. It ends with Elvis firing the Colonel later as the two continue to argue in Elvis's suite. Parker counters that he quits and will submit a bill for money owed.

quote of the day

"People keep saying that my manager has a good thing in me, taking 25 percent of my earnings. He sure has. And I've got myself a good thing in him. We both make money. He knows how to drive a hard bargain for me. And he works night and day."

—Elvis Presley on Tom Parker

GOING TO THE COLONEL

Q: What popular group reportedly asked Colonel Tom Parker to manage them after the death of their own manager?

A: The Beatles

4 September

(1948) Thirteen-year-old Elvis acquires his parent's marriage certificate and makes some amendments. He fills in September 4, 1948, to the date of application, lists the date of marriage at September 11, 1948, and as the nuptial participants his own name and that of "Magdline" [Magdeline] Morgan, a girl his own age who he knows from the First Assembly of God Church. When Ms. Morgan learns of the document, almost fifty years later, she's very surprised, saying, "It was just a very sweet relationship. At that time, if you just held hands, it was very serious. And we did hold hands a lot."

quote of the day

"Female mostly."

—*Elvis responding to the question: "What kind of girls do you prefer?"*

COTTON PICKIN' FOR DOLLARS

When Elvis was ten years old, he and some friends worked in a cotton field where they were paid one dollar for half a day's work. They quit after two weeks, deciding the pay was too low.

History

(1957) Elvis begins three days of recording sessions at Radio Recorders in Hollywood. Elvis records "Treat Me Nice," which is to be the flip side of the "Jailhouse Rock" single. The only other song completed is "Blue Christmas," scheduled for release on a later Christmas album. The usual group of Memphis/Hollywood musicians participate in the sessions. When recording is finished, Scotty Moore and Bill Black each send Elvis a registered letter resigning from his back-up band. The earlier promise to allow Scotty and Bill to record some instrumentals of their own upon completion of Elvis's sessions has now been refused by Colonel Parker. The trio has been together since 1954, but when Elvis's popularity took off, and he began spending more time on films, Scotty and Bill found themselves making lower salaries. By "resigning" they could find other work and still work with Elvis on a contractual basis.

5 September

quote of the day

"If I had to drop it all, I could do it, but I wouldn't like it."

—*Elvis Presley*

HOLLYWOOD NAME CALLING

Elvis and Dewey Phillips exchanged barbs in 1957. Elvis called Dewey a "low life," and Phillips responded by pegging Elvis as a "Hollywood Snob."

Today in

6 September

(1965) The *Memphis Press-Scimitar,* publishes an article this week advising readers of Elvis's financial situation. The hometown entertainer stands to make $2.7 million for the four films of 1965, plus 50 percent of the profits of each film. Compared with other top Hollywood actors, each of whom makes an average of two movies a year, Elvis is in a class by himself. According to the report, most Elvis movies gross about $5 million of which $500,000 is profit. Of that amount, Elvis stands to make an additional $250,000 on films. Include the royalty income from his records ($1.25 million), music publishing ($400,000), and merchandise ($60,000), and Elvis stands to top the $5 million income mark, not too bad a living for 1965!

quote of the day

Whenever Elvis appeared at the Hilton, all those nice little flyers and flags and decorations were put up by some hotel personnel and a lot of fans who happened to be around. We worked our butts off putting that stuff up, sorting menus, postcards, and heaven knows what else. After working, working, working for several days prior to Elvis's opening, we got our reward...drum roll...a pancake breakfast!!! When we told Elvis he howled and said, "Yeah, that would be the Colonel all right."

—Sandi Miller, a friend of Elvis's during the '60s and '70s.

BREAKING UNCLE SAM

Elvis already earned over $100,000 a month by the time he was drafted into the army. His two-year army stint cost the US government an estimated $500,000 in tax revenue!

History

(1977) In Memphis, an attorney for the Elvis Presley Estate, Beecher Smith III, files an application with the board of adjustment for a zoning variance to allow the bodies of Elvis and Gladys Presley to be moved from Forest Hills cemetery to a plot on Graceland property. Although the request will not be heard for three weeks, it is eventually granted. The bodies of both Elvis and Gladys are moved from Forest Hill Cemetery to Meditation Gardens on the Graceland estate on October 2, 1977. On November 27, 1977, the gardens are opened to the public. Elvis's father and paternal grandmother, Vernon and Minnie Mae Presley, are also interred at Meditation Gardens.

7 September

quote of the day

"Someone asked me this morning, what did I miss about Memphis, and I said, 'Everything!'"

—*Elvis upon his return from the army*

WORLD-WIDE FAMILY TIES

A fan from Ireland once described her visit to Graceland as "just like going to see your dad's grave."

Today in

September 8

(1974) Near Twin Falls, Idaho, Elvis is in the crowd as Evel Knievel attempts to blast across the seventeen-hundred-foot-wide Snake River Canyon in a small self-made rocket. Unfortunately for Knievel, Elvis, and the other fans, the rocket's drag shoot deploys as the rocket gains speed off the ramp, and he misses his mark by a wide margin. Other celebrities in the audience include John Wayne, Steve McQueen, Dustin Hoffman, and President Ford's two sons. Two years from now in 1976, amid rumors of Elvis booking performances in Great Britain, Evel Knievel's promoter, John Daly, suggests a "British Spectacular" starring Elvis Presley and featuring Evel Knievel. The idea never comes to fruition.

quote of the day

"When he started he couldn't spell Tennessee. Now he owns it."

—Bob Hope on Elvis

TRUCK BED BOXING

Q: To promote an Elvis movie, some small-town theaters set up a boxing ring in the back of a pick-up truck and hired locals to spar while being driven around town. Which movie was promoted in this unique way?

A: Kid Galahad

History

9 September

(1970) Today Elvis begins his first tour since the fifties. Other than the first show in Phoenix, this tour is booked by the Concerts West Company, which has paid, at the Colonel's insistence, $1 million up front. Tickets for all locations cost an extravagant $10.00, $7.50 and $5.00, but over 15,000 are sold. Elvis basically takes his Vegas show on the road, even bringing along comedian/emcee Sammy Shore. Elvis hires the Hugh Jarrett Singers (Jarrett is a former member of the Jordanaires). Elvis and crew arrive in Phoenix aboard three planes, one for Colonel Parker, one for the musicians and road crew, and a customized Fairchild for Elvis. The entourage checks into the Townhouse Hotel where Elvis has booked the entire tenth floor for himself. A bomb threat delays the show by half an hour, but at 9:00 PM Elvis takes the stage. He's on the road again.

quote of the day

"That's my idol, Elvis Presley. If you went to my house, you'd see pictures all over of Elvis. He's just the greatest entertainer that ever lived. And I think it's because he had such a presence. When Elvis walked into a room, Elvis Presley was in the fucking room! I don't give a fuck who was in the room with him, Bogart, Marilyn Monroe."

—Eddie Murphy

TEDDY BARE

The third issue of *Playgirl* magazine published a cartoon that presented a nude Elvis, discreetly covered by a toy teddy bear. The caption had Elvis singing, "I want to be your Teddy BARE."

Today in

10 September

(1967) Elvis is in Nashville recording at RCA Victor's Studio "B." A familiar group of musicians joins Elvis for the sessions, including Scotty Moore on guitar. When Scotty has trouble with the intricate guitar introduction to the song "Guitar Man," Jerry Reed, the song's composer, is contacted. Reed, who is fishing nearby, has never met Elvis and readily agrees to participate in the recording sessions. He arrives with a three-day beard and a lot of apprehension. Reed's addition turns out to be inspirational, however, as he turns out blistering guitar work on "Guitar Man" and "Big Boss Man."

quote of the day

"Elvis could do everything, from a very quiet sensual moan and groan to a high panic scream and was willing to do it within the context of a three-minute song, with no inhibitions whatsoever."

—*Elvis's bassist Norbert Putman*

HOON DOG

British protesters against the 2003 Iraq war carried placards with a message for Britain's Defense Secretary Geoff Hoon: "You ain't nothing but a Hoon Dog, lying all the time."

History

11 September

(1956) Elvis's rise to fame is apparent all over the magazine world. This month's edition of *Rod Builder and Customizer* magazine publishes an article titled "Rock 'N' Roll Drag" reporting that Elvis once held a part-time job cleaning garages and of his early desire to own a hot-rod. The current issue of *Coronet* has an article titled "The Craze Called Elvis," covering his September 9 appearance on the Ed Sullivan show. *Songs That Will Live Forever* magazine features Elvis and Pat Boone on its cover.

quote of the day

"I sang then with a big heavy rhythm—what I called a rockabilly beat."

—Elvis on his early style of singing

WOULDN'T YOU REALLY RATHER HAVE...

Elvis took the test for his first Tennessee driver's license in his uncle Travis's 1940 Buick. He passed the first time.

September 12

(1948) Elvis's name appears today for the first time in a newspaper. The *Tupelo Journal* Sunday edition publishes a list of newly elected student council members for Milam Junior High. Last week, which was the first week of school, Elvis was elected to represent his homeroom. The Presleys also know the results of last school year's General Achievement Test, in which Elvis scored an acceptable 70 percent average. His high scores came in diction (79%) and physical education (80%), while lower scores were earned in arithmetic (64%), social studies (62%), and literature (61%).

quote of the day

"I would lie awake wondering what I was going to do. I really wasn't much good at anything. At school I'd been only an average student. I mean I didn't flunk, but I didn't do too good, either. I couldn't figure out how I was ever going to make something out of myself."

—Elvis Presley

WALK A MILE IN MY SHOES

Upon graduation from high school in 1953, Elvis hitchhiked over two hundred miles to Meridian, Mississippi, to enter a country music talent contest. He finished runner-up.

History

13 September

(1973) Around this time, as told by Red and Sonny West and Charlie Hodge in *Elvis: What Happened?*, a teenager reportedly overdosed on Hycodan (a potent cough suppressant) while visiting at Elvis's Palm Springs home. *Teddy Bear* magazine later published a different account of the incident from someone who claims that West and Hodge were not even there. According to *Teddy Bear*, Elvis was suffering from a head cold and was, indeed, taking Hycodan. The eighteen-year-old woman was at the Palm Springs home with some mutual friends. The woman "tasted" the cough syrup after Elvis commented it tasted terrible. Later the woman consumed wine, said she didn't feel well, and went to the bedroom to lie down while Elvis watched television with the others. When Elvis went to check on the woman, he found her unconscious. An ambulance was called and she was treated. Elvis phoned the woman's mother who told him her daughter was on tranquilizers and should not drink wine.

quote of the day

"Gossip is little talk for little minds."

—*Elvis Presley*

THE MONSTER WITHIN

A comic book called *Invasion of the Elvis Zombies*, by artist Gary Panter, has Elvis being eaten by female fans only to be brought back to life as a hybrid of himself, King Kong, and Godzilla.

14 September

(1970) Today Elvis is scheduled for a performance in Mobile, Alabama, at the Municipal Auditorium. The last time Elvis performed in Mobile was 1955 when he and his smaller entourage stayed at one of the city's premiere hotels, the Admiral Semmes. Elvis and company once again check into the Admiral Semmes only to find that over the years the place seems to have fallen on hard times and had turned into, as Elvis calls it, "the dump of dumps." Elvis complains to Joe Esposito, insisting other quarters be found. But when Joe tries to find another hotel he's told there isn't a room in town, more than once being asked, "Don't you know Elvis Presley's in town?"

quote of the day

"It is not the critic who counts ... the credit belongs to the man who is actually in the arena."

—message on an inspirational wall-hanging Elvis once had hanging at Graceland

I SCREAM YOU, YOU SCREAM, WE ALL SCREAM...

Q: While staying at a hotel in Jacksonville, Florida, Elvis wanted ice cream and called to find out what flavors were available. On being told there were 28 to choose from, which flavor did he choose?

A: All of them. He reportedly ate a scoop of each.

History

(1956) The *Billboard* charts report "Don't Be Cruel" as number one on the "Top 100" for the week ending September 5. It remains at number one for seven weeks. In its "Vox Jox" column, *Billboard* tells the story of three hundred irate rock 'n' roll fans marching on radio station WEIL in Elizabeth, Kentucky, when the station announced it was breaking Elvis records. The protest of the protest results in a compromise. WIEL now devotes fifteen minutes each day to nothing but Elvis, and fifteen minutes to the show "For All Those Who Don't Like Elvis Presley."

15 September

quote of the day

"You're puttin' too much into your singin', though you're not vulgar. But you keep that kind of activity and you won't live to be thirty!"

—Gladys Presley's response when Elvis asked if she thought he was vulgar on-stage in 1955

ARCHIVING A LEGEND

Q: Since 1955, a university in Tennessee has kept copies of every piece of news coverage regarding Elvis Presley. The collection continued even after Elvis's death. Can you name the university?

A: Vanderbilt

16 September

(1963) The Memphis City Commission is presented with a motion to rename the portion of U.S. Highway 51 from Parkway to the Mississippi state line the "Elvis Presley Highway." This portion of highway passes in front of Graceland. Also at this meeting, the commission rules out previous suggestions to name the Fairground Coliseum and a new football stadium for Elvis Presley.

quote of the day

"I remember Elvis as a young man hanging around Sun Studios. Even then, I knew this kid had a tremendous talent. He was a dynamic young boy. His phraseology, his way of looking at a song, was as unique as Sinatra's. I was a tremendous fan, and had Elvis lived, there would have been no end to his inventiveness."

—B.B. King

COLLECTOR'S ENDORSEMENT

In 1961 Elvis bought a special-edition Ford Thunderbird Landau from Hull-Dobbs Ford in Memphis after seeing a television ad for the car. He was photographed sitting in the car. When a wheel cover on the T-bird was damaged, Ford refunded the entire $6,000 purchase price of the car figuring it an insignificant amount compared to the photo of Elvis at the wheel of a Ford product.

History

(1974) Elvis begins one of his legendary buying sprees. This one will last ten days, in which he will purchase more than a dozen vehicles for friends, family, strangers, and staff. He also buys his younger cousin, Billy Smith, a three-bedroom 1975 Woodcrest double-wide trailer so that Billy and his family can live comfortably on the Graceland grounds. Elvis's relationship with Billy, who is eight years Elvis's junior, was always close and now seems to become more so. Billy and Elvis remain close until Elvis's death.

17 September

quote of the day

"Well, I guess they're just like myself. They're very thankful for it. We've always had a common life. We never had any luxuries, but we were never really hungry, you know, and I guess they're just, you know, they're real proud, just like I am."

—Elvis when asked how his parents felt about his early success

SALES AGENT'S DREAM

A lot of people have Elvis to thank for putting a roof over their heads. He bought houses not only for girlfriend Linda Thompson, but also for her parents and even her brother, Sam. Memphis Mafia member Jerry Schilling's mother died when he was a baby, so Elvis bought him a house saying, "I wanted to be the one to give you a home." And when he bought a house for Graceland's cook, Mary Jenkins, Elvis threw in a car each for real estate agent Portia Fisher, and her mother, as thanks for closing the deal.

Today in

18 September

(1974) Recent press coverage in the *Memphis Press-Scimitar* shows photos of Elvis participating in a karate demonstration. The accompanying article reports he is involved in producing a film on karate, to be titled *The New Gladiators,* which he will also narrate. The project began in 1973 as the idea of Elvis's karate instructor and bodyguard, Ed Parker, and George Waite, an entrepreneur and karate black belt. In the beginning Elvis is only to provide financial backing, but Waite eventually convinces him to appear in and narrate the film. A director is hired in Bob Hammer, who has filmed commercials for Parker's tournaments before. After about a year of sporadic work on *The New Gladiators*, the unfinished movie is shelved, never to be released in its entirety.

quote of the day

"Maybe one day we'll do one right."

—Elvis, *commenting on the making of* Harum Scarum

MAFIA FRINGE BENEFITS

Technically, every member of the Memphis Mafia had "jobs." Although the salaries of the entourage seem modest, Elvis covered almost every other expense they incurred, from cars to dentists and often houses.

History

19 September

(1958) At Ft. Hood, Texas, it's 7:00 PM and Elvis's unit boards an army troop train (made up of four separate trainloads of soldiers) embarking for the Military Ocean Terminal in Brooklyn, New York. Vernon, Grandma Minnie, Red West, Lamar Fike, Eddie Fadal, and Anita Wood are at the Ft. Hood station to see Elvis off. Aboard the train, Elvis shares the rail car with Charlie Hodge, an army friend and vocalist for Red Foley's Foggy River Boys, and Tennessee army buddies Rex Mansfield and Bill Norvell.

quote of the day

"I'm looking forward to going to Germany. I'm looking forward to seeing the country and meeting a lot of people, but at the same time I'm looking forward to coming back here, because here is where I started."

–Elvis Presley

SEA CRUISE

When Elvis arrived at the Military Ocean Terminal in Brooklyn, he boarded the *U.S.S. Randall* to head to Germany for his eighteen-month stint with the US Third Armored Division. Prior to boarding the Randall, Elvis walked up and down the gangplank eight times for the benefit of the assembled photographers. Elvis received a ten-day cruise courtesy of the United States government, landing at Bremerhaven, Germany, on October 1.

Today in

20 September

(1977) The Memphis Development Foundation pays a $151,000 commission to sculptor Eric Parks of Unionville, Tennessee, to create a twenty-five-foot tall, fifty-ton bronze statue of Elvis to overlook the Mississippi River in Memphis. By this October, the Foundation will have filed a lawsuit against Factors, Etc., asking for damages of $8,400,000 because the company allegedly is attempting to restrict the foundation's attempts to raise money for the Elvis Memorial. Factors, Etc., Inc. was the largest mass-merchandising company in the world. They laid claim to the Presley name within forty-eight hours of Elvis's death when Colonel Parker convinced Vernon Presley to sign a contract making Factors the distributor of all authorized Elvis-related products except music and films. Parker engineered a deal wherein he received 75 percent of the profits and left only 25 percent to the Presley estate. Verily, a sweet deal for Parker.

quote of the day

"Oh, dear God ... Nothing has changed. This won't change anything."

—Tom Parker's words to Joe Esposito upon Esposito's call informing the Colonel of Elvis's death

JUST A LITTLE RESPECT...

At Elvis's funeral, Tom Parker wore a Hawaiian shirt and a baseball cap. At the cemetery he avoided the grave site and sat by himself on a police motorcycle.

History

(1964) Up until now Elvis has held the title "Honorary Chief Deputy Sheriff" of Shelby County, Tennessee, (where Memphis is located). Today, County Sheriff Bill Morris appoints Elvis as "Special Deputy Sheriff" and he is fingerprinted and photographed to receive his ID card and badge. Elvis tells Sheriff Morris he's "always been interested in law enforcement." True to form Elvis has his badge set with rubies and diamonds.

September

quote of the day

"Elvis wanted to be an example to young people. Some say that because he used drugs, he couldn't. But they overlook the fact that he never used illegal drugs. The drugs were always prescribed by his physician. He was a very decent and sincere man."

—Richard M. Nixon

OH CAPTAIN, MY CAPTAIN

By 1970 Elvis was no longer satisfied with an honorary police title. He persuaded then-Sheriff Roy Nixon to commission him as a special deputy with full law enforcement powers. In 1976, Elvis received a promotion to Memphis Police Captain. His law enforcement commission gave him full authority of arrest powers and privilege to carry firearms.

Today in

22 September

(1952) Red West recalls in *Elvis: What Happened?* when Elvis started his senior year at Humes High School that two incidents occurred that solidified the two boy's relationship. Both incidents involve groups of bullies picking on Elvis because of his hairstyle. The first time three seniors wait for Elvis along Manassas Street. In the second, a group of Red's football teammates pin Elvis against a restroom wall and attempt to cut his hair. In both incidents, Red sides with Elvis and defuses the situation.

quote of the day

"If you really want to please me, search for God and the truth."

—Elvis to his friends in the Memphis Mafia

BY ANY OTHER NAME

Q: Name at least one other moniker by which the "Memphis Mafia" was known.

A: "El's Angels," "Presley Punks," and "The CB's" ("Cherry Busters").

History

(1971) There are growing rumbles in the media that Colonel Parker may be testing the waters to find a buyer for Elvis's management contract. The *Los Angeles Citizen News* publishes the headline: "Elvis Presley to Dump Parker?" and the British music weekly *New Musical Express* runs an article suggesting that Parker is engaged in talks with Gordon Mills, Tom Jones's current manager. Despite evidence of correspondence between the Parker and Mills offices, the Colonel and his assistant, Tom Diskins, deny any such activity, albeit in language suggesting something may indeed be in the works.

23 September

quote of the day

"I consider it my patriotic duty to keep Elvis in the 90 percent tax bracket."

—Colonel Tom Parker upon Elvis's being drafted into the army

YOU CAN'T GO HOME AGAIN

Reportedly, Colonel Tom Parker turned down countless lucrative offers to have Elvis tour abroad because he himself was an illegal immigrant without a passport.

24 September

(1965) It's late September and Elvis is readying to head for home in Memphis. Before he leaves, he moves from his Perugia Way house into a rented, single-story house at 10550 Rocca Place. The modern, ranch-style home is near the Bel Air Hotel in an area known as Stone Canyon. Elvis has divided his time between Hollywood and Graceland for most of the sixties. Most of his California residences are described as bachelor pads that basically served as hotels. The house at 565 Perugia Way, which once belonged to the Shah of Iran, is where Elvis played host to the Beatles on August 27. Elvis will remain at Rocca Way when he's in Hollywood until 1967, when he buys his first Los Angeles home at 1174 Hillcrest Road in the Trousdale Estates section of Beverly Hills.

quote of the day

"Elvis's house has balls."

—Michael St. Gerard, the actor who played Elvis in ABC-TV's Elvis

THE WRITINGS ON THE WALL...

As they do at Graceland and other former residences of Elvis around Memphis, fans write messages about their devotion to Elvis on the iron gate of 1174 Hillcrest Road, which some have deemed the "West Coast Wall of Love."

History

(1954) Elvis heads for the O.K. Houck Piano Company, a music store on Memphis's Union Avenue, to trade in his old guitar for a new one. He purchases a 1942 Martin D-18, paying $175. Elvis later tells *Memphis Press-Scimitar* reporter Bob Johnson how the music store's owner gave him eight dollars for his old, beat-up guitar and promptly threw it in the trash, about which Elvis tells Johnson, "Shucks, it still played good." Elvis customizes his guitar by having his name spelled out in metal letters at an angle to the guitar body just below the strings.

25 September

quote of the day

"Prices for Elvis Presley belongings have skyrocketed in the past twenty years. With increases averaging across the board a whopping one hundred fold. It's true! Things selling for $100 in 1979 may now fetch $10,000 and in some cases closer to $20,000."

—Jerry Osborne, from Guernsey's Official Auction Catalog

ELVIS EVERYWHERE

Q: Elvis impersonators can earn up to $100,000 a week in Las Vegas! What is the official term for these performers?

A: Elvii

Today in 26 September

(1956) It's "Elvis Presley Day" in Tupelo. A banner announces "Tupelo Welcomes Elvis Presley Home." Elvis drives his white "Miami" Lincoln into town. He heads to the Tupelo Fairgrounds where the annual Mississippi-Alabama Fair and Dairy Show is in full swing. After a press conference and meeting with various relatives, Elvis performs two shows in the fairground's stadium. Tomorrow's *Tupelo Journal* headline says it all: "20,000 Persons, Mostly Screaming Teenagers, Welcome Presley Home:' Elvis entertained for forty-five minutes in each show. More than a hundred special police, including fifty highway patrol officers, protected Elvis from hysterical fans. The National Guard was assigned the task of keeping the peace in the front of the stage, which was only five feet high."

quote of the day

"I was a nobody, a small town kid in a big city, without a dime in my pocket, not too good in class, kinda shy ... and the other guys wore GI haircuts. I wanted to look older, be different. I guess mostly I wanted to be noticed. My hair, the black shirt and pants I wore did it. But don't think I didn't take a lot of kidding from my friends. Still, I stuck with it. I guess I always knew if you want to stand out in a crowd you gotta be different."

–Elvis Presley

GET THE NAME RIGHT, SON

When Dewey Phillips, who is often credited with being the first DJ to play an Elvis record on the air, first introduced "That's All Right" on his show he introduced the artist as "Elton Preston!"

History

(1957) Elvis and his entourage arrive in Tupelo in a caravan of Cadillacs. This year they are in town to perform at a benefit concert to raise money for the "Elvis Presley Youth Recreation Center." There is only one performance, at eight o'clock, at the fairgrounds stadium where, as usual, this year's annual Mississippi-Alabama Fair and Dairy Show is being held. Elvis takes the stage wearing the jacket of his famous gold suit and navy blue trousers. For this appearance, Scotty and Bill are being replaced by Nashville session musicians Walter "Hank" Garland on guitar and Chuck Wiginton on bass. D.J. Fontana is on drums. The show nets the charity $22,800 as 12,000 fans pack the stadium.

September

quote of the day

"Man, they [a live audience] knocked me out. I was a little nervous for the first three songs, but then I thought, 'What the heck, get with it man, or you just might be out of a job.'"

—Elvis Presley

BUSTING THE CARNEYS

Elvis spent $600 (an enormous amount at the time) in one hour at a ball toss game at the Mid-South Fair in 1957. He threw the dolls he won into the crowd of screaming fans.

Today in

September 28

(1974) Elvis is in College Park (just outside of Baltimore) for his second appearance of the fourth tour of 1974. It is the second show to be held at the University of Maryland Fieldhouse. Elvis arrived in Baltimore yesterday aboard the Playboy Jet, which he's leased from Hugh Hefner. Critics note that Elvis's weight has increased dramatically since closing in Las Vegas earlier in the month. The weight gain seems to limit Elvis's movement on-stage. At one point he addresses the subject to the audience telling them, "It's a bullet proof vest in case some fool tries to blow my belly button off."

quote of the day

"Elvis is fat, and there's no hiding it. His cheeks are puffy and he has a double chin."

—A 1976 Memphis Press Scimitar *Elvis concert review* entitled: *"Fat and Forty—But Also Sold Out"*

THE FOOL'S GOLD SANDWICH

Elvis once flew his private jet to Denver in the middle of the night to get a "Fool's Gold" sandwich. The Fool's Gold is a whole loaf of bread, hollowed out and filled with bacon, peanut butter, and jam. It's a specialty of the Colorado Gold Mine Company restaurant and cost $49.95.

History

29 September

(1956) Today's *Billboard* reviews a new facet of Elvis's career in an article entitled "Presley Juggernaut Rolls—Merchandising Campaign Expected to Top $20 Mil Sales by Year End." According to the report, H.G. Saperstein & Associates, in conjunction with Elvis and the Colonel, have eighteen licenses producing thirty products, including, hats, T-shirts, blue jeans, kerchiefs, headscarves, sweaters, bobbysox, canvas sneakers, shirts, blouses, belts, purses, billfolds, wallets, charm bracelets, necklaces, rings, ear rings, pins, magazines, gloves, mittens, statues, bookends, a guitar, lipstick, cologne, stuffed hound dogs, stationary, buttons of all types, and a soft drink. To date, sales are estimated at four million charm bracelets, 120,000 pairs of jeans, and 240,000 T-shirts. The Elvis Presley Fan Club now boasts 200,000 members.

quote of the day

"Elvis has always been there. I always expected him to be a part of American culture that I would share with my children."

—Dave Marsh, from his book Elvis.

ELVIS FOR KIDS

The true Elvis fan who may wish to introduce the youngsters to Elvis can buy a copy of *Shake Rag: From the Life of Elvis Presley* by Amy Littlesugar and Floyd Cooper. It's an illustrated children's book telling the story of Elvis's childhood and his discovery of his passion for music.

30 September

(1968) As he often does, Elvis goes to the Memphian Theater for exclusive showings of current movies. Tonight's midnight showings are *Charly*, starring Cliff Robertson and *The Heart Is a Lonely Hunter* starring Alan Arkin. *Charly* doesn't last long until Elvis asks for the next film. To round out the usual two-film matinee, Elvis watches *The Hell with Heroes*, last night's feature. B.J. Thomas, the singer and songwriter, is Elvis's guest at tonight's showings. Elvis is a fan of Thomas and has recorded several of his hits, "I Just Can't Help Believin'," "It's Only Love," and "Tomorrow Never Comes." Elvis also sang Thomas's "Hooked on a Feeling" in concert and mentions him by name during the Las Vegas concert featured in *Elvis—That's the Way It Is*.

quote of the day

"Oh God, I hope they bring Elvis back."

—*Female character in the Will Smith film* Independence Day *as alien spaceships draw near*

ELVIS GOES TO THE MOVIES

In the Nicholas Cage film *Con Air*, a character exclaims, "If that aircraft's carrying thirty prisoners, then I'm Elvis Presley." When the plane lands on the Vegas strip, Cage says, "Well, Viva Las Vegas."

October

1 October

(1960) Elvis wraps up production of *Flaming Star*, his sixth film, at Twentieth Century Fox studios in Hollywood. The film took two and a half years to bring to the screen and endured numerous title changes. In 1958 the announcement was made that Marlon Brando and Frank Sinatra were set to play the two brothers who are the main characters in the film. After negotiations with the two stars break down, it isn't until 1960 that Elvis is signed as the star. When the film opens in December of this year, newspaper advertisements incorrectly promise the movie has "four new songs." In fact only two new songs are introduced in *Flaming Star*, "Flaming Star"—sung over the opening credits and "A Cane and a High Starched Collar"—sung in the Burton's cabin during the first few minutes of the film. "Britches" and "Summer Kisses, Winter Tears" were both cut from the movie.

quote of the day

"I've made a study of poor Jimmy Dean. I've made a study of myself. And I know why girls, at least the young ones, go for us. We're sullen, we're brooding., we're something of a menace. I don't understand it exactly, but that's what the girls like in men. I don't know anything about Hollywood, But I know you can't be sexy if you smile. You can't be real if you grin."

—Elvis Presley

FLAMING APARTHEID

Flaming Star was banned in 1960's South Africa because Elvis portrayed a mixed-race character.

―――――― History ――――――

October 2

(1954) Elvis, Sam Phillips, and his assistant, Marion Keisker, in Phillip's car, followed by Scotty, Bill, and the instruments in Scotty's wife's car, drive to Nashville for Elvis's only regularly scheduled appearance on the *Grand Ole Opry*. The *Opry* originates from Ryman Auditorium and is broadcast locally over WSM radio from 8:00 to 11:00 PM, central time. It is also carried over the CBS radio network to forty states. Elvis performs between 10:15 and 10:30 PM on the Hank Snow segment, sponsored by Kellogg cereals. Also appearing on this segment are the Davis Sisters and Eddie Hill. During rehearsals, Elvis tried out his new release, "Good Rockin' Tonight," but Jim Denny, Opry manager, persuades him to sing "Blue Moon of Kentucky" instead. It's the only song Elvis performs on the air. Two other performers and cereal commercials use the rest of the fifteen-minute segment.

quote of the day

"Elvis would hear us worrying about our debts; being out of work and sickness and so on. He would say, 'Don't you worry none. When I grow up, I'm going to buy you a house and pay everything you owe at the grocery store and get two Cadillacs; one for you and Daddy and one for me.' Little as he was he'd look up at me holding onto my skirt and you know, I'd believe him!"

—Gladys Presley, 1955

GOOD ON HIS WORD

Variety's banner headline for an October 1956 issue read simply: "Elvis: A Millionaire in One Year."

Today in

3 October

(1945) Today Elvis makes what is generally regarded as his first public appearance as a performer during "Children's Day" at the Mississippi-Alabama Fair and Dairy Show. This year the fair runs October 2–6 in Lee County at the Tupelo Fairgrounds. Vernon is working today, so Gladys accompanies her son on the school bus to the fairgrounds. The "Radio Talent Show" is broadcast on WELO radio as part of the station's *Black & White Jamboree Show* emceed by Mississippi Slim. As his performance for the contest, Elvis sings "Old Shep" into the microphone without benefit of accompaniment. Elvis misses out on the first-prize $25 war bond and trophy, which goes to one of his classmates.

quote of the day

"My daddy never made much money, but I don't remember ever wanting something real bad that he wouldn't try to get for me."

—*Elvis Presley*

OVERALL UNIFORM

In his sixth grade class photo, Elvis was the only kid wearing overalls, the South's uniform of poverty.

History

(1976) About 2:00 AM, Elvis is spotted riding out of Graceland on his red Harley-Davidson show motorcycle. He's dressed head to toe in black leather with a black helmet. Over a dozen fans give pursuit, and when he stops for gasoline at Vicker's, he chats for a half hour. Elvis has been impressed with motorcycles for years, sometimes riding friends around the Tennessee countryside. Upon taking a spin on Jerry Schilling's Triumph 650 in 1960, he is so impressed he decides to buy nine Triumphs, one for each member of his California entourage at the time.

4 October

quote of the day

"Like income taxes, you mean?"
—Elvis response when asked the question, "Have you made any contributions to culture?"

THE KING ON WHEELS

Q: In six of his movies, Elvis portrays either a professional driver or a character whose wheels are most important. Can you name the "Films with Wheels"?

A: *Viva Las Vegas, Clambake, Speedway, Spinout, Roustabout,* and *G.I. Blues*

Today in

5 October

(1966) Today Elvis begins shooting *Easy Come, Easy Go*, his twenty-third film, and another for producer Hal Wallis. Exterior locations for the movie are shot at the harbor of the Long Beach Naval Station, the pier and harbor in Santa Monica, and an estate in the Hollywood hills. The navy ship in the opening scene is the minesweeper *U.S.S. Gallant*. Pat Priest, who portrays the character Dina Bishop in the film, is more well-known as Marilyn Munster in the popular 1960's television sit-com *The Munsters*. Upon its release in 1967, *Easy Come, Easy Go* reaches number fifty in *Variety's* list of top-grossing films for that year, eventually taking in $1.95 million.

quote of the day

"One thing I gotta do is go after more serious material. Anyway, I'm real tired of playing a fella who gets into a fight, then starts singing to the guy he's just beat up."

–Elvis Presley

FOR SERIOUS FANS ONLY

Q: Not exactly an Elvis trivia lightweight? Try this one: What number was on the side of the ship on which *Easy Come, Easy Go's* navy Lieutenant Ted Jackson was stationed?

A: 489

― History ―

(1958) Elvis is on the third day of a three-day pass from army duties in Germany. Yesterday, as Elvis, Lamar Fike, and Red West strolled in a park near their hotel, the group was spotted by German photographers, one of whom is in the company of sixteen-year-old Margit Buergin. The photographers urge Elvis to have his picture taken with the blond, blue-eyed Ms. Buergin who is later dubbed by the press as the "German Junior Edition of Bridgette Bardot." Elvis immediately begins dating Margit. He sees her several times a week for the next few months, usually at his place or her home in Frankfurt. The relationship sours after Margit poses for a pin-up style photograph that appears in the military's *Overseas Weekly* magazine.

6
October

quote of the day

"I've eaten things in the army that I never ate before. And I've eaten things that I didn't know what it was, but after a hard day of basic training, you could eat a rattlesnake."

—Elvis Presley

BY APPOINTMENT ONLY

At Elvis's German private residence, 14 Goethestrasse, he placed a sign on the door, in German, reading: "Autographs between 7:30 - 8:30 PM"

―――― Today in ――――

7 October

(1955) Elvis is in the middle of a weeklong tour of small venues in Texas with a *Louisiana Hayride Jamboree*. The tour's emcee is Horace Logan, the *Hayride*'s director who, years later, will claim that "he made Elvis a star" by signing the young singer to the *Louisiana Hayride* a full year before Elvis signed a contract with Colonel Tom Parker. Tonight, while the rest of the troupe relaxes on an evening off in Austin, Elvis, Horace Logan, and Tillman Franks, who booked the *Jamboree* tour, catch a Greyhound bus to Houston for the Bob Wills and his Texas Playboys show at Cook's Hoedown Club. Bob Wills is a Country Music Hall of Fame member who is credited as being the first to introduce drums into country music (which they kept hidden behind a curtain when playing the Grand Ole Opry).

quote of the day

"Country music was always a part of the influence on my type of music. It's a combination of country music, gospel, rhythm and blues. As a child, I was influenced by all that."

—Elvis Presley

BEATING THE DRUMS

In 1955, Elvis recorded "Mystery Train" at Sun studios. There were no drums on the original recording; they were added at the last minute by Johnny Bernaro, the drummer for the Dean Beard Band, who played drums on several of Elvis's Sun recordings but was never credited.

History

(1971) The first serious full-length profile of Elvis is published: *Elvis: A Biography,* by Jerry Hopkins. The initial printing is 25,000 copies. Excerpts from the book appeared in two issues of *Look* magazine in May and in the first issue of *The Journal of Popular Music,* published at Bowling Green University.

8 October

quote of the day

"I never expected to be anybody important. Maybe I'm not now, but whatever I am, whatever I will become, will be what God has chosen for me. Some people can't figure out how Elvis Presley happened. I don't blame them for wondering that. Sometimes I wonder myself.... But no matter what I do, I don't forget about God. I feel he's watching every move I make, and in a way it's good for me. I'll never feel comfortable taking a strong drink, and I'll never feel easy smoking a cigarette. I just don't think those things are right by me. I just want to let a few people know that how I live is by doing what I think God wants me to. I want someone to understand."

—Elvis Presley

THE SPIRITUAL SELF

Elvis enjoyed reading spiritual books and literature. He once copied these words from *The Kahlil Gibran Diary For 1973:* "If I wasn't tough I wouldn't be here. If I wasn't gentle I wouldn't deserve to be here."

Today in 9 October

(1973) Elvis's petition for divorce is finalized. A judge of the Santa Monica Superior Court grants a modified property settlement. The settlement states Elvis agrees to leave in Priscilla's hands everything from the original agreement plus $725,000 to discharge any further claims on community property. Priscilla also receives one half of the proceeds of the sale of the couple's Holmby Hills home, plus 5 percent of the total outstanding stock in Elvis Presley Music, Inc. and White Haven Music, Inc., plus alimony of $4,200 a month for twelve months, plus $4,000 a month for Lisa Marie until maturity or marriage, an additional $6,000 for ten years, and joint custody of Lisa Marie. Upon leaving the courthouse Elvis kisses Priscilla and drives off.

quote of the day

"Did you see the bone structure in her face? It's like the woman I've been looking for all my life."

—Elvis commenting to Charlie Hodge upon meeting Priscilla in Germany

NEVER, NEVER LAND

Graceland met Neverland in 1994 when Lisa Marie married Michael Jackson in a secret ceremony in the Dominican Republic. The two had met years before, when Elvis took his daughter to a Jackson Five concert. It is reported Lisa Marie believed she had found someone who was capable of handling her celebrity, as he did his own. The couple split in 1996.

History

10
October

(1967) Production begins this week for Elvis's twenty-sixth film, *Stay Away, Joe*. Some scenes are shot at MGM studios in Culver City but location scenes are shot in Arizona where film headquarters sets up in Flagstaff. In Sedona, thirty-five miles south of Flagstaff, several scenes are shot. The exterior for the parent's ramshackle house is constructed right outside of Sedona. In town, the exterior and interior of the First National Bank of Arizona are used. The local rodeo grounds are featured toward the end of the movie. Elvis also appears in scenes shot on Sedona's downtown Main Street and a local used car lot. The more scenic shots are filmed at the Tazigoot National Monument outside of Cottonwood, twenty-five miles southwest of Sedona.

quote of the day

"The only thing worse than watching a bad movie is being in one."

–Elvis Presley

THE BRIGHTEST STAR

Q: Elvis starred in numerous feature films between 1956 and 1969 during which he became the highest paid movie star on earth. How many feature films did he make?

A: Thirty-one

Today in

11 October

(1976) Elvis is spotted with Linda Thompson, who's come to Graceland to accompany Elvis on his next tour. Thompson has been Elvis's "serious" love interest since 1972 when she moved into Graceland. When Elvis was admitted to Baptist Memorial Hospital for eighteen days in 1973, Thompson stayed with him in the same room. Some estimate Elvis spent over a million dollars on jewelry for Linda during their romance. It's been reported that just before breaking off the relationship, Linda ran up $30,000 in charges on Elvis's credit cards. Thompson claims she left Elvis because she grew tired of watching him "self-destruct" on drugs. According to the book *Are You Lonesome Tonight?*, in July of this year Elvis had security-man John O'Grady "throw Linda out of Graceland."

quote of the day

"When I'm pushed to a certain point, I have a very bad temper, an extremely bad temper. So much to the point I have no idea what I'm doing. And then I don't like myself later."

–Elvis Presley

OUT OF THE FRYING PAN

Linda Thompson broke off her relationship with Elvis in November 1976. That same month he met Ginger Alden, who was nineteen years his junior. Ginger claims that early in 1977 Elvis proposed and the two were engaged to be married that same year. It was Ginger who discovered Elvis's body on the day of his death.

History

(1969) Elvis returns to Los Angeles after a week-long Hawaiian vacation with family and friends. During the stay in Hawaii, some of the group decide to continue the vacation in Europe. Those on their way abroad are Elvis and Priscilla, Jerry and Sandy Schilling, Joe and Joanie Esposito, and Patsy and Gee Gee Gambill. Anybody who doesn't have a passport scrambles to acquire one. Plans change dramatically, however, when the Colonel prohibits Elvis from visiting Europe on the reasoning it will insult his European fans for him to come there as a tourist rather than an entertainer. After some minor objections, Elvis gives in to the Colonel and the vacationers are redirected to the Bahamas, where the Colonel has contacts and, he says, they will enjoy the gambling.

12 October

quote of the day

"If nobody recognized me or asked for an autograph...I think I would miss it."

—Elvis Presley

TROUBLE IN PARADISE

The group going to the Bahamas (in lieu of Europe) stayed at the Paradise Island Hotel in Nassau. The trip is a washout with rain and hurricane winds, so they left after only a couple days.

Today in

13 October

(1961) Elvis is living in a rented Mediterranean-style home at 1059 Bellagio Road. His current love interest is actress and *Follow that Dream* costar Anne Helm. Elvis recently broke off a relationship with another *Follow that Dream* alumnus, Joanna Moore. Ms. Moore's behavior may be the reason for Elvis's departure. According to Joe Esposito, Joanna came to the Bellagio Way house late one evening claiming that Elvis had gotten her pregnant. She allegedly told Joe and Charlie Hodge that she had taken an overdose of sleeping pills. Elvis was asleep, so Joe and Charlie rushed the young actress to the UCLA Medical Center emergency room. At the ER, Ms. Moore's stomach was pumped, but there are no signs of a pregnancy. Joanna never comes around Elvis again.

quote of the day

"Well, I would like to play a dramatic role, but I don't—I'm not ready for that either, really. I haven't had enough experience in acting; and until I'm ready for it, it would be foolish to undertake something very dramatic."

–Elvis Presley

A MATTER OF PREFERENCE

Q: Elvis costarred with many actresses during his film career. His favorite was Shelley Fabares, who appeared with him in *Girl Happy*, *Spinout*, and *Clambake*. Which one, according to numerous reports, was his least favorite?

A: Mary Tyler Moore, from *Change of Habit*

History

14
October

(1964) This week Elvis begins production of *Tickle Me,* his eighteenth film. The film is being made by Allied Artists, one of the first movie production companies started outside of the old studio system that controlled the Hollywood film industry since the 1920's. The company is a joint partnership of several of Hollywood's more successful actors including Paul Newman and Sidney Poitier. Allied Artists is struggling financially, having produced several money-losing movies. As a result, even though Elvis is under contract, the Colonel agrees to an unprecedented cut in Elvis's salary from his normal $1 million to $750,000, including half of the box office. *Tickle Me* single-handedly saves Allied Artists from financial ruin, becoming the third-highest grossing film in the company's history.

quote of the day

"I can't go on doing the same thing year after year. The inspiration simply isn't there."

—*Elvis on Hollywood*

SAVING ALLIED ARTISTS

In 1966, *Variety* reported that *Tickle Me* actually earned $4 million during its first ten days of release, a million dollars more than original estimates and more than enough to keep Allied Artists solvent.

Today in

15 October

(1973) It's six days since Elvis's and Priscilla's divorce decree was finalized and four days since Elvis's return to Memphis. He's been experiencing breathing difficulties since his return and even has Dr. Nick's office nurse, Tish Henley, providing home care at Graceland. Today, the breathing difficulties not improving, Dr. Nick admits Elvis to Baptist Memorial Hospital where he undergoes extensive testing. Congestive heart failure is almost immediately ruled out, leaving Dr. Nick and the team of physicians puzzled. Dr. Nick eventually reveals that the daily "acupuncture" treatments Elvis was receiving in California included injections of Demerol, a powerful pain medicine. From then on Elvis's treatment focuses on what amounts to narcotics addiction, and Elvis remains in the hospital with Linda Thompson at his side for two weeks.

quote of the day

"There was a guy that said one time...he said, 'You never stood in that man's shoes, or saw things though his eyes. Or stood and watched with helpless hands, while the heart inside you dies."

—Elvis from the Las Vegas stage, 1970

HOLLYWOOD HIGH-LIGHTS

During the early days in Hollywood, Elvis's entire entourage took pills just to keep up with each other. In those days, nobody considered possible addiction, and doctors routinely prescribed pills like Dexedrine just to help people lose weight.

History

16 October

(1954) This evening Elvis makes his first appearance on *Louisiana Hayride*. He and the band appear early in the show in a segment reserved for new talent. Elvis's first *Hayride* appearance is captured on tape. The band is introduced by Frank Page, the show's producer, who acts as emcee for the broadcast. Page motions for the boys to come on-stage and announces, "Elvis Presley, let's give him a nice hand. Elvis, how are you this evening?"

"Just fine. How are you, sir?," is the nervous response.

Page begins to ask, "Are you all geared up with your band ..."

"All geared up ..." Elvis interrupts.

"... to let us hear your songs?" Page concludes.

"Ah, well, I'd just like to say how happy we are to be down here. It's a real honor to get a chance to appear on *Louisiana Hayride*. We're gonna do a song for ya..."

Realizing he had stepped all over Page's introduction, Elvis asks, "You got anything else to say?"

"No! I'm ready!" Page answers to the brash enthusiasm.

"We're gonna do a song for ya we got out on Sun Records, it goes something like this ... " are Elvis's next words. The rest is music history.

---- Today in ----

17 October

(1946) Jesse Dee Presley, Elvis's grandfather, has long since moved to Louisville, Kentucky, and Grandma Minnie continues to have none of it. Today, Jesse files for divorce in Louisville from Minnie Mae on the grounds of "desertion" because she insists on remaining in Mississippi. Grandma Minnie, stubborn as ever, counter-sues her husband, demanding a two-hundred-dollar divorce settlement. The divorce will eventually be granted and Grandma Minnie will receive the money. Jesse eventually re-marries and remains in Louisville, even trying his hand in the music business for a time.

quote of the day

"All my life I've always had a nice time. We never had any money or nothing, but I've always managed to…. I never had any luxuries, but we always … we never went hungry, you know. That's something to be thankful for, even if you don't have all the luxuries, because there's so many people who don't."

—Elvis Presley

IS THAT BROOKLYN OR LOS ANGELES

Elvis nicknamed Grandma Minnie "Dodger" when he was five years old. During a temper tantrum, little Elvis threw a baseball at his grandmother, just missing her head because she dodged the ball.

October 18

(1956) At about 5:00 PM, Elvis pulls his white Lincoln Continental into Hopper's Gulf service station at Second and Gayoso Streets in Memphis to have gas fumes checked. A crowd of teenagers gathers and Ed Hopper, age forty-two, asks Elvis to leave, then shoves him into his car. Elvis starts swinging and leaves Hopper with a black eye. A second attendant at the station, Aubrey Brown, age twenty-one, joins in the fray. The police are called and all three men are charged with disorderly conduct and assault. Elvis is later acquitted of all charges, but Hopper and Brown are found guilty of assault and receive fines. Within a week Gulf Oil fires Hopper, even though Elvis tries to intercede on his behalf.

quote of the day

"I've never turned down a reporter. I've never turned down a disc jockey. I have never been sassy to one. In fact, I've never been sassy to anyone."

–Elvis Presley

WHAT ARE THE ODDS THAT'S ELVIS?

In 1956 Elvis bought a Lincoln Continental Mark II. The car was so rare the dealership ran an ad saying that if you saw one on the road, the odds were one in two-thousand Elvis was behind the wheel.

19 October

Today in

(1970) In Beverly Hills, Elvis goes to Schwartz and Ableser Fine Diamonds and Jewelry to pick up twelve pendants specially ordered at $90 each. They are the original TCB pieces made to order from a design created by Elvis and Priscilla and purchased as gifts for each member of the current entourage. The fourteen-carat gold charm bears the letters "TCB" over a zigzag lightning bolt. Elvis later gives various explanations of the symbolic meaning of the design (one alludes to the Captain Marvel comic books Elvis read as a young boy), but its meaning is borrowed from a line in Aretha Franklin's song "Respect," which says: "Taking care of business—in a flash."

quote of the day

"He had total love in his eyes when he performed. He was the total androgynous beauty. I would practice Elvis in front of the mirror when I was twelve or thirteen."

–k.d. Lang

FIT FOR A KING

One of Elvis's most prized possessions was a pendant given to him by the members of his entourage in 1967. It was a gold "tree of life" pendant with all their names engraved on it.

History

20 October

(1955) Elvis is appearing in a show in Cleveland that's been put together by local DJ Bill Randle. Randle is filming the show to, as he puts it in his column in the *Cleveland Press,* make a picture for Universal in which he'll be, "supported by Pat Boone, the Four Lads, Bill Haley and his Comets, and the phenomenal Elvis Presley. Called *Top Jock* [or *A Day in the Life of a Famous Disc Jockey*], the film will run about fifteen minutes when it hits your movie house." The film was never completed and the master copy was lost until 1992 when it was sold various times. Allegedly there are eighteen minutes of Elvis performing five songs. PolyGram, a major European music conglomerate, now owns the film.

quote of the day

"If I had to find one place to live—just one—and it couldn't be Graceland, then it would be Hollywood."

—*Elvis Presley*

ELVIS ON BROADWAY

Q: Actor Christopher Walken wrote and starred in a play on the New York stage, wherein Elvis ambles around in limbo tormented by look-alikes on his way to the next life. What is the title of the play?

A: Him

Today in
21 October

(1965) Bill Black, Elvis's bass player from 1954 to 1957, dies of a brain tumor at Memphis's Baptist Memorial Hospital at age thirty-nine. He leaves behind his wife of twenty years, Nancy, and three children. In 1955, Bill, Scotty Moore and Elvis were briefly known as The Blue Moon Boys. They performed together on the *Louisiana Hayride* show and in many one-night stands across the South. Black sometimes added some fun to performances by riding his bass across the stage. He played Eddie the bass player in 1957's *Loving You*. Bill Black and Scotty Moore left Elvis in 1957 after a salary dispute (Elvis was making millions and they still held $100-a-week salaries). Bill went on to form The Bill Black Combo.

quote of the day

"Like when you dive into the water and you hear the rush—it would cancel out all the sound onstage."

—Scotty Moore describing early audience noise

LEGEND TO LEGEND

The stand-up bass that Bill Black used on his recordings with Elvis is today owned by Paul McCartney, a rather famous bass player himself. On Wings's 1979 album *Back to the Egg*, McCartney played Bill Black's bass, which still has the name "Bill" on the lower left, on the song "Baby's Request," a song Paul originally wrote for the Mills Brothers.

History

(1956) Elvis's popularity becomes more prominent everyday. He's becoming a hot topic, especially among the print media. The premiere issue of *Teenage Rock and Roll Review* magazine features Elvis on the cover. The accompanying article, titled "Here's Elvis Presley," is supposedly written by Elvis. Elvis is also featured in this month's issue of *House and Garden* magazine in the article "The War of the Generations." *Cowboy Songs, Country Song Roundup,* and *Song Hits* magazines all make Elvis the cover story for their current issues.

22 October

quote of the day

"Elvis, who rotates his pelvis...gave an exhibition that was...tinged with the kind of animalism that should be confined to dives and bordellos."

—US Daily News

HAIRY SITUATION!

In October of 1956, sixteen-year-old Robert Phernetton was expelled from school in Romeo, Michigan, for "having an Elvis Presley haircut."

―― Today in ――

October

(1956) This week, *Variety* runs a front-page banner headline exclaiming "Elvis A Millionaire in One Year." The story reports Elvis stands to make $450,000 in record royalties, $250,000 in movie deals, $100,000 in television appearances, and $200,000 in personal appearances. It is also expected that Elvis merchandise will sell over $40 million in the next fifteen months. According to *Variety*, other deals in the works include 18,000 ice cream locations and 30,000 hamburger stands selling large hot dogs ("hound dogs") and "Presley Burgers."

quote of the day

"*He was generous beyond his means. He gave away most everything he had.*"

—Joe Moscheo of the Imperials

THE HAND THAT FEEDS YOU ――

The largest single contribution ever made to the Motion Picture Relief Fund was $50,000, from Elvis Presley.

―――――――――――――― History ――――――

(1966) According to Colonel Tom Parker, Elvis's recent motion picture soundtrack albums have lacked "pep," consequently affecting sales figures. The Colonel pushes for more "up-beat tempo" songs for the album accompanying Elvis's cinematic release in *Spinout*. Upon the album's release, however, the best songs do not come from the film at all but are three cuts from an earlier Nashville recording session, including a rousing, hand-clapping cover of the Clover's 1953 "Down in the Alley" and the Dylan number "Tomorrow is a Long Time." Sales reach over 300,000, a slight improvement over the last two soundtrack albums.

24
October

quote of the day

"After my first picture for Hal Wallis, it's non-musicals for me!"

–Elvis early in his career in Hollywood

CLASSICAL PIANIST ―――――――――――

In addition to the hundreds of gospel and pop songs Elvis taught himself to play on the piano, many people are surprised to know he also could play Beethoven's "Moonlight Sonata" and Debussey's "Clair de Lune."

Today in

25 October

(1975) Almost certainly in need of cash because of recent purchases of airplanes, cars, racquetball courts, and jewelry as well as a sizable payroll that includes virtually every member of his family, increasing medical bills, expensive upkeep on his various houses, and unchecked gifts to friends, relatives, even casual acquaintances, Elvis borrows $350,000 from the National Bank of Commerce in Memphis, putting up Graceland as collateral. The loan is to be repaid in two equal installments in November of 1976 and 1977.

quote of the day

"Roses are red, violets are blue. When a chicken gets into your house, You should say shoe, shoe. When you get married, and live in a shack, Make your children's clothes out of 'toe sacks.'"

—*Poem written by eleven-year-old Elvis Presley*

ELVIS ECONOMICS

In the 1994 presidential election campaign George Bush Sr. described Bill Clinton's recovery plan as "Elvis economics that would lead to 'Heartbreak Hotel.'" The sarcasm backfired when commentators pointed out that more people tuned in to watch Elvis sing "Heartbreak Hotel" than those who watched the Republican National Convention, and Elvis's estate still earns a fortune from "Heartbreak Hotel." *USA Today* said, "Now that's a record you can run on."

History

(1976) Elvis is performing in Dayton, Ohio. Around the same time, *The Star*, a grocery store tabloid, publishes an article by Sonny and Red West's "tell-all" book collaborator, Steve Dunleavy, that includes portions of a surreptitiously taped conversation between Elvis and Red. The article's headline reads "Elvis' Dramatic Plea to His Ex-Bodyguards: Don't Write that Book About Me." Elvis is devastated by the report, feeling that what has transpired between he and the Wests is nothing more than a private quarrel among friends that has now totally reeled out of control.

26 October

quote of the day

"You can surround yourself with people [who are] your so-called equals, and there can be dissention, there can be jealousy ... I have my own way of learning ... It's more important to surround yourself with people who can give you a little happiness."

—Elvis, responding to a reporter's question about why he surrounded himself with people who seemed "beneath him"

"CRAZY" ABOUT ELVIS

Elvis once had bracelets made for all the members of his inner circle. He had their names inscribed on top with nicknames underneath. The boys got together and got Elvis his own bracelet, the nickname was "CRAZY."

Today in

27 October

(1956) Elvis is in New York City for his second appearance on *The Ed Sullivan Show*. While Elvis attends rehearsal for the appearance, Colonel Parker makes his way to the Times Square Paramount Theater where *Love Me Tender* will shortly premiere. As the theater prepares to unveil a forty-foot cardboard likeness of Elvis to commemorate the event, the Colonel passes out "Elvis For President" buttons. After rehearsal Elvis attends a press conference where he is described as "polite, personable, quick-witted and charming." Responding to reporter's questions about his affects on teenagers Elvis replies, "My Bible tells me that what he sows he will also reap, and if I'm sowing evil or wickedness it will catch up with me. If I did think I was bad for people, I would go back to driving a truck, and I really mean this." After the press conference, Elvis gets inoculated with the new Salk polio vaccine as part of a public service announcement for the March of Dimes.

quote of the day

"The trouble with going to see Elvis Presley is that you're liable to get killed."

—Detroit Free Press

HEARTBREAK HOTEL

While Elvis was touring in Florida in 1955 he met songwriter Mae Axton in Jacksonville. Axton promised she'd give Elvis his first million-seller. Thanks to a newspaper article about a suicide in a hotel, she and Tommy Durden made good on the promise. They wrote Elvis's first chart-topper in twenty-two minutes.

―――――――――――――――― History ――――――――――――――――

28 October

(1968) Elvis begins filming *The Trouble with Girls (And How to Get into It)*, his thirtieth film, at MGM studios in Culver City. The movie has been in various stages of production for nine years. In 1960, Elvis's name was mentioned as a costar of the movie, with Glen Ford getting the lead role. In 1964, the project was again discussed with Dick Van Dyke to receive top billing. Bobbie Gentry, who eventually has her own fling with Elvis, was also considered for a costarring role at one time. In the early years, the movie was titled *Chautauqua*, an antiquated term for a combination minstrel show, concert, and lecture gathering that was popular early in the twentieth century.

quote of the day

"Elvis was not an actor. We did not sign him as a second Dean or second Brando. We signed him as the number one Elvis Presley."

–Hall Wallis

MAKING THE CUT

There are a number of movie roles Elvis was either offered or considered for that he never made for various reasons. Among them: *Midnight Cowboy:* Elvis was up for the role of the title character that eventually went to Jon Voight in the Oscar-winning film. *A Star Is Born:* Streisand wanted Elvis. Parker wanted top billing and $1 million. *Sweet Bird of Youth:* The Colonel turned down the role because the character was a gigolo; Paul Newman got the part. *West Side Story:* Robert Wise wanted Elvis to play Tony.

Today in

29 October

(1963) Elvis is filming *Kissin' Cousins,* his fourteenth film. The movie is being made under Elvis's previous contract with MGM. The budget to complete the film is only $800,000, of which Elvis is to receive $500,000. The film's total budget is a mere $1.7 million, which includes advertising, film prints, and distribution costs. The setting for *Kissin' Cousins* is supposed to be Tennessee's Great Smoky Mountains. In fact, most of the movie is shot at MGM studios with a few scenes done around Big Bear Lake, about eighty miles east of Los Angeles.

quote of the day

"When I sat down to write a book about Elvis Presley, I watched all 33 of his movies—including the ones that are all but unwatchable. I felt that to understand what happened to Elvis, I really had to look at what happened to his career. And those movies are undeniable proof of Hollywood's general disdain for his talents ..."

—Pat H. Broeske, *author of* Down at the End of Lonely Street, *in* Writer's Digest *magazine*

KISS 'EM GOODBYE

On the set of *Kissin' Cousins,* especially when the role required him to wear a blond wig, Elvis was so embarrassed by the role he didn't want to come out of the dressing room. Even by this time, Elvis sometimes got physically sick when he read his scripts.

History

30 October

(1956) Today the press reports that Elvis has signed a new, twenty-year contract with RCA calling for $1,000 a week in lieu of royalties, which currently stand at $430,000 with Elvis receiving 5 percent of the sale price of each record (out of 90 percent shipped) in royalties as a singer. The twenty-year period comes as the result of changing terms of the contract from two years plus a one-year option to a five-year contract with a five-year option. At the end of ten years there will be another ten-year option. The reports indicate this is the Colonel's idea to cut down on the amount of federal income tax on royalties. The Colonel allows, by way of comment through his office, the royalties are the same, but the length of contract time is changed, which he won't discuss.

quote of the day

"From a strictly Marxist-Leninist viewpoint, Elvis Presley is a typical example of capitalist exploitation."

—Harper's *magazine, 1957*

BY THE NUMBERS

Elvis's Estimated Lifetime Income (1935 – 1977) : $4.3 BILLION

Today in

31 October

(1961) Principal filming begins of *Kid Galahad*, Elvis's tenth film, in Hollywood. The interior scenes are filmed at United Artist's studios, but Elvis and a film crew spend a month on location in Idyllwild, California, a hundred miles east of Los Angeles in the San Jacinto Mountains. Sonny West and Elvis bury the hatchet after a several-month riff just in time to be hired on as a stunt man for the film. During filming, Elvis dates popular starlet Connie Stevens, one of the few times he steps outside the costar arena.

quote of the day

"How can you help but put your heart and soul into this?"

—Elvis commenting on love scenes in his films

FIGHTING WORDS

Elvis played a struggling boxer in *Kid Galahad* and in most of his films ended up on the right side of some kind of scuffle. When he decided to go back on tour, Elvis decided the karate uniform, the "ghi," was just the costume look he needed. Designer Bill Belew made a number of ghis, both black and white, and found a macramé sash interwoven with karate symbols for Elvis to wear on-stage.

November

Today in

1 November

(1960) Forty-six-year-old Memphis police inspector Fred Woodward, a personal friend and sometimes security man for Elvis since his launch into show business, dies of a heart attack while supervising school children at an afternoon Memphis Symphony youth concert at Ellis Auditorium. Elvis rushes to St. Joseph's Hospital as soon as he hears about his friend. Reporters are at the hospital, but Elvis seems oblivious. Obviously distraught, he is overheard telling Mrs. Woodward, "He was a great guy, a good friend. He was supposed to come out to my house tonight."

quote of the day

"I've also tried to help the guys in law enforcement around the country. They're on the front lines."

—Elvis Presley

UNDERCOVER ELVIS

Elvis held honorary law enforcement titles and commissions all over the United States, among them: Honorary Deputy Sheriff, Shelby County, Tennessee ID#39 / Deputy Sheriff, Shelby County / Honorary Policeman, Monroe, Louisiana / Special Deputy Sheriff Badge #6 ID#293, Shelby County / Lieutenant, Denver, Colorado Police Department / Investigator, Colorado Organized Crime Strike Force / Captain, Memphis Police Department / Federal Narcotics Officer / Deputy United States Marshall.

History

(1959) The "Cold War" rages in the East German city of Leipzig. Today, fifteen enthusiastic Elvis fans, who call themselves "The Elvis Presley Hound Dogs," receive prison terms ranging from six months to four-and-a-half years for participating in a protest march through Leipzig shouting derogatory remarks about East German music in general and communist party boss Walter Ulbright in particular. The youth's inflammatory mantra was, "Long live Elvis Presley!" They are also accused of singing Elvis songs.

2 November

quote of the day

"Elvis Presley's death deprives our country of a part of itself. He was unique, irreplaceable. More than twenty years ago, he burst upon the scene with an impact that was unprecedented and will probably never be equaled. His music and his personality, fusing the styles of white country and black rhythm and blues, permanently changed the face of American popular culture."

—President Jimmy Carter, 1977

ELVIS PRESLEY: COLD WAR PROPAGANDA PROVOCATEUR

Eastern Europe's communist party was very sensitive to Elvis's army service and his presence in West Germany in 1959. In November of that year, when Elvis went on special training maneuvers in Grafenwohr near the Czechoslovakian border, his proximity to the communist East caused the Eastern block some anxiety. The East German newspaper *Neues Deutschland* described Elvis as "a Cold War weapon," and in the Soviet press he was accused of being part of the West's "ideological battle" to subvert communist youth.

Today in

3 November

(1972) This week the documentary film *Elvis on Tour* opens across the United States. In most places the second film on the bill is *Elvis: That's the Way it Is*. The film receives reviews that are mixed to say the least. *Variety* calls the picture "a bright entertaining pop music documentary." The *Los Angeles Times* says, "Both off stage and on, Presley comes across as an assured, relaxed, thoroughgoing pro who knows exactly what he's doing and enjoys it immensely." According to the *New York Times:* "The film strips away the storybook myth to find underneath a private person who is indistinguishable from the public one, except for the fact that he dresses with somewhat less flamboyance."

quote of the day

"Sometimes every knock can be a boost. When everybody agrees on something and someone says, 'I like that,' they start talking about something else. When there's no controversy, there's no news. When they quit talking about you, you're dead."

—*Elvis Presley*

HE'S A GOOD FELLA, AND THOROUGH

Q: 1972's *Elvis on Tour* won a Golden Globe Award for Best Documentary—thanks in part, no doubt, to its montage supervisor, who soon after became a successful director. Can you name him?

A: Martin Scorcese

4 November

(1956) An interview in the *Los Angeles Times* with *Love Me Tender* producer David Weisbart (who also produced one of Elvis's favorite films, *Rebel Without A Cause*) quotes Weisbart as saying, "He [Elvis] will surprise a lot of people who go to see him because his presence is just a gimmick. Actually he plays an acting part in a legitimate story and does so very well." Elvis originally believed his first film role would be the part for which he screen tested, *The Rainmaker,* an idea nixed by Colonel Parker because the part was too small. With *Love Me Tender* Elvis managed to establish himself as a Hollywood money maker in the film's relative success and the screen-song that reached number three on *Variety's* "Top 100." Elvis's *Love Me Tender* character's dying words in the film are, "Everything's gonna be all right," which proves prophetic for Elvis's film career.

quote of the day

"I'd like to become a good actor. That's my ambition."

—*Elvis Presley*

SHARP DRESSED MAN

The famous Hollywood film costume designer Edith Head wrote in her autobiography, *Edith Head's Hollywood,* that Elvis's movie wardrobe presented no challenge as it could be reduced to "basic uniform" standards: For casual scenes—a shirt open at the neck and tight pants. Time for romance?—dark pants, dark shirt, and a lighter jacket. According to Edith, "There was always a striking contrast between his shirt and his jacket."

Today in

5 November

(1971) Today Elvis begins a longer-than-usual tour schedule, fourteen shows in twelve days. Starting today, J.D. Sumner and the Stamps Quartet permanently replace the Imperials as Elvis's male back-up vocalists. Jackie Kahane also becomes the resident comedian / emcee for the rest of Elvis's shows. Starting with this appearance in the tour, in Seattle, Washington, the matching cape and jumpsuit costumes become an on-stage trademark. In the future, Elvis will wear a cape when he takes the stage. More frequently, he will use it for dramatic effect as he bows gracefully to the audience before he leaves the building.

quote of the day

"I've made some wonderful friends in the so-called grandmother group. They write the greatest letters. I even try to see them when possible. They're real fun people."

—Elvis Presley

PLEASE DON'T LOSE THE SLEEPY DROOP —

In 1975 Elvis had cosmetic surgery around his eyes, even though most everyone close told him he didn't need it. One of his oldest friends, cousin Billy Smith, thought it ruined his looks as it changed the "sleepy droop" look of his face.

History

(1954) Today is the official date that Elvis, Scotty, and Bill sign a contract with the International Broadcasting Corporation, owners of the *Louisiana Hayride*. The agreement calls for the trio to appear on the show for fifty-two consecutive Saturday nights in Shreveport or wherever the I.B.C. designates. (They are allowed to miss one Saturday night every three months with fifteen days prior notice.) For the contract's term, pay will be at union scale for Shreveport, Louisiana: eighteen dollars for the band leader (Elvis), and twelve dollars each for the musicians (Scotty and Bill). Because Elvis is a minor (nineteen years old) Vernon and Gladys are also required to sign the contract.

6 November

quote of the day

"I couldn't even go down to the creek with the other kids and swim. That's why I'm no swimmer today."

—Elvis on his mother's protectiveness of him as a child

A DANGEROUS GIFT

Q: On his eleventh birthday Elvis wanted a bicycle but Gladys worried he'd get hit by a car. What present did she give him instead?

A: A Guitar

––––––––––––––––––––––––––––– *Today in* –––––––––––––––––––––––––––––

November

(1973) In the month since Elvis's and Priscilla's divorce is finalized, the rumor mill remains hard at work. According to "inside sources," Elvis and singer Bobbie Gentry are to be married on New Year's day of 1974. Elvis and Ms. Gentry met when she attended a party in his suite in Las Vegas a few months ago. Elvis is also rumored to be set to begin filming two movies: *Death Wish,* a detective thriller, and a picture about karate for Hal Wallis and Paramount. (*Death Wish* is made in 1974 with Charles Bronson in the lead role. The karate film never comes to fruition.)

quote of the day

"Colonel Parker had a golden goose and he kept wanting to turn out the same eggs."

–Mike Stoller, songwriter and Elvis friend

HEADS ABOVE THE REST

Mainliner, the in-flight magazine for United Airlines, once ran an article titled "America: 1955-1960." The accompanying artwork shows a drawing of Elvis above such fifties luminaries as Martin Luther King, Jr., *I Love Lucy,* a 1955 Thunderbird, and *Sgt. Bilko.*

(1948) Elvis is enrolled in the eighth grade at Memphis's Humes High School. In the meantime, Tom Parker is becoming one of the top managers in the country music field. His sole client, Eddie Arnold, has five number-one hits this year alone. It is now that Parker persuades Arnold to quit the Grand Ole Opry for what he feels are more lucrative opportunities, including television, Las Vegas bookings, and motion pictures. Only last month Tom Parker (who was an enlisted man in the army) received an honorary Colonel's commission from Louisiana Governor Jimmie Davis, which he begins using as a title, first as a joke, later as if it is his legitimate due.

8 November

quote of the day

"The mean streak in Parker saw kids who were idolizing his client as a multitude of marks who only deserved to be short-changed and humiliated."

—Dick Vellenga in Elvis and the Colonel

YOU'RE GETTING SLEEPY...

Colonel Tom Parker was an amateur hypnotist. He often hypnotized staff members, getting them to act like chickens and once had the entire Memphis Mafia barking like dogs. Theories abound that Parker kept Elvis hypnotized for twenty years, a very unlikely assertion.

Today in

9 November

(1956) Today Elvis is in Las Vegas where he recently arrived by train with Bitsy Mott and Gene Smith. Vernon wires $1,000 in cash to the New Frontier Hotel, where the group is staying, to cover expenses of the trip. Over the next ten days Elvis takes in most of the shows Vegas has to offer. He is accompanied by a frequent date, Dottie Harmony, a blond Las Vegas dancer who later makes several visits to Graceland. Elvis makes four trips to see the Billy Ward and His Dominoes show because he is a huge fan of lead singer Jackie Wilson's version of "Don't Be Cruel." He also attends the Riviera's late performance by Liberace in the Clover Room and has the opportunity to visit Liberace backstage.

quote of the day

"The world seems more alive at night. ... It seems like God ain't watching."

–Elvis Presley

DUSK TO DAWN

Elvis was the consummate night owl. He recorded most of his music as he lived, from dusk until dawn.

History

10 November

(1976) It's Wednesday afternoon in the Memphis suburb of Whitehaven when Elvis goes to Jim Ellis Chevrolet to buy a new Corvette. The car costs $10,403.99 and Elvis writes a personal check drawn on the National Bank of Commerce in Memphis (account #01-143875-0210, check #210). The car is a gift for long-time friend and Memphis Mafia member Lamar Fike. Elvis is renowned for giving high-end automobile as gifts. During one weekend in 1974, he made five trips to a Memphis car dealership, buying their entire stock of Lincoln Continental Mark IVs, at a cost of over $60,000. He gave away each of the cars. One local car dealer gave Elvis a plaque proclaiming him "The World's Greatest Car Buyer," which bore all thirty-one names of the cars' recipients. One of the last cars Elvis bought as a gift was for his back-up singer Kathy Westmoreland, a Lincoln Continental in the summer of 1977.

quote of the day

"Don't worry, I just bought it for you."

—Elvis to Minnie Person as she admired a Cadillac but related to Elvis there was no way she could afford it

CAR DEALER'S DREAM

Despite the huge quantities in which Elvis bought cars, he never haggled over the price.

Today in

11 November

(1957) Tonight at eight o'clock Elvis performs at Hawaii's Post Bowl in Pearl Harbor for 10,000 military personnel, civilians, and their families stationed at Schofield Barracks Army Base. Last night, Elvis performed his first Hawaiian show at Honolulu Stadium. Scotty, Bill, D.J., and the Jordanaires are all on-hand to perform. There are a variety of introductory acts coming from the show at the Queens Surf Hotel. The acts include an orchestra, comedians, hula dancers, and even jugglers and sword twirlers. Elvis makes his appearance wearing the famed gold jacket, black shirt, and black pants. He later describes the Hawaiian audience as "one of the most well-behaved of my career."

quote of the day

"I enjoy rock 'n' roll. As long as it sells, I'll continue doing it, as long as that's what people want. And if they change, if it dies out, I'll try to do something else. And if that doesn't work, I'll just say, well, I had my day."

–Elvis Presley

TROPICAL TRIVIA

Q: Two of Elvis's movies have the name of the 50th State in the Union in the titles. What are they?

A: 1961's *Blue Hawaii* and 1966's *Paradise, Hawaiian Style*

12 November

(1954) This week's *Billboard* votes Elvis, just five months after his first recording session, number eight on the "Most Promising C&W Vocalist" chart in the annual disc jockey poll. Consequently, Elvis quits his job driving a truck for Crown Electric. Not only is his rising popularity demanding more and more of his time, he also makes more money in one or two nights than he makes in a week driving for Crown. Scotty and Bill also quit their jobs. Scotty has a wife and two kids to support. Bill is not only married and has a child, he also holds a solid union job. The moves certainly show confidence of future success on the trio's part.

quote of the day

"If the media would stop handling such nauseating stuff, all the Presleys of our land would soon be swallowed up in the oblivion they deserve."

—The Catholic journal *America* circa late 1950's

WORDS OF FORECAST

Many have heard of the restraining order issued by a Jacksonville, Florida judge in 1956 prohibiting Elvis from making "offensive gyrations" during his performance. In compliance, Elvis wiggled his pinky finger in lieu of his hips or legs but still caused frenzy in the crowd. What many don't know is he altered his trademark departure statement to express his opinion of the order and "Thank you very much" somehow came out, "Fuck you very much," inaudible to the fans but heard clearly by his friends in the wings.

Today in

13 November

(1970) This week the documentary *Elvis: That's the Way it Is* opens across the country. The film, Elvis's first documentary and thirty-second film, draws mixed reviews from the press. The *Hollywood Reporter* says: "Elvis is perhaps the only performer today who will bring into movie theaters enough people to make a documentary of himself pay off." *Variety* agrees, sort of: "Presley is the Pied Piper of the rock era ... Presley explodes on screen." The *Los Angeles Herald-Examiner* is less sure about the film, calling it "a very inadequate documentary. Easy exploitation, stock sell stuff. A hack job ... the camera follows but does not penetrate." The British magazine *Films and Filming* seems downright insulted by the movie, commenting: "If [Dennis] Sanders [the film's director] has wished to show the Presley followers as morons he has succeeded admirably."

quote of the day

"I'd like to think I've improved over the last fifteen years. But I don't want to take away from my early hits."

—*Elvis Presley*

THE KING'S BEST

Q: What was was Elvis's biggest-selling album during his lifetime?

A: The motion picture soundtrack to *Blue Hawaii*

History

14 November

(1955) Despite the fact that negotiations for a recording contract with RCA have not come together, the Colonel appears to be looking into the future when he writes William Morris Agency rep Harry Kalchheim that he is "interested in making a picture with this boy. However, we must be very careful to expose him in a manner befitting his personality, which is something like the James Dean situation." Parker later elaborates on his thought in wondering if Warner Brothers may have shelved any plans for a James Dean film that might suit Elvis. "Believe me," he tells Kalcheim, "if you ever follow one of my hunches, follow up this one and you won't go wrong."

quote of the day

"People shout 'quiet!' and then all of a sudden you're supposed to be acting a part. It's enough to make your legs slide out from under you. Whenever I get excited I stutter a little bit. I have a hard time saying any words that start with W or I. Well, I can tell you I really had a hard time with the Ws and Is that day."

—*Elvis on his screen test*

THE UNIVERSITY OF ELVIS

In 1992 the University of Mississippi taught a course called "Blue Hawaii: The Polynesian Novels and Hawaiian Movies of Melville and Elvis."

15 November

(1952) Today seventeen-year-old Elvis makes his singing debut in front of an audience made up entirely of strangers. Even in Tupelo, in 1945, he had the support of his fellow students and mother. Today, Elvis and his friend Ronald Smith, a student at South Side High School, sing a duet on "Til Then" and "60 Minute Man" during the annual amateur benefit show for the South Side High marching band. In the crowd is Ronald Smith's girlfriend, Barbara Hearn, who Elvis will eventually date in the fall of 1954.

quote of the day

"I guess I must've sat there at least three hours. I sang everything I knew—pop stuff, spirituals, just a few words of anything I remembered. I was an overnight sensation. A year after they heard me the first time, they called me back!"

—Elvis Presley

ALL IN THE FAMILY

Gladys Presley is known for having a superb singing voice. She also was an accomplished harmonica player.

History

16 November

(1956) Gladys Music, Inc. registers with ASCAP (the American Society of Composers, Authors and Publishers), so Elvis can have a song published with each of the two major songwriting societies. Elvis Presley Music, Inc. is already a member of BMI (Broadcast Music Incorporated). Some songwriters are members of one society, some the other. BMI was originally formed in the 1940's to fill an exclusivity left by ASCAP to traditionally black, hillbilly, and folk music, which left the majority of country and rhythm-and-blues songwriters members of BMI. The dual membership gives Elvis and his partners at Hill and Range (originally an exclusively BMI company) both greater business leverage and much broader song selection. When Elvis needs money in the 1960's, he will sell part of his ownership in Gladys Music to Hill and Range.

quote of the day

"There's no law that says a singer has to stick to one kind of music all his life. I think I'll be singing rock 'n' roll for a long time, but I also hope I'll be singing other styles, too."

—Elvis Presley

THE BEAT OF A DIFFERENT DRUMMER

When Elvis, Scotty, and Bill recorded their very early songs, Bill told his band mates, "They'll run us out of town!" In the early years the trio did suffer some amount of prejudice and abuse. Some radio executives wanted Elvis expelled from the country music charts because he sang "mongrel" music. None of them prevailed. Elvis did.

Today in

17 November

(1970) Elvis is in concert at the Coliseum in Denver, Colorado. At the venue the boys notice him chatting with the off-duty police officers more than his entourage or anyone else. Elvis shows the cops his ever-growing collection of police badges and is sorely disappointed when they can only come up with an "honorary" badge to add to the effort. Elvis does make plans to come back to Denver to collect a real badge soon, however, and he invites the Denver police officers to come out to see him the next time he plays Las Vegas.

quote of the day

"I've tried to be the same all through this thing ... And I always considered other people's feelings. I didn't kick anybody on the way."

—Elvis Presley

ATTENTION ALL CARS: ELVIS LOCATION PLEASE

When Elvis drove out the gates of Graceland the event was announced over the Memphis Police radio frequency, and he'd be tracked through the city. A patrol car was always near in case Elvis required "back up."

History

18 November

(1963) After some uncharacteristic pessimism about the value of a soundtrack for the movie *Fun in Acapulco* from Colonel Parker earlier in the year, an LP is released right on time this month. Producer Hal Wallis is all for the album, feeling the soundtrack and movie complement each other in the record shops and at the box office. The soundtrack includes two "bonus tracks" recorded in May at a Nashville session. Despite the bonus tracks and significantly improved sound quality, the present downsized market takes its toll and sales are disappointing as the Colonel unfortuitously predicted.

quote of the day

"Most people do not realize how Elvis still sells records at a phenomenal rate. Last year Elvis sold eight million records world-wide."

–Ernest Jorgensen, 1997

BLUES IN THE HOUSE AND A BIG RED IN THE YARD —

Q: The last album Elvis made in his life was recorded at Graceland in the den (now known as the Jungle Room) in 1976, with a mobile RCA recording truck known as "Big Red" parked in the yard. What is the title of that album?

A: Moody Blue

Today in

19 November

(1966) It's Saturday and workers begin putting up the Nativity scene in front of Graceland. This is usually a sure sign that Elvis is expected home soon. Since he's been in Hollywood, Elvis's bedroom at Graceland was remodeled. The bedroom walls are now covered with gold flocked wallpaper. The windows are now covered with black drapes and a white rug covers the floor. The headboard of the bed is now a glitter-black. Two televisions, provided courtesy of RCA Victor, are now located in the ceiling above the oversized bed, and another TV is at the foot of the bed.

quote of the day

"I don't know. I wasn't there."

—A typical Graceland tour guide's answer to questions regarding Elvis's drug use or sex life

MY HOW YOU'VE GROWN

Elvis made many additions and renovations to Graceland, including a garage and racquetball court. When Elvis moved in, the Graceland mansion covered 10,266 square feet. When he died, it had grown to 17,552 square feet.

History

(1972) Elvis is relaxing in a penthouse suite at the Hawaiian Village Hotel after a concert tour in the Hawaiian Islands. Today he holds a press conference in the Hawaiian Village's Rainbow Rib Room to announce that an upcoming concert, planned for worldwide telecast next year, will be a benefit for the Kui Lee Cancer Fund. The charity is named for Hawaiian composer Kuiokalani Lee. Lee is the composer of "I'll Remember You," which Elvis recorded in 1966. At the press conference Elvis and Colonel Parker kick off the benefit by donating a check for $1,000. The *Elvis: Aloha From Hawaii* TV special during which Elvis sings "I'll Remember You," raises over $75,000 for the Kui Lee Cancer Fund.

20 November

quote of the day

"First I found [Elvis] to be a gentleman and then a gentle man. I found he could be sensitive to small issues. For someone of his stature there is very little for him to notice, ya know? He's so insulated by the people who surround him and by his own popularity. And yet Elvis will still find little things. He'll take the time to be gentle with people."

—Bill Bixby, in Elvis: A Biography *by Jerry Hopkins*

HAPPY FATHER'S DAY

Elvis's gifts of automobiles is legendary. In the 1999 film *Father's Day*, Billy Crystal's character gives Robin Williams's character the keys to his car, to which Williams quips, "How Elvis of you."

―― Today in ――

21 November

(1955) In Memphis, RCA executives Steve Sholes and Coleman Tily, Hill and Range Music Publishers attorney Ben Starr, Hank Snow, Tom Diskin, and Colonel Parker all converge on Sun Studios for the sale of Elvis's Sun contract and all of his Sun master recordings. The transaction is formally signed off on by Tily for RCA, Sam Phillips for Sun, Elvis, Vernon, the Colonel, and Bob Neal, who still holds some management rights on Elvis. The contents of Elvis's RCA contract call for a minimum of eight sides per year, two one-year options, and a 5 percent royalty, with the purchase price of the contract recoupable from one half of that royalty and a $5,000 non-recoupable bonus. A further agreement with Hill and Range grants Elvis a 50-50 song publishing partnership. This deal grants Elvis another $6,000 of which he receives $4,500 after the Colonel's standard 25 percent.

quote of the day

"Johnny, someday I'm going to be driving Cadillacs."

—Elvis, to his friend Johnny Slack in 1952

"YOU GOT A MANAGER, SON?"

Tom Parker first met Elvis in February 1955 in a Memphis coffee shop. His first words to him were, "You got a manager, son?" By spring Parker had Elvis booked on a Jamboree Attractions tour. By November, Elvis was signed with RCA Victor and the Colonel was in, to the tune of **25 percent.**

History

22 November

(1958) While Elvis's army unit is on maneuvers near Grafenwohr, West Germany, he meets nineteen-year-old Elisabeth Claudia Stefaniak. Elisabeth, a German by birth, is the adopted daughter of one of Elvis's fellow servicemen. Elvis and Elisabeth date for a time, and Ms. Stefaniak is asked to accompany the Presleys back to their Bad Nauheim home, where she is invited to become the family's secretary. Elisabeth receives $35 a week and takes up residence with Elvis's family at Goethestrasse 14. In June of 1960, Elisabeth will marry Elvis's G.I. buddy Rex Mansfield. The couple will eventually author the book *Elvis the Soldier,* in which Elisabeth tells about her relationship with Elvis and how Minnie Mae Presley introduced her to Rex and how she dated him, a relationship that everyone except Elvis seemed aware of.

quote of the day

"I look forward to our marriage and a little Elvis. I have never and never again will love anyone like I love you."

—Elvis, to Anita Wood, the girl back home when he shipped out to Germany with the army

MONSIEUR PRESLEY, ZEE SHOW MUST GO ON!

On army leave in Paris, Elvis lodged at the Hotel Prince de Galles. A hotel waiter described the mademoiselles going in and out of Monsieur Elvis's suite like a "door revolving." One evening the manager of the Lido nightclub had to phone Elvis to ask for his girls back so they could start the floor show—the entire chorus line was in his room.

Today in

23 November

(1976) Jerry Lee Lewis appears at the Graceland gates in the early morning hours waving a gun and demanding to see Elvis. According to the *Memphis Press-Scimitar*, "Witnesses were quoted as saying [he] was screaming and cursing ... and police reported the singer was sitting in his car with a loaded .38 caliber Derringer resting on his knee when they arrived." This is the second night in a row Lewis has shown up. Last night he told Elvis's cousin, Harold Lloyd, he and Elvis have been "trying to get together a long time." Elvis watches the drama from the house on closed-circuit television. Jerry Lee is arrested for his hijinks. Perhaps not coincidentally, Lewis is also a patient of Dr. George Nichopoulos, from whom it is reported he could obtain prescriptions for vast amounts of legal pills.

quote of the day

"Elvis created the template for what the celebrity rock-star persona had to live up to."

—Marilyn Manson

BIG BROTHER E

Besides regular television, Elvis had monitors in his bedroom from which he could watch, via closed-circuit, what was going on in other parts of the house and down at the gates, where fans were always waiting. Today, elvis.com offers Elvis insiders a twenty-four-hour live internet view of Graceland's front lawn as Elvis would have seen it from his bedroom window.

24 November

(1965) *Harum Scarum*, Elvis's nineteenth film, opens across the United States. The film's director, Gene Nelson, had been given only fifteen days to shoot the movie. Elvis even offered to "play sick" to get Nelson more time. Even Colonel Parker seemed stunned by *Harum Scarum*'s flimsy production, telling MGM executives it would take "a 55th cousin of P.T. Barnum" to sell the film. Reviews give credit for any hope for the film to Elvis: The *Hollywood Reporter* says Elvis "continues to handle himself naturally., no different in manner or appearance than his earliest films." *Variety*'s review says: "With anybody but Elvis Presley ... this would be a pretty dreary affair. Elvis, however, apparently can do no wrong." The *Hollywood Citizen-News* puts it more simply: "The cinematic farce just doesn't come off."

quote of the day

"Regardless of what you do, there's gonna be people that don't like you. There was only one perfect man and that was Jesus Christ, and people didn't like him ... I mean, if everybody liked the same thing, we'd all be driving the same car and married to the same woman and it wouldn't work out."

—Elvis Presley

SHEIK ELVIS

Q: *Harum Scarum* opens with Johnny Tyrone (Elvis) acting in a desert adventure movie, titled *Sands of the Desert*. What does Johnny do to free the heroine?

A: Knocks out a leopard with a karate chop.

Today in

25 November

(1956) After driving all night, Elvis arrives in Louisville, Kentucky, and checks into the Seelbach Hotel. He is scheduled for 2:00 and 8:00 PM shows at the Jefferson County Armory. Earlier in the month, Louisville's police chief Carl Heustis announced a local "no-wiggle" ban directed toward Elvis. The chief says he will not permit "any lewd, lascivious contortions that would excite the crowd." Police appear at both shows to enforce the ban. The FBI also becomes involved in the Louisville shows because Bill Haley and the Comets are also on the bill. According to a Louisville police radiogram to FBI Headquarters in Washington, there is fear this "simultaneous booking" will result in a riot by teens. As a result, a hundred Louisville police officers and sixty ushers are on hand for Elvis's performances.

quote of the day

"Advice to teenagers? All I can say is if I do anything wrong, don't copy me."

—*Elvis Presley*

BEATING THE RIOT DRUMS

Once during an early Elvis concert in Kansas City, the crowd became so frenzied that drummer D.J. Fontana was thrown into the orchestra pit.

History

(1977) This week an inventory of Elvis's estate is filed with the Memphis probate court. Elvis's checking account at the National Bank of Commerce contains a balance of $1,055,173. There are several savings accounts with balances ranging from $35 to $39,000. There is $150 million due from RCA in the form of royalties. Also, outstanding loans totaling $255,000 are owed by Dr. George Nichopoulos. Elvis owned two houses, Graceland and his Palm Springs getaway, valued at $1 million. The household inventories list fifty guns, a 1971 and a 1973 Stutz Blackhawk, a Ferrari, a 1955 Cadillac and four other new vehicles. There are six golf carts, two pick-up trucks, a two-ton truck, and six motorcycles. Two airplanes are listed, the "Lisa Marie," a Convair 880 and the "Hound Dog" a nine-passenger Lockheed Jetstar.

26
November

quote of the day

"I don't regard money or position as important. But I guess if you're poor, you always think bigger and want more than fellows who have most everything from the minute they're born."

—Elvis Presley

PLAY ON, SWEET MELODY...

Q: The record player in Elvis's Graceland bedroom still has the record he last played. It's a pressing of what group singing some of Elvis's favorite gospel songs?

A: J.D. Sumner and the Stamps

Today in

November 27

(1959) In Germany, Elvis's cosmetologist, flown in from Johannesburg, South Africa, arrives at Bad Nauheim where Elvis puts him up at the Rex Hotel. Laurenz, who had been contacted by Elisabeth Stefaniak in early October, advertised that his special blend of flowers, herbs, and other ingredients rejuvenate the skin and stall the aging process. Over the next four weeks, Elvis receives daily massages and treatments to his skin, face, and shoulders from Laurenz. Elvis also consumes huge doses of Laurenz's special vitamins. Elvis's relationship with Laurenz ends abruptly in several weeks when Elvis's friends alert him that Laurenz is making homosexual advances toward them.

quote of the day

"It's human nature to gripe, but I'm going ahead and doing the best I can. One thing the army teaches is boys to think like men."

—Elvis Presley

HEARTBREAK HOTEL-MEN'S ROOM

Elvis once wrote out the "TCB Oath" while traveling on an airplane. The oath consisted of noble personal goals. Among them are "strive for shaper skills," "greater respect towards others," and "freedom from constipation."

History

(1971) A paternity suit brought against Elvis by one Patricia Parker finally comes to court. Results of blood tests that were ordered last January are presented at this hearing. The test results are kept confidential, but one source confirms that of the three specific areas checked for compatibility, none of the tests prove Elvis could have fathered Ms. Parker's baby. The "S" factor test reportedly proves it an impossibility Elvis could have fathered the child. The suit is eventually dismissed with Elvis being completely absolved.

November

quote of the day

"Well, sir, you got to accept the bad along with the good ... I know that I'm doing the best I can."

—Elvis, to Hy Gardner during an interview

WHO'S YOUR DADDY?

Elvis had a lot of paternity suits filed against him, the first in 1956 from a girl in Ohio. Elvis was exonerated in every one.

———————————— Today in ————————————

November

(1959) This week the National Academy of Recording Arts and Sciences announces the second annual Grammy Award winners for 1959 during a one-hour NBC-TV special. *(Now and Then There's) A Fool Such as I* becomes Elvis's first-ever Grammy nomination for "Record of the Year." Also *A Big Hunk O' Love* receives two nominations, for "Best Performance by a Top 40 Artist," and "Best Rhythm and Blues Performance." Bobby Darin *(Mack The Knife)* and Frank Sinatra dominate the voting, and Elvis doesn't win any Grammys.

quote of the day

"Elvis is still my favorite singer."

—King Buhmibol Adulyadej of Thailand

ELVIS RIGHT IN YOUR NEIGHBORHOOD!

The book *Elvis & You: Your Guide to the Pleasures of Being an Elvis Fan,* by Laura Levin and John O'Hara, lists over 250 Elvis fan clubs spanning every continent.

30 November

(1975) This week Elvis flies from Memphis to Las Vegas on the maiden flight of the "Lisa Marie." Elvis bought the Convair 880 jet for $1.2 million this month and has since spent an extra $750,000 to have it customized. The plane is finished in white, with red and blue trim, with the name "Lisa Marie" on the side near the cockpit. On the tail is the "TCB" insignia with the lightning bolt. The jet requires a crew of four. Lisa Marie is equipped with a $14,000 queen size bed, a conference room, four television sets, a bar, leather swivel chairs, and a pair of couches.

quote of the day

"Hi Babies, Here's the money to pay the bills. Don't tell no one how much money I sent. I will send more next week. There is a card in the mail. Love, Elvis"

—*an early telegram from Elvis to his parents*

I'D RATHER BE RICH

Elvis once told producer Felton Jarvis that he sometimes gave people things to show them life would be the same after they got it as it was before.

December

History

(1975) This week Elvis opens his "Pre-Holiday Jubilee" at the Las Vegas Hilton. These concerts are re-schedules from the August Hilton shows that were cancelled. This is one of the engagements filmed for the *Elvis in Concert* documentary. These performances are only once daily at 10:15 PM except Saturdays when an 8:00 PM show is added with the second moved to midnight. Tickets are $22.50 per person. During the engagement everyone seems to notice Elvis's good mood and general well being after taking a three-month hiatus. In several of the shows from this run Elvis takes audience requests and performs songs not on the regular routine, including "Little Sister," "Help Me Make it Through the Night" and "Blue Christmas."

1 December

quote of the day

"You never heard anybody ask 'Elvis who?'"

—Charles Kuralt

LAS VEGAS CHRISTMAS WISH LIST

After Elvis cancelled shows in August of 1975, he made it up to the Las Vegas Hilton by holding his "Pre-Holiday Jubilee." Although the months of November and December were typically the slowest time of year for Las Vegas hotels and casinos, Elvis shows were a sellout. So happy were they with the business, the Las Vegas Hilton approached Colonel Parker about extending Elvis's engagement through the new year. Parker explained there was no way Elvis would spend the holidays away from Graceland.

Today in

2 December

(1955) This week's *Billboard* announces that Elvis, "one of the most sought after warblers this year, signed two big-time contracts," one with RCA and one with Hill and Range, the music publisher under which newly formed Elvis Presley Music, a BMI company, will operate. Reports say RCA plans to market Elvis's "platters in all three fields—pop, R&B, and c&w. However, RCA ... plans to cut the warbler with the same backing—electric guitar, bass fiddle, drums and Presley himself on rhythm guitar—featured on his previous Sun waxings."

quote of the day

"A hard-working stripper who tried anything like it would find herself a guest of the county."

—Variety

BAR SET TOO HIGH?

By the end of 1955, big-name artists refused to go on a bill with Elvis.

3 December

(1968) The TV special *Elvis* airs on NBC-TV from 9:00 to 10:00 PM (EST). It receives generally good reviews and seems to restore Elvis's credibility as an entertainer following eight years of increasingly mediocre movies. The show's producer, Bob Finkel, wins a Peabody Award for the special. Ratings for the week place *Elvis* at number 1, beating even the widely popular *Rowan & Martin's Laugh-In*. Elvis receives a Nielson rating of 32, with a 42 share. In the "Multi-Network Area (MNA)" survey, the special receives a rating of 33.2 percent of the audience, beating the *Laugh-In* share of 31.1 percent.

quote of the day

"It was the finest music of his life. If there was music that bleeds, this was it. Nothing came easy that night, and he gave everything he had—more than anyone knew was there."

—Greil Marcus, on Elvis's performance in Elvis the '68 Comeback Special, from Mystery Train: Images of America in Rock 'n' Roll Music

TELECIDE

There were fourteen television sets at Graceland, and Elvis often had one tuned to each available program at the same time. He took his TV viewing very seriously, and is known to have committed "telecide" on several occasions by shooting the picture tube out of a set whose broadcast he didn't particularly like.

4 December

(1956) Elvis is showing Marilyn Evans, the Las Vegas showgirl who's visiting, around Memphis when they stop by Sun Studios. There they find Carl Perkins working on his latest song, "Matchbox." Also on hand is Jerry Lee Lewis who is backing Perkins's session. Lewis's first single, "End of the Road," has just been released by Sun. For the next three hours, the three performers, later joined by Johnny Cash, another Sun artist, run through a succession of gospel and popular songs. Portions of the jam are captured on tape by Sam Phillips. Someone notifies the *Memphis Press-Scimitar*, which dispatches a photographer and reporter to cover the impromptu event. This gathering comes to be known as "The Million Dollar Quartet."

quote of the day

"10-inch shellac, the 45, the EP, the 8-track tape, the cassette tape, the LP, the CD, the DAT, the VHS, and the laser. Elvis has lasted through all of these."

—Don Wardell, RCA Executive

TRUE TO HER ROOTS

Despite Elvis's stardom and wealth, Gladys Presley still hand-washed her family's laundry with a tub and washboard. She also did all of the family's ironing by herself and all of the sewing on Vernon's and Elvis's clothes.

History

(1971) Elvis returns to Memphis from Los Angeles for his usual Christmas break. During this vacation, as he has many times in years past, Elvis rents a local movie theater, the Memphian located at 51 South Cooper, for midnight showings of movies he wants to see. Tonight he's watching the current James Bond film, *Diamonds Are Forever*. Other movies Elvis enjoys watching over and over include *Dirty Harry* and *Straw Dogs*. When he goes to the movies, Elvis wears a variety of clothing styles from football jerseys to wide gold belts. The one accessory he always wears is his pistol over his left hip.

5 December

quote of the day

"Is it true you shot your mother?"

—*Television host Hy Gardner interviewing Elvis on July 1, 1956*

THE NEW KILROY?

During the Persian Gulf war in the 1990's, American soldiers left their mark all over the theater of operations. You could tell where they'd been by looking for the graffiti "Elvis Was Here."

— Today in —

6 December

(1970) Elvis is in Los Angeles, where he personally delivers a check to Police Chief Ed Davis for $7,000 to be used in a police community relations program. Elvis also makes a gift of a custom-made frontier model Colt .45 revolver to the chief. The only stipulation Elvis has is that no publicity be generated about the gift. Elvis's cash donation is the largest single donation to LAPD's program. The money is used to buy toys for needy children, uniforms for the police marching band, and special flak jackets for explosive-sniffing dogs.

quote of the day

"I know this—all good things come from God. You don't have to go to church to know right from wrong. Sure, church helps, but you can be a Christian so long as you have a Christian heart."

—Elvis Presley

THE SPIRIT OF THE SEASON

The big reason Elvis loved the holidays was because it's the season of giving. In 1961, he started a Christmas tradition of distributing checks to over fifty charities, donating more than $100,000 every year.

History

(1960) It's Pearl Harbor Day. Colonel Parker reads an editorial in the *Los Angeles Herald Examiner* written by the editor of the *Honolulu Advertiser*. The article, which is sent to every major newspaper in the United States, asks citizens for donations to construct a memorial to the *U.S.S. Arizona,* one of the battleships sunk at Pearl Harbor nineteen years ago with a loss of 1,102 service men and women. The Colonel immediately calls the *Advertiser* to volunteer Elvis's services. The result is a charity concert held in March of 1961 at Bloch Arena in Hawaii that raises over $65,000 for the memorial.

7 December

quote of the day

"Gratitude ... for what this country has given me. And now I'm ready to return a little. It's the only adult way to look at it."

—*Elvis when asked about his feelings upon receiving his draft notice.*

GRATITUDE, LOST

When the U.S. Park Service, a division of the Department of the Interior, took over custody and management of the *U.S.S. Arizona* Memorial at Pearl Harbor, Hawaii, they removed a plaque from the memorial commemorating Elvis's help and donations to its construction.

Today in

8 December

(1954) This week Columbia Records recording artist and up-and-coming country performer Marty Robbins cuts his version of "That's All Right." This is the first complete cover version of a song recorded by Elvis. (Bill Monroe had re-recorded "Blue Moon of Kentucky" in September, starting in his original style, then switching to something closer to the Presley version.) Although Robbins's recording is more country than Elvis's, it is closer to the Elvis version than to the original by Arthur "Big Boy" Crudup.

quote of the day

"Before Elvis there was nothing."
—John Lennon

"And after him not much."
—Lex Raaphorst, an Elvis fan from Holland

THE LAST TEMPTATION OF ELVIS

The Last Temptation of Elvis, a tribute album recorded in 1990 as a charity benefit, has covers of Elvis songs from some very popular entertainers including Paul McCartney singing "It's Now Or Never," Bruce Springsteen's version of "Viva Las Vegas," and the Pogues doing "Got a Lot O' Livin' to Do."

History

9 December

(1963) Producer Hal Wallis sends a message to Colonel Parker about what he feels could be a problem in Elvis's upcoming appearance in the Wallis production of *Roustabout*. Wallis tells the Colonel Elvis looks "soft, fat, and jowly with a hairdo that makes him look as if he's wearing a wig that is painted too black." "I will appreciate it," Wallis writes, if you will have a talk with Elvis, as this is a very serious concern for both us and him, as it could have a very detrimental effect on his entire career." Elvis will not be permitted to bring his own hairdresser on the *Roustabout* set. The Colonel responds, "You must strongly impress on your people in production that they should only convey your desires … because if Elvis is not sure what someone is supposed to do and they ask him how he likes it, he naturally is going to tell them what he likes, regardless of the picture."

quote of the day

"When Elvis reached his teens, he… grew his hair long and added sideburns. Elvis favored the ducktail look and knew if he went to a barber shop, the barber might take it upon himself to cut his hair in the popular crew cut style. As a result, Elvis chose to go to the local beauty parlor instead."

–Jim Curtin, *from* Elvis: Unknown Stories Behind the Legend

G.I. ELVIS

Q: What did Elvis do to prepare himself for life in the military?

A: In the weeks before his induction, Elvis received a series of progressively shorter haircuts

Today in

10 December

(1976) New girlfriend Ginger Allen has been with Elvis for almost two weeks now, accompanying him to shows since Linda Thompson's departure. Now a few days into an engagement at the Las Vegas Hilton, Ginger tells Elvis it's time she return home to see her family. Elvis responds by dispatching his plane to fly Ginger's mother, father, brother, and brother's wife, and her two sisters to Las Vegas. Today's *Memphis Commercial Appeal* publishes an interview with Ginger's mother in which she confirms Elvis did give her daughter a Lincoln Continental, although "she doesn't think it was an engagement gift."

quote of the day

"I'm looking forward to spending this Christmas in a new way. I'm looking forward to possibly seeing some people that are gonna be shocked. I just hope they're not gonna be hurt, but I know they're gonna be shocked!"

—*Elvis, in 1960 after getting fourteen-year-old Priscilla's parent's permission to have her visit Graceland for the holidays*

BLUE... BLUE, BLUE, BLUE... CHRISTMAS

On Christmas day in 1971, Elvis learned of Priscilla's extra-marital affair with Mike Stone. When Elvis confronted Priscilla with the revelation, she asked for a divorce.

―――――――――――――――― History ――――――――――――――――

11 December

(1973) Around this time Elvis is feeling exhausted and sick so doctors admit him to Baptist Memorial Hospital for tests. His nurse, Clara Lee Mayhew, is charged with his care, making sure that he is comfortable, receives his medicine, and has privacy. It's the day before Elvis is scheduled to undergo tests, and Nurse Mayhew discovers he's missing from his room. Frantically searching the hospital, she overhears singing coming from the children's ward. She finds Elvis, clad in a white robe, sitting among the kids singing "Blue Christmas." Besides the impromptu holiday concert, he makes sure gifts are sent to every child in the ward.

quote of the day

"Every time I felt low, I just put on an Elvis record and I'd feel great, beautiful."

–Paul McCartney

IT'S THE THOUGHT THAT COUNTS!

Tom Parker rarely, if ever, gave Christmas presents. He broke the trend in the 1960's when he sent the Memphis Mafia wrapped packages. The boys couldn't believe their eyes upon opening the gifts to find—a stuffed animal. The next year he sent cash! Eighty dollars—to be split seven ways.

Today in

12 December

(1976) It's closing night of a two-week run in Vegas at the Hilton. The sold-out shows have seen ups and downs in Elvis's performances. Elvis has an ankle injury, which is causing pain. Vernon was admitted to the hospital with chest pains but released the next day. It all culminated with Elvis announcing at Friday night's show, "I hate Las Vegas." Of tonight's performance *Memphis Press-Scimitar* reporter Bill Burk writes: "One walks away wondering how much longer it can be before the end comes," and asks, "why the King of Rock and Roll would subject himself to possible ridicule by going on-stage so ill-prepared."

quote of the day

"Elvis, right now I want to pray for you. He said, 'Please do,' and started weeping."

—Rex Humbard, televangelist, upon meeting Elvis in his dressing room after a show at the Las Vegas Hilton

THE PROPHET

An early girlfriend of Elvis's, June Juanico, gave him his first copy of Kahlil Gibran's *The Prophet*, about Eastern concepts of spirituality, in 1956. Elvis read and re-read the book many times during his life, calling it his "unwinder."

History

(1963) Today Elvis buys almost fifty tickets to the premiere of *Cleopatra* starring Elizabeth Taylor. The tickets—meant as a Christmas present for Priscilla, family, and friends—are quite a hot item and very hard to come by. The tickets are $12.50 each, which is very expensive at this time. On the day of the premiere showing, Elvis apologizes to everyone and tells them he won't be able to attend because of other important matters he must see to. Unbeknownst to Priscilla, Elvis's "business" is a trip back to Hollywood to spend a few days with Ann-Margret.

13 December

quote of the day

"Elvis was a wonderful kisser. How do you describe soft lips, slightly parted, not too much, but just perfect. And he sometimes opened his mouth about three inches–sucked off part of my nose."

—June Juanico, from Elvis in the Twilight of Memory

QUEEN FOR A DAY

The Memphis Mafia divided Elvis's female love interests into two categories. "Lifers" were the women with whom Elvis had long-term relationships, like Anita Wood, Priscilla, and Linda Thompson. His "fleeting" romances were known as "Queen for a Day."

Today in

14 December

(1976) With Christmas only days away, Elvis is home at Graceland entertaining Lisa Marie by reminiscing about his favorite Christmases. He recalls snowball fights and snowmen when Lisa Marie interrupts, telling her father she doesn't know what snow is. Daddy-Elvis immediately summons the crew of the *Lisa Marie*, his private jet, and takes a plane ride to a place with snow-covered mountains, where they land at a nearby airport. On the ground Elvis picks up two handfuls of snow and sets it in his daughter's hands telling her, "That's exactly what snow is!" Lisa Marie only asks, "Why didn't you tell me that it was like ice?" The two head back to the plane. The snow adventure costs Elvis $30,000.

quote of the day

"Goodbye, darling, goodbye. I love you so much. You know how much I lived my whole life just for you."

—Elvis, at his mother's funeral

A BLUESY CHRISTMAS

RCA found themselves one song short during production of Elvis's Christmas album, so they asked composers Leiber and Stoller to come up with something. "Santa Claus Is Back in Town" resulted and became one of Elvis's most popular and recognizable Christmas tunes.

―――――― History ――――――

(1956) Elvis is in Shreveport, Louisiana, to perform in what will be his last *Louisiana Hayride* appearance. The dressing room area of the Hirsch Youth Center is more crowded than usual because fellow *Hayride* members want to give Elvis their best wishes. A backstage pre-show press conference is disrupted, as usual, by enthusiastic fans trying to get to Elvis. At showtime, more than 9,000 screaming fans are in the audience. This performance, lasting from 8:30 to 11:30 PM, is a benefit for the Shreveport YMCA. Elvis, Scotty, Bill, D.J., and the Jordanaires are the night's closing act. It's a rousing conclusion to the end of Elvis's two-year association with the *Louisiana Hayride*, the show that was one of the first to recognize his talent.

15
December

quote of the day

"The boy is a show business freak. He'd better save his money while it's pouring in. Chances are in a year or two from now no one will remember him."

— Miami Herald

THE MANY SINGING STYLES OF ELVIS

Elvis aficionados identify various "singing styles" Elvis used very well. Among them:
Soft, Airy, Falsetto-Like ("I'll Remember You")
Macho, Dark, and Solemn ("Peace in the Valley," "I Was the One")
Classic (Italian) Tenor ("Long Tall Sally," "Lawdy Miss Clawdy")

Today in

16
December

(1957) The Memphis draft board announces that Elvis will soon be receiving his official draft notice, and every major branch of the military (except the marine corps) rallies for his service. The navy wants to create a specially trained "Elvis Presley Company" with a unit made up of all his Memphis friends, the opportunity to perform while off-duty, and offers an admiral's housing facility. The air force plans an Elvis tour of recruitment centers. The army wants to put Elvis in a special services assignment where he could visit bases world-wide, record when he wanted, and perform off-duty. Ultimately, Elvis joins the army and refuses any special treatment.

quote of the day

"We had a Christmas party here. I had a lot of guys from over at the post, you know. I had as many of the boys here as possible at my home ... to kind of make them feel at home around Christmastime. And we had a little Christmas party and on New Year's we had another little party and it seemed nice. It was better than last year!"

—*Elvis, while stationed in Germany in 1959*

DRAFT BOARD DAYS

Q: When Elvis was drafted into the army in 1957, he did ask for, and received, a deferment of sixty days so he could finish production of a motion picture. What film was it?

A: *King Creole*. In Elvis's request to the draft board he mentioned leaving the production would cost Twentieth Century Fox $350,000 dollars.

History

17 December

(1965) This week Elvis continues his long-established annual Christmas custom by personally donating checks for more than $55,000 to Memphis charities. He attends a ceremony in the auditorium of the Memphis Publishing Company to distribute the gifts. This year Elvis also donates to charities in Mississippi, Omaha, and Los Angeles. Remembering those in the service, Elvis also gave $5,000 to the USO for use by the four servicemen's clubs in Saigon, South Vietnam. All totaled, Elvis's Christmas giving for 1965 is pretty close to his generous standard: $101,350.

quote of the day

"There is a lot of difference in Christmas today and when we were growing up in East Tupelo. Honestly, I can't say that these are any better!"

–Elvis Presley

SANTA CLAUS IS DRIVIN' 'ROUND TOWN! —

In 1963 on Christmas Eve Elvis drove his new Rolls Royce all over Memphis, hand delivering his annual gifts to various charities, perhaps causing a bigger stir than Santa himself.

Today in

18 December

(1948) The Presleys are preparing to spend their first Christmas in Tennessee when Gladys comes up with an idea she thinks will make the holidays really special. She tells her family they are going home, to Tupelo, for Christmas. Having only been in Memphis for three months with Vernon still unemployed leaves the three with only two options—walking or hitchhiking. Vernon, Gladys, and Elvis start their trip in good spirits, with mother and son discussing the family they miss and the foods they'll eat. Vernon, however, needs a new pair of shoes so the walk becomes tedious. Just when Vernon is about to put a stop to the whole idea, a trucker happens by and rides the Presleys all the way to Mississippi, where they pick up another ride to Old Saltillo Road, where they spent Christmas.

quote of the day

"My gosh, you're guarded better than the president!"

—Billy Carter, upon visiting Elvis at Graceland in the 1970's

KING FOR A DAY (UH, NEXT YEAR)

On December 18, 1973, then-Georgia Governor and future President Jimmy Carter signed a proclamation naming January 8, 1974, as "Elvis Presley Day" in the state of Georgia. Elvis had performed to 85,715 fans in five appearances at Atlanta's Omni in 1973, grossing more than $800,000.

History

19 December

(1962) Vernon and Dee fly to New York to meet seventeen-year-old Priscilla Beaulieu, who is arriving on a flight from Germany. Vernon and Dee accompany Priscilla back to Memphis and their Hermitage Road home. There, Elvis picks her up and drives to Graceland, where the annual Christmas display awaits. Some reports say Priscilla misses the first two days of her Tennessee holiday because of pills Elvis gave her to help sleep on the first night. Regardless, the rest of Priscilla's vacation is spent with Elvis playing tour guide showing her the places where he grew up. The couple also roller skates, goes to movies at the Memphian, and dines out at Chenault's Drive-In. This Christmas, Elvis gives Priscilla a toy poodle puppy she names Honey.

quote of the day

"My Mama and I used to plan Christmas for days, even when we had no money at all!"

– *Elvis Presley*

A LIVING DOLL

Q: A popular Christmas gift set in 1997 brought two American favorites together in doll form. Name the famous pair.

A: Elvis and Barbie

Today in

20 December

(1958) Today Elvis faces two unsettling issues: it's his first Christmas without his mother, and he's in Germany for the holidays, which he's always believed should be spent at home. He goes to Frankfurt to buy himself a Christmas present and decides on a used white BMW 507. The two-seater sports car costs $3,750 and was previously owned by German race car driver Hans Stuck. After bringing the car back to his house, Elvis has the racing engine, which is impractical for his needs, replaced with a touring engine. He also has the car painted red, to alleviate the problem of lipstick messages. Elvis is the only soldier who can afford a car on base and consequently his is the only soldier-owned vehicle there. At the same time he bought his BMW, he picked up a black Mercedes Benz for his father.

quote of the day

"If I could have one wish granted it would be to talk again with my mother. There are times I dream about her. She's always happy and smiling. Sometimes we embrace, and it's so real I wake up in a cold sweat."

–Elvis Presley

WHEN IN ROME

The German media nicknamed Elvis's **BMW 507** *"Der Elviswagen."*

History

(1970) Elvis arrives in Washington, D.C. and delivers a hand-written letter to President Richard Nixon that says in part, "I would love to meet you just to say hello if you're not too busy." He then checks into a Washington hotel. Later he and his accompanying friends, including California Senator George Murphy, tour the Bureau of Narcotics and Dangerous Drugs. Bureau Deputy Director John Finlator is Elvis's guide. During his tour, Elvis asks Finlator for a federal narcotic officer's badge, but he's summarily turned down. That afternoon Elvis receives an invitation to the White House to meet President Nixon. During the meeting, Elvis brings up his keen interest in a narcotic's officer's badge and mentions this morning's request. The President immediately orders that Elvis receive a badge. Elvis is so overcome, he gives the President a Tennessee bear hug.

December

quote of the day

"Elvis was a narc, wearing sequins after dark. And every pill he'd eat, was one less on the street. Elvis ate 'em all for you and me."

—*Pinkard & Bowden, country comedy singers from the song: "Elvis Was a Narc."*

SPECIAL AGENT ELVIS

The photographs of Richard Nixon and Elvis meeting are the most requested items from the National Archives. Elvis's Bureau of Narcotics and Dangerous Drugs badge became one of his most prized possessions, and he carried it the rest of his life.

Today in

December

(1966) Yet another example of Elvis's generous spirit occurs when he reads a newspaper story about an elderly black woman whose wheelchair had deteriorated with age. The paper mentions a fund that is being raised by the lady's friends to buy her a new one. Springing into action, Christmas-spirit Elvis goes out and buys a new electric wheelchair. He makes the gift even more special by delivering it himself. To ensure a Merry Christmas for all, Elvis also gives the woman an additional two hundred dollars.

quote of the day

"The beautiful thing about Elvis was he turned everybody into everybody. It doesn't matter "is the guy black or white" anymore, and maybe even you can do it; it sparked a dream."

—Keith Richards

MERRY McCHRISTMAS

One Christmas Eve at Graceland Elvis preceded handing out gifts to his entourage by complaining that it had been a lean year. Once the envelopes were distributed, each Memphis Mafia member found McDonald's gift certificates inside. After some startled looks and panic, Elvis laughed and gave out the genuine Christmas bonuses they all expected.

History

23 December

(1959) This winter comedian Bob Hope sends members of his staff to Bad Nauheim, Germany, to try to get Elvis to sign on in the annual U.S. Troop Christmas Tour. Elvis politely declines, telling Mr. Hope's men he is in the army to serve and not sing. Colonel Parker hears of the news and is much less diplomatic. Elvis is on maneuvers and unavailable, so Parker contacts Bob Hope himself. Insisting all of Elvis's business transactions go through him, the Colonel demands of Bob Hope, "Why should Elvis work for the army for free when we can get $50,000 for a single night's show?" When Mr. Hope tells the manager he does indeed intend to pay for Elvis's appearance, the Colonel resorts to his customary no-cooperation tactic of upping the price to $125,000. Hope insists no entertainer is worth that much and Colonel Parker maintains his image.

quote of the day

We're here to entertain you and make you happy. Till we meet again, may God bless you. Adios."

—Elvis, while closing a show

BIG BOSS MAN

In many of Elvis's business dealings, Tom Parker walked away with a bigger income than his star. As a result of Parker's short-sighted, self-serving and ethically questionable deals, when Elvis died he left behind an estate worth only $7 million. In contrast, John Lennon, who died three years after Elvis, left a fortune of $200 million.

Today in

24 December

(1959) It's Christmastime in Germany, and the army's third armor division, of which Private Presley is a member, throws a special Christmas party for one hundred and fifteen German orphans from the Steinmuehle Orphanage. In the holiday spirit, Elvis decides to do something he's never done and plays Santa Claus for the children. The orphans love the party referring to Santa Elvis as their "foster father." The sentiment brings Elvis to tears and he hugs each child in turn, thanking them in German. The orphanage's director, Hermann Schaub, later publicly thanks Elvis, saying that in the orphanage's history no one has ever treated the children so well.

quote of the day

"Christmas is my favorite holiday. I believed in Santa Claus until I was eight years old. Some of the kids at school told me there was no such thing. Mama explained it to me in such a way that Christmas didn't lose its magic."

—Elvis Presley

WAY TO GO, JIMBO

On Christmas Eve of 1956, Elvis and Dorothy Harmony bought a monkey from a Memphis pet shop. They named the monkey "Jimbo." On the way back to Elvis's house, Jimbo did his "monkey business" all over Dorothy and the car. Dorothy's outfit, a white dress and red leather jacket, was ruined. Elvis had to pull over at a gas station and have Dorothy take Jimbo to the ladies room to clean up while he worked on his white leather upholstery. Merry Christmas, Jimbo!

History

(1966) It's Christmas Day and Elvis formally proposes to Priscilla Beaulieu and gives her a diamond engagement ring as a Christmas gift. Elvis's personal Christmas cards this year show Elvis and Priscilla in front of Graceland's Nativity Scene. It is signed "Elvis and Priscilla." The Christmas card from Elvis and the Colonel shows Elvis in a red jacket, leaning on a chair.

December

quote of the day

"Elvis had his old boyish grin on his face and his hands were behind his back. 'Sit down, Sattnin', and close your eyes.' I did. When I opened my eyes, I found Elvis on his knees before me, holding a small black velvet box. 'Sattnin',' he said. I opened the box to find the most beautiful diamond ring I'd ever seen. It was three-and-a-half karats, encircled by a row of smaller diamonds, which were detachable—I could wear them separately. 'We're going to be married,' Elvis said. 'You're going to be his. I told you I'd know when the time was right. Well, the time's right.' He slipped the ring on my finger. I was too overwhelmed to speak; it was the most beautiful and romantic moment of my life."

—Priscilla Beaulieu Presley, from Elvis and Me

MERRY CHRISTMAS

Q: The first Christmas gift Elvis ever gave to Priscilla was a gold and diamond watch. What was her gift to him?

A: A set of bongo drums

Today in

26 December

(1964) The entourage presented Elvis with a special Bible as a Christmas gift. The present has an inscription of the "tree of life" motif drawn on the front page. On each one of the branches is one of the guys' names, and at the bottom is one of Elvis's favorite Bible verses: "Know the truth, and the truth shall set you free," written in English, Hebrew, and Latin. Because Elvis notices his hairdresser, friend, and spiritual confidant Larry Geller's name doesn't appear on the tree, he refuses to accept the gift until it is added. Around now Elvis is acknowledging his Jewish ancestry (his maternal grandmother, Martha Tackett, was Jewish) and begins wearing a Jewish "chai" around his neck. He also has a Star of David symbol added to Gladys's grave marker.

quote of the day

"I am not the only boy to lose his mother and I am well aware that there are so many others, but I can never show the grief I feel inside. And Christmas, which meant so much to us, because Mama made it such a wonderful, big, happy occasion, brings back that grief."

–Elvis, 1961

MAMA'S CHRISTMAS WISHES

After Gladys's funeral in August of 1958, Elvis went through some of her possessions in her Graceland bedroom. In a drawer he found her unfinished Christmas list. Shedding a tear that marked the paper, Elvis folded the list and placed it in his wallet. He carried the list with him for the rest of his life.

(1960) Today, of all the countless accolades bestowed upon him, Elvis receives a rare and distinguished honor. The Los Angeles Indian Tribal Council, because of their admiration of his portrayal of a mixed American Indian character in the film *Flaming Star*, want to initiate him as a blood brother of the Los Angeles Indian community. This is a very big honor usually reserved for full-blooded Indians who have distinguished themselves in the community. Because Elvis is known worldwide and has brought attention to the cause of the forgotten and often abused Indian race, Chief Wah-Nee-Ota, leader of the council, presents Elvis with a chief's bonnet as their tribute to him and his contributions to their cause.

December

quote of the day

"Home means all the relatives and friends getting together and all of us talking and laughing and singing and playing and enjoying ourselves. Like Christmas, everyone was at Graceland. And the boys, they have wives and children and families, just everyone. We had a great time. We had turkeys and a huge Christmas tree, of course. And lots of presents."

–Elvis Presley

HOMEMADE CHRISTMAS CHEER

In the early years, the Presleys created their own Christmas atmosphere. Vernon and his brother Vester would hunt for a tree to chop down and take home. Gladys and Elvis then decorated the tree with berries, popcorn on a string, and, with color paper, made chains. To the Presleys, theirs was a marvelous tree!

Today in

28 December

(1970) This afternoon Elvis serves as best man at the wedding of Delbert B. "Sonny" West to Judy Jordan, who is described as "an actress" by the press. Priscilla is the Matron of Honor. The ceremony is held at Trinity Baptist Church in Memphis. After their marriage, Sonny and Judy move into a two-bedroom apartment converted out of a garage at Graceland. Charlie Hodge, who had been living in the garage, moves to a basement apartment next to the TV room.

quote of the day

"I wish I could just do that [walk away from the life he was leading]. It's too late for that. There are too many people. There are too many people who depend on me. I'm too obligated. I'm in too far to get out."

—Elvis Presley

NO TIME CLOCK NECESSARY

All of the members of the Memphis Mafia were on call 24/7. No matter what the hour, Elvis would call his friends to play racquetball, do some target shooting, even fly to Las Vegas.

History

(1954) Today's *Memphis Press-Scimitar* reports, "Elvis Presley, the 19-year-old Memphian whose first two records ... won him quick acclaim, has signed a management contract with Bob Neal, WMPS folk music disc jockey, it was announced yesterday." Starting next year, Bob Neal begins to book dates inside of the WMPS listening area on an exclusive basis. He uses contacts in the *Louisiana Hayride* network to book Elvis at venues as far away as west Texas and eastern New Mexico. The article shows a photo of a bow-tied young Elvis and also announces the release of his third single for Sun Records.

29 December

quote of the day

"He shimmied, squirmed and wriggled the mob into a panic which took the efforts of police, sailors and firemen to restrain."

—The Commercial Appeal

FIRST OF MANY

Second manager Bob Neal arranged for Elvis to buy one of his first cars in 1954. Since Elvis lacked credit, he bought the 1951 Lincoln Continental on Neal's. The car had 10,000 miles on it. Elvis had "Elvis Presley - Sun Records" lettered on the doors.

Today in

30 December

(1966) In preparation for the closing of escrow on the ranch in Mississippi, Elvis purchases seventeen horses that today he's boarding in the stables at Graceland. He can be seen frequently riding his favorite, a palomino named Rising Sun, around the Graceland grounds and even out to South Bellevue Boulevard. Even after riding most of today, Elvis gets more saddle time in on New Year's Eve when he can't get into the party at the Manhattan Club in Memphis because of the fans crowding the area. Consequently, he returns to Graceland and rides until six o'clock in the morning.

quote of the day

"Animals don't hate and we're supposed to be better than them."

–Elvis Presley

PRETTY AS A PEACOCK

Elvis's menagerie at Graceland is famous. Among the birds on the estate were ducks, chickens, mynah birds, and a tom turkey named Bowtie. Elvis also had some peacocks on the grounds, but they were "re-located" to the Memphis Zoo after one of them scratched Elvis's Rolls Royce while watching its own reflection in the finish.

History

31 December

(1970) Before flying home to Memphis for his annual New Year's Eve Party, Elvis is in Washington, D.C. taking a special tour of FBI Headquarters. The agent giving the tour sends a memo to J. Edgar Hoover, the FBI's director, quoting Elvis as saying he admires Hoover and is disappointed to not be able to meet him. The agent also reports Elvis remarked "in private comments, that he, Presley, is the 'living proof that America is the land of opportunity' since he rose from truck driver to prominent entertainer almost over night." The agent also notes Elvis's offer to serve in an undercover capacity in any way he can. Hoover later sends Elvis a note in reply saying, "your generous comments concerning the Bureau and me are appreciated, and you may be sure we will keep in mind your offer to be of assistance."

quote of the day

"PHILOSOPHY FOR A HAPPY LIFE"
SOMEONE TO LOVE,
SOMETHING TO LOOK
FORWARD TO, AND
SOMETHING TO DO"
E.P.
1972

—Elvis, found written on a scrap of paper in his handwriting

EVERY ONE PRECIOUS

Elvis lived a total of 15,197 days.

About the Author

JOHN BOERTLEIN is a life-long Elvis fan. His collection of Elvis memorabilia spans decades going back to the 1960's. He is an avid collector of Elvis recordings and attended Elvis's second-last live performance at the Cincinnati Coliseum on June 25, 1977. Sharing Elvis's interest in law enforcement, Boertlein spent over twenty years as an officer with the Cincinnati Police Department. He is the author of *Howdunit: A Writers Guide To How Crimes Are Committed And Solved* (Writer's Digest Books). He is currently a freelance writer and resides in Ohio with his special lady friend and his son and daughter.